INDUSTRIAL PRODUCTIVITY
A Psychological Perspective

This book introduces the manager and the student to the major ways in which psychology can aid organisational productivity. In particular, the authors examine the way in which the work environment can affect the individual's willingness and capacity to produce effectively. Thus topics such as the nature of the work itself, financial incentives, work groups, physical aspects of the worker's environment and individual differences in response to work are considered. The book deals with ergonomic considerations of machine design and with psychological aspects of problematic work adjustment, such as absence, job turnover and stress and conflict at work; and it also considers methods of job redesign aimed at alleviating some of the problems found at work.

Michael M. Gruneberg is Senior Lecturer in Psychology at the University College of Swansea. He was co-convenor of the NATO conference on 'Changes in the Quality of Working Life' and was also co-convenor (with David Oborne) of the international conference on 'Psychology and Medicine' held at Swansea in 1979.

David J. Oborne is Lecturer in Psychology at the University College of Swansea. He has contributed papers to learned journals in various areas of psychology and ergonomics. He was senior convenor of an international conference on 'Ergonomics and Transport' in 1980.

INDUSTRIAL PRODUCTIVITY

A Psychological Perspective

Michael M. Gruneberg
and
David J. Oborne

A HALSTED PRESS BOOK

John Wiley & Sons
New York – Toronto

Published in the U.K. by
THE MACMILLAN PRESS LTD
London and Basingstoke

*Published in the U.S.A., and Canada
by Halsted Press, a Division
of John Wiley & Sons, Inc.,
New York*

Printed in Hong Kong

Library of Congress Cataloging in Publication Data

Gruneberg, Michael M.
  Industrial productivity.

  "A Halsted Press book."
  Bibliography: p.
  Includes index.
  1. Labor productivity—Psychological aspects.
I. Oborne, David J. II. Title.
HD57.G74   658.3′14′019   81–7521
ISBN 0–470–27194–9   AACR2

Contents

Acknowledgements

We would like to thank Mrs Maureen Rogers and Miss Jackie Scholz for the typing of the original manuscript, and for the pleasing appearance of the final copy.

Preface

This book is intended to introduce the manager and the
student to the major ways in which psychology can aid
organisational productivity. In particular, this book will
look at the way in which the work environment can affect
the individual's willingness and capacity to produce effectively. Thus topics such as the nature of the work itself,
financial incentives, work groups, the physical context of
work and individual differences in response to work will be
considered. The book will also deal with psychological aspects of problematic work adjustment, such as absence, job
turnover and stress and conflict at work, and will consider
methods of job redesign aimed at alleviating some of the
problems currently found at work. Because the book is intended as an introduction to the area, no attempt is made
to cover all relevant topics; rather the aim is to cover
many of the major factors which affect and are affected by
efficient productivity at work.

It will become apparent to the reader that a number of
factors have been shown to aid productivity. Locke *et al.*
(1980), for example, note that on average financial incentives, when introduced, improve productivity by 30 per cent
compared with goal-setting, which improves productivity on
average by 16 per cent and job redesign, which improves
productivity by 17 per cent. The reader must be careful,
however, not to make the assumption that financial incentives are therefore more useful than goal-setting and job
redesign. Each incentive is likely to have value under
certain conditions only, to be effective for different
periods of time and to have different kinds of problems
associated with its operation. Each factor, therefore,
should be considered on its own terms, rather than in relation to other factors. This, of course, is not to deny
that different factors interact. For example, various studies
have found that financial incentives have increased productivity considerably, but have had to be abandoned because
of problems created in other parts of the organisation
where financial incentives were not appropriate.

Of course, no introductory book of this kind can answer all the problems of a psychological kind which face the manager and workforce. Nor is it claimed that psychology is all-important or indeed even the most important aspect of improved organisational productivity. There can, however, be little dispute that for many organisations it is an important factor, and this book aims to make readers aware of the extent to which psychologists have been engaged in problems of organisational efficiency, so that they can make an informed judgement of the usefulness of psychology to their own particular situation.

1 Introduction and Historical Background

As our whole society depends for its well-being on the mass
production of a vast range of goods and services, it is
clear that understanding how production can be made more
efficient is of considerable importance to everyone, regard-
less of whether they are employers, employees or consumers
of the products of organisations.

For any particular organisation, one major concern is not
so much how much material is produced, but how efficiently
resources are used in the production process - productivity.
However, a number of writers have pointed out how difficult
it is to give an adequate account of productivity. Ruch and
Hershauer (1974), for example, note that the simplest
possible definition of productivity is 'output per unit of
time' where output may be measured in units of production,
service, money or some other measurable criterion. In other
words, Ruch and Hershauer note that, at its simplest, productivity can be regarded as the ratio of output to input,
as measured by hours. Unfortunately, this approach does not
necessarily take account of the factors (other than improved
efficiency of the employees) which may cause an increase in
output over time, such as investment in new machinery.
Furthermore, even an increase in output may not be econcmic-
ally justified. For example, if a car firm invested $10
million in a new plant that resulted in an increased production of one car per month, this would not be considered
a satisfactory state of affairs. Nevertheless, as Ruch and
Hershauer point out, in some situations a simple approach
to productivity is appropriate where, for example, the
organisation is concerned with the better utilisation of
manpower, *per se*.

One major problem with the concept of productivity as far
as the psychologist is concerned, is that output is sometimes extremely difficult to measure, particularly in
situations where there is no 'simple' product, such as in
teaching or in research, where quality is more important
than quantity, or, for example, in group working, where
the critical product cannot easily be attributed to any
individual within the organisation. Further, psychologists

often point out that 'short term' measures of productivity
may be misleading, for example, if high output in the short
term is 'bought' at the expense of 'worker well-being' and
satisfaction, then short term gains may be more than out-
weighed by long term losses in the form of industrial
conflict, absence behaviour and large-scale turnover.

As was noted above, the nature of the concept of
'productivity' is a complex one. The appropriate definition
will depend on the context in which it is used. As this book
focuses on the psychological aspects of productivity, however,
the term will generally be used in relation to the more
efficient use of human resources. The book will begin by
examining the theoretical and historical background to the
motivational aspects of organisational behaviour (Chapters
1 and 2). It will then examine those aspects of the work
itself which affect productivity (Chapter 3), aspects of
the work context which are important (Chapters 4 and 5),
individual differences in work motivation (Chapter 6), and
problems associated with organisations and their environment, such as absence, turnover, stress and conflict
(Chapter 7). Chapter 8 will look at a number of methods for
redesigning work to take account of some of the problems
noted in earlier chapters. The final chapter will look at
various methods of assessing performance. Whilst all of the
chapters are relevant to an understanding of industrial
productivity, Chapters 3-8 cover material of more direct
practical applicability.

HISTORICAL BACKGROUND AND PRESENT-DAY THEORIES OF WORK BEHAVIOUR

Man's attempt to increase the productivity of his fellow
man is of course as old as history itself. Among the
incentives used have been the lash, starvation, monetary
incentive, good marriage prospects, and freedom from
slavery. Present-day thinking on how to motivate people to
work can perhaps partly be attributed to F. W. Taylor (1911)
with his highly influential theory of scientific management.
Following Taylor, and in reaction to his theories, came the
human relations school, whose primary focus was on human
relationships in work. More recently, the focus has been in
terms of achieving satisfaction from the work itself, and
has as its major exponent Frederick Herzberg. The basic
philosophies of these approaches will be considered in turn.

SCIENTIFIC MANAGEMENT

Frederick Taylor, the founder of scientific management, was
an engineer whose concern for increased productivity led
him into a number of studies at the Bethlehem steel works.
His philosophy of management, published in *The Principles
of Scientific Management* in 1911, was based on these studies
although there is some controversy as to who actually carried
out the original studies and how they did so (Wrege and
Perroni, 1974).

The basic experiment reported by Taylor involved improvements in shovelling pig-iron into railway wagons. Using
principles of selection, time and motion, equipment redesign
and incentive payments, Taylor demonstrated the success of
his approach in the most spectacular way. He selected an
employee, Schmidt, and using these methods increased his
loading capacity by 400 per cent, from about twelve to
about fifty tons of pig-iron per day.

Much of the criticism against Taylor revolved round his
view of the importance of monetary incentives in improving
productivity. Such an approach is seen by many not only as
potentially manipulative of workers, but also as a degrading
approach to man, particularly as Taylor regarded man as
naturally lazy and needing financial incentives to overcome
his natural inclinations. In Taylor's defence, however, Fry
(1976) points out that he did appreciate that other
motivators than money might play a role in motivating workers,
but it is fair to argue that these other motivations did
not play any part in his theory of scientific management.
The role of money as an incentive is today of considerable
emotional significance, because to see man in purely
economic terms is to play down the importance of higher-
order needs for autonomy and self-actualisation. As Fry
points out, however, in the days in which Taylor was
advocating his theories, money was of greater significance
to the welfare of the average worker. It was because poverty
was still prominent that needs for growth and self-
actualisation had to take second place to the need for food
and shelter. Only with changing technology and increased
wealth does it become possible to look at work in terms of
higher-order satisfaction.

It is undoubtedly true that, after Taylor, money went
out of fashion as a motivator of increased productivity, at
least amongst organisational psychologists. A recent review
by Locke *et al.* (1980), however, suggests that for lower-
level workers at least, money is still a most important
motivator. Locke found average performance improvements in
the order of 30 per cent in studies reporting the effects

of payments systems, a percentage increase greater than any other form of incentive considered. Whilst it is fallacious to argue that this shows money to be the best incentive, (because studies examining financial incentives are conducted in different circumstances from those examining other motivators) such findings undoubtedly point to the importance of money as a major incentive to higher productivity, as Taylor argued.

A second major feature of Taylor's approach was to undertake a proper analysis of the job, rather than use the rough and ready methods then employed. His technique basically involved selecting the most skilled employees, analysing the movements they made, and timing the units of movement. From this, useful movements are then retained and useless movements rejected. Similarly, equipment was redesigned to capitalise on the best way of carrying out the job. This, of course, is the basis of time and motion study and, like the approach to monetary incentives, has resulted in strong hostile reactions. In particular, his method of devising work methods was based on the assumption that there was one best way to tackle a job, and that workers should be trained in this method. Those who could or would not fit in should be sacked. In other words, he ignored individual differences in ways of working. Whilst such an approach might work for very simple labouring tasks it was, as Rose (1978) points out, totally inapplicable to higher-order jobs where dexterity and attention are important. In ignoring individual differences, Taylor was again applying the approach of the engineer to human beings.

A third prong of Taylor's approach was to select the right men for the job, and where necessary dismiss those who proved to be incompetent or incapable of working at the required rate. In his selection of the right men for pig-iron handling, Taylor wrote, 'Now one of the first requirements of a man who is put to handle pig-iron as a regular occupation is that he shall be so stupid and phlegmatic that he more nearly resembles in his mental make-up the ox than any other type.' Even allowing for Fry's defence of Taylor, there does seem to be something less than egalitarian about Taylor's approach to organisational behaviour.

Taylor's scientific approach also contains other important aspects which have since been shown to be related to productivity. In particular, in setting goals for productivity, Taylor was a clear forerunner of present-day workers such as Locke, and in his insistence on adequate training in job performance, he also has had an influence which runs on to the present day. Indeed, despite his dated approach to people as machines, his identification of the importance of money, goals, selection, training and job analysis has been of major significance and should not be dismissed because of his manifest faults.

THE HUMAN RELATIONS APPROACH

In sharp contrast to Taylor's emphasis on economic man, the human relations school led by Elton Mayo came to emphasise the importance of human relationships at work, and sought to understand man at work in terms of how he related to those around him.

The human relations movement arose through work carried out by Mayo and his colleagues (Roethlisberger and Dickson, 1939) at the Hawthorne plant of the Western Electric Company in the 1920s. The first series of experiments, the illumination experiments, were started very much in the Taylor tradition, assuming that changes in physical features of the work situation would affect productivity. The expectation of the experiments was, of course, that improvements in illumination would improve productivity. What they found, in fact, was that practically any change in illumination increased productivity. In one experimental situation, for example, illumination was reduced until the group could hardly see what it was doing, but productivity still increased. Findings at such variance from expectation obviously needed an explanation and the next series of studies was set up to investigate what factors, other than physical working conditions, were affecting output in this strange way.

To investigate the problem further, a small group of girls was selected to assemble relays in what has become known as the relay assembly test room experiment. The girls were isolated from the rest of the factory. A number of changes were introduced including an incentive payments scheme, rest pauses, shorter working hours and so on, with a resultant increase in productivity over a two year period. Whilst the Hawthorne experimenters acknowledged the importance of money, the fact that productivity went up practically no matter what changes were made, including withdrawal of privileges, led the experimenters to conclude that social factors were of particular importance in increasing productivity. In particular, the investigators argued that friendly supervision and social relationships were of critical importance in increased productivity.

The importance of social factors, however, is by no means clear. During the experiment two girls engaged in talking to such an extent that they had to be dismissed and replaced by two other girls. Supervision became friendly after the

new girls started producing at a higher level. Friendly
supervision was thus the result, not the cause, of higher
productivity. Furthermore, the dismissal of the two girls
for talking is an indication of the disruptive effects on
productivity of social interaction under some circumstances.
A number of commentators have indicated that the role of
monetary incentives and worries about security in the context of the ongoing recession were considerably underplayed
in relation to the relay test room experiment.

Nevertheless it is reasonable to argue on the basis of a
further Hawthorne experiment, the bank-wiring observation
room experiment, that the Hawthorne studies did succeed in
demonstrating the importance of social factors on productivity. In this study there was clear evidence of social
pressures being brought upon individuals to produce at less
than the maximum level of their capabilities. Individuals
who exceeded norms were regarded as rate busters who were
a threat to the group. Hickson (1961), in a later study,
also noted how individuals under some circumstances
restricted their output if, for example, they felt that
management might reassess what was reasonable output
following higher productivity. (See Chapter 4).

It is, of course, hardly surprising that social factors
such as peer group pressure, group norms, friendly supervision and relationships affect productivity, although their
actual effects are often complex. The importance of the
Hawthorne study, despite its considerable limitations, was
to point to factors other than economic ones as important
to man in a working environment. The human relations school
was born which sought to improve the social situation, in
many cases drawing the erroneous conclusion that improvements
in the social situation would lead to increased job satisfaction, which in turn would lead to increased productivity.
The naivity of this approach can be seen in the relay test
room, where girls had to be dismissed for talking too much.
Again the emphasis of social factors and the underemphasis
of monetary award is clearly fallacious in relation to the
relay assembly test room experiment, where incentives in
terms of monetary reward almost certainly led to increased
productivity.

HERZBERG AND THE TWO-FACTOR THEORY OF MOTIVATION AND SATISFACTION

Although a number of writers have pointed to the importance
of the job itself as a critical factor in job behaviour and
attitudes, it was undoubtedly the work of Frederick

Herzberg which focused attention on this area. Herzberg *et al.* (1959) attacked the human relations view of human relationships as being of critical importance in job attitudes and motivation to work. He argued that factors such as social relationships were context factors which, when deficient, gave rise to feelings of dissatisfaction, but did not lead to job satisfaction when adequate. On the other hand, when intrinsic job aspects are satisfactory, for example, achievement in the job, they lead to job satisfaction. Their absence, the argument goes, does not lead to dissatisfaction, but rather to no satisfaction. In other words Herzberg argues that the causes of satisfaction and dissatisfaction are separate and distinct, and that only intrinsic job aspects motivate individuals to work well. The extrinsic aspects, when they are deficient, cause dissatisfaction, but when present do not motivate individuals to perform well, except possibly in the short term. Herzberg's emphasis on the job itself as a source of motivation and satisfaction has had considerable influence right up to the present day and his theories will be considered in greater detail, therefore, in the next chapter. Its considerable historical significance, however, is in seeing man as an individual in his own right, capable of, and wanting to achieve autonomy and to be self-fulfilling.

Few present-day workers would allow that any one of the historical approaches to human behaviour in industry has all the answers. Most accept that both the context and the content of the job are of critical importance in understanding industrial behaviour. Furthermore, there is a growing appreciation of individual differences in people's reactions to the various facets of the job. Of major significance too, is the emphasis on how the effects of each factor are contingent on a host of other factors in order to operate effectively as motivators or satisfiers. Money, for example, is unlikely to be an incentive where there is lack of trust, fear of unemployment following improved productivity, where there is no relation between effort and reward, and so on.

2 Theoretical Considerations

In considering psychological aspects of productivity, a major concern is how and why people are motivated to productive activity. This chapter will concern itself, therefore, with theoretical approaches to the question of motivation. As, however, the present book is intended to focus on *empirical* work on the psychological aspects of the productive process, only a brief account of the main theories of motivation will be considered. More detailed accounts can be had from, for example, Campbell and Pritchard (1976). Campbell and Pritchard have divided motivation theories into two; content and process theories. Content theories are concerned with what it is in the individual that sustains behaviour, in other words, what specific needs motivate people. Process theories, on the other hand, try to explain the process by which behaviour is sustained. This is done by giving an account of the way variables such as values, needs and expectations interact with what the job has to offer, to affect the individual's willingness to work. Some of the theories are concerned with job satisfaction, on the assumption that individuals are motivated to work to the extent that productivity can be improved by satisfying certain of the individual's needs, values or expectations. The validity of this assumption is considered at the end of the chapter. The various theories are considered in turn.

MASLOW'S NEED HIERARCHY THEORY

Possibly the most influential early need theory was that of Maslow (1943) who postulated a hierarchy of needs. The basic notion of the theory is that needs at a particular level in the hierarchy must be satisfied before needs at the next higher level start to motivate the individual. The need levels described by Maslow are:

(1) physiological needs

(2) security needs

(3) social needs

(4) esteem needs

(5) self-actualisation needs

An illustration of the theory might be seen by looking at
the behaviour of a man newly shipwrecked on a desert
island. The first step would be to find food and water,
then to build a shelter for defence. The next stage is
perhaps to search the island for inhabitants, both in order
to establish how secure he is and possibly to make social
contacts. Only after these basic needs are fulfilled is it
possible to pay attention to higher-order needs for self
fulfilment. In a job context, this would imply that only
after pay and security are satisfied will the employee
seek satisfaction from the work itself.

Intuitively appealing as the needs hierarchy theory is,
it has been subject to a considerable number of criticisms.
Perhaps the major criticism, for example by Locke (1976),
is that there is a lack of substantial evidence for a
hierarchy. However, whilst there might be no direct
evidence for Maslow's theory, there certainly is some
evidence which supports the theory. For example, Mann and
Williams (1962), in a study of job restructuring, found
that whilst satisfaction with the job itself, with
responsibility and with the opportunity to develop skills
all increased, overall job satisfaction did not, because
job restructuring led to great insecurity and fear of
losing jobs. In other words, a failure to satisfy lower-
level needs made the satisfaction of higher-order needs
difficult. Other supportive evidence for Maslow arises
from findings on the relationship between occupational
level and motivation. Those in lower-level jobs are more
likely to be motivated more by lower-order needs such as
money, whereas those at higher levels are more interested
in fulfiling higher-order needs for achievement (Centers
and Bugental, 1966). This may be because those in lower-
level jobs receive less money and therefore seek to
satisfy this need before they are in a position to look
for a job which gives satisfaction in its own right. On
the other hand, it might be that those in lower-level jobs

do not have the kind of job which can be satisfying in its own right and therefore seek financial satisfaction as compensation.

HERZBERG'S TWO-FACTOR THEORY

Related to Maslow's needs hierarchy theory is Herzberg's famous two-factor theory of job satisfaction. Herzberg distinguishes two classes of factor involved in job attitudes. The first class, motivators, includes factors which, if present in the working situation, lead to satisfaction, but which, if absent, do not lead to dissatisfaction. Such factors include the achievement of something worthwhile, recognition and advancement, and they correspond to the higher levels of Maslow's hierarchy of needs. These higher-order factors are separate and distinct from the second group, hygiene factors, which, when inadequate, lead to job dissatisfaction, but which, when adequate, do not lead to job satisfaction. Among the hygiene factors are pay, security, social relationships, and physical working conditions, and these correspond to the lower-order needs in Maslow's hierarchy.

In splitting the factors involved in job satisfaction in this way, Herzberg argues that the causes of job satisfaction and job dissatisfaction are separate and distinct. An analogy might be with the concepts of pleasure and pain. For the normal healthy individual, the mere absence of pain is not pleasurable of itself, although over the short term, of course, it may be that the relief of pain is considered pleasurable. Similarly, hygiene factors such as pay do not normally lead to feelings of satisfaction when they are adequate, except in the short term when they are newly introduced. On the other hand, when they are bad, they do lead to job dissatisfaction.

The thrust of Herzberg's argument is that such factors as pay and working conditions are context factors which have little to do with deriving satisfaction from the job. They are necessary conditions for, but do not of themselves produce, job satisfaction. On the other hand, job satisfaction is produced by the job itself allowing the individual to 'grow' psychologically, that is, achieve a worthwhile aim, achieve recognition for his efforts and so on, so that he can regard himself as a worthwhile individual. Herzberg argues that the absence of such motivators on the job does not, of itself, lead to dissatisfaction, but merely to a failure to achieve satisfaction.

Herzberg relates the concept of job satisfaction to the concept of mental health. Like job satisfaction and dissatisfaction, Herzberg argues that mental illness is not the obverse of mental health. The causes of mental illness are to be found in the strain imposed by the environment, whereas mental health involves reaction to factors involved in psychological growth. The mentally healthy individual will seek psychological growth from his job, and Herzberg (1966) implies that those who seek satisfaction from hygiene factors have characteristics which add up to neurotic personalities.

For Herzberg, much of the importance of the distinction between the two sets of factors lies in the implications for motivation. His argument is that only where the motivation to work comes from within can one really speak of motivation to work, and this motivation from within comes from seeking satisfaction from 'motivators'. Giving individuals rewards in the form of hygiene factors such as pay is making them 'move' because of external stimulus, and the problem with this is that it has constantly to be re-applied, as when one has to kick the dog every time one wishes him to move.

Evidence for and against the theory
What, then, is the evidence for Herzberg's theory? The basic study reported in his book *The Motivation to Work* (1959), investigated engineers and accountants, and one criticism of Herzberg has been that his conclusions are based on far too narrow a sample of the working population. To be fair to him, however, a large number of studies using his technique of data collection have generally confirmed his findings, for a great variety of samples. The basic technique employed by Herzberg is known as the critical incident technique in which workers are asked to think of a time when they felt exceptionally good or exceptionally bad about their present job or any other job they had had. These incidents were then classified and the results are shown in Figure 1.

The results show clearly that the hypothesised motivators are given more frequently, but not exclusively, when talking of satisfying incidents. Similarly, the hypothesised hygiene factors are given more frequently, but not exclusively, when talking of 'bad' incidents. Yet it is undoubtedly true that much of the controversy surrounding Herzberg's theory arises because of Herzberg's own ambiguity in interpreting his results. For example, Herzberg (1966, p.74) states:

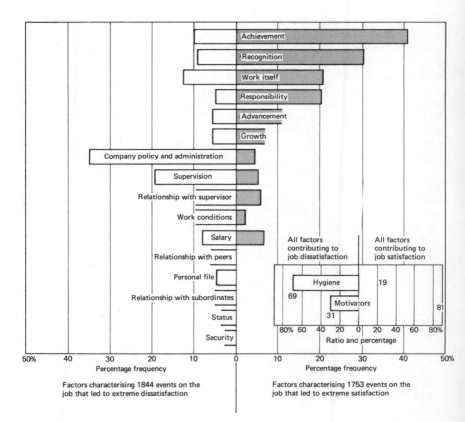

(Source Frederick Herzberg, 'One more time: How do you
motivate employees', *Harvard Business Review*, Jan/Feb
1968).

Figure 1. Motivating employees

'When the factors involved in the job dissatisfaction
events were coded, an entirely different set of factors
evolved. These factors were similar to the satisfiers
in their unidimensional effect. This time, however,
they served only to bring about job dissatisfaction
and were rarely involved in events that led to
positive job attitudes.'

Even a look at the diagram presented by Herzberg shows
that the term 'rarely' in this context is highly suspect.
'Salary', for example, extends considerably into
'satisfiers', 'recognition' extends considerably into

'dissatisfiers'.

King (1970) and Gardner (1977), in reviewing the work undertaken on Herzberg's theory, take up the point about the ambiguous way in which Herzberg states his theoretical position. King lists five possible interpretations of the theory, from the view that motivators contribute only to satisfaction and hygienes only to dissatisfaction (theory 1, the 'strong' theory), to the view that motivators contribute more to satisfaction than do hygienes and vice versa for dissatisfaction (theory 5, the 'weak' theory). Certainly, even on Herzberg's own results, it is difficult to see how the strong theory can be maintained. It might be added that such attempts have been made by arguing that satisfiers 'in the wrong place' are due to sampling error, but such a position does seem difficult to justify.

In fact, Herzberg does allow for the possibility that some individuals do gain satisfaction from hygiene factors. Those individuals are regarded by Herzberg as being unfortunates who 'have not reached the stage of personality development at which self-actualising needs are active'. From this point of view they are fixated at a less mature level of personal adjustment (Herzberg, 1966, p.80) and again (p.81), 'a hygiene seeker is not merely a victim of circumstances, but is motivated in the direction of temporary satisfaction'.

However, it could be argued that in many situations where psychological growth is not possible on the job, because it is dull and routine, a search for hygiene factors such as money is a healthy adjustment and in no way indicative of a neurotic personality. Furthermore, many studies have shown that it is not only the individual, but the culture from which the individual comes, which determines what he will seek from his job, and for some groups, money is seen as the most important aspect of the job. To take account of one's social relationships is not normally considered poor adjustment.

Besides this criticism, a large number of theorists have challenged Herzberg on a number of other issues. One of the most serious charges is that Herzberg's theory is method-bound, that is, when using the critical incident technique, the results tend to confirm the weak form of his theory at least. Using other methods, however, there have been consistent failures to confirm Herzberg's theory. The main argument against the critical incident technique is that it may induce respondents to blame unsatisfactory events on others, for example, their supervisor (hygiene factor), whilst taking credit themselves for the good things that happen, for example, claiming responsibility (motivator). Herzberg denies this by arguing that, in fact, when employees wish to make themselves look good they do sometimes blame motivators. Thus they claim that they have no responsibility, uninteresting work and so on. Herzberg's central argument is that the incidence of this kind of response is much less than is the response of dissatisfaction caused by hygiene factors. Actually, this argument of Herzberg's can be turned round and used to disprove the 'strong' theory of the two-factor model, which claims that only hygiene factors contribute to job dissatisfaction.

Another problem with the critical incident technique is that bad motivators may not occur as critical incidents. Being bored with one's job, for example, is not something that necessarily occurs at a critical point in time, it occurs from day to day. In other words, there is often no incident which makes the job boring, it is merely the repetition of what has gone before. Unless it can be shown that the aspects of motivators which cause dissatisfaction can be captured by the critical incident techniques, then, as King (1970) points out, other methods of establishing Herzberg's theory are required. As noted earlier, however, attempts to verify Herzberg's theory using other techniques have met with almost universal failure.

It must be pointed out that Herzberg was well aware of the possibility of methodological criticism of the critical incident technique. His reason for using the technique in the first place was the mistrust shown by a large number of psychologists of job satisfaction questionnaires, with their susceptibility to bias. Unfortunately, the fact that there are problems with other techniques does not necessarily lessen the problems of Herzberg's own technique.

Perhaps the major problem with Herzberg's theory is the evidence that motivators are important in both satisfaction and dissatisfaction (for example, Wall and Stephenson, 1970). Herzberg (1966, p.84) notes that satisfiers can act as dissatisfiers. He claims this occurs where there are failures in advancement, recognition, lack of responsibility and uninteresting work. Herzberg's explanation for this is that they are really failures of hygiene factors. For example, the respondent who declares that his unhappiest time on the job occurred when his boss did not recognise his work, is often saying that he lacks the comfort and security of an accepting supervisor. Herzberg provides no evidence for this and it is difficult to see what evidence he could provide. It might also be asked whether the converse could hold, that when individuals complain about

the lack of security and consideration provided by their
supervisors, they are really complaining that he is
undermining their chances of higher-order achievement!
Certainly we would argue that the evidence on motivators as
dissatisfiers, in particular, makes it difficult to accept
Herzberg's theory as an adequate account of job attitudes.

Whilst few people appear to allow that Herzberg has
provided evidence which unambiguously supports his theory,
there is little doubt that his emphasis on the importance
of motivators rather than hygiene factors as contributing
to job satisfaction is justified and has wide acceptance
(for example Locke, 1976). Furthermore, his argument that
those who do gain satisfaction from hygiene rather than
motivator factors are missing out on life is readily
accepted by researchers such as Locke, who see such
individuals as having values which conflict with their real
needs. One might argue, however, that in reality the
present opportunities for psychological growth on the job
are so limited and confined to so few people that it is
perhaps fortunate that so many seek only hygiene
satisfaction from the job.

It must not be thought that Herzberg's emphasis on
motivators means that he regards the adequate provision of
hygiene factors as unimportant - prevention of pain is as
important in its way as the provision of pleasure. In its
way, ensuring adequate hygiene factors is as essential for
well-being at work as the provision of motivators. Indeed,
Herzberg argues that it is only when hygiene factors such
as pay are adequate that one can begin to structure a job
so that motivators come to play a part in the individual's
satisfaction with his job.

In conclusion, it must not be thought that Herzberg's
theory is valueless, despite its defects. His emphasis on
intrinsic aspects of the job is in part a healthy reaction
to the 'human relations' school, which saw human relationships at work as the central area of concern for
organisational psychology. Whatever the defects of his
theory, thanks to Herzberg, no one will ever again be able
to ignore the importance of analysing characteristics of
the work itself in coming to an understanding of job
attitudes and motivation.

As far as its implications for motivation in industry
are concerned, Herzberg's theory has been of the greatest
importance in stressing the need for job redesign which
allows the individual to fulfill his higher-order needs.
Herzberg argues that job enrichment involves giving the
opportunity for greater responsibility, recognition,

advancement, and learning on the job. It also involves
removing controls on the individual, increasing his
accountability for his own work, giving him whole and
meaningful pieces of work, and giving new and more
challenging tasks. It would be fair to say that Herzberg
has been the major begetter of the job enrichment approach
to job redesign (see Chapter 8), whatever the limitations
of his theory.

PROCESS THEORIES

As previously noted, the theories of Maslow and Herzberg
have been described by Campbell and Pritchard (1976) as
content theories since they are basically interested in
identifying the factors which make for job satisfaction and
dissatisfaction. In contrast, there are a number of
theories called process theories, which aim to describe the
interaction between variables in their relationship to job
satisfaction and motivation.

Process theorists see job behaviour as being determined
not only by the nature of the job and its context, but by
the needs, values and expectations that individuals have
in relation to their job. For example, some individuals
have a greater need for achievement than others and where
a job gives no opportunity for achievement, such
individuals are likely to be more frustrated than those
whose need is less. Process theories, no less than
Herzberg's theory of job satisfaction, thus attack the
view that increases in job satisfaction simply arise by
giving individuals more of a variable that normally leads
to satisfaction - for example, more money. If an individual
expects a £10.00 pay rise, then a rise of £5.00 might well
be positively dissatisfying. Yet whilst all process
theorists agree that job attitude depends on the relationship between the individual and his work environment, there
are considerable differences of view as to which process
is of importance. At least three classes of theory have
been put forward; that job attitudes and behaviour are
determined by the extent of the discrepancy between what
the job offers and what the individual expects; what the
individual needs; and what the individual values.

EXPECTATIONS AND EQUITY THEORY

That expectations about our environment affect how we
behave is, of course, well known to everyone. One

important aspect of expectations is that they give to the
individual a frame of reference by which he judges the
world about him. If events in the world do not fit his
frame of reference, he is often unhappy and sometimes
changes his interpretation of the world in order to
accommodate awkward facts. In a job, we use frames of
reference when deciding, for example, what is reasonable
pay. We relate what we are getting to what others are
getting and if we find ourselves getting too little, we
become dissatisfied. This is the central notion of equity
theory which argues that we have a concept of what is just
reward for our efforts. What is just depends on the
individual assessing his inputs in terms of education,
skill, danger, effort and so on, and the job outputs in
terms of financial reward, satisfaction with the work, and
so on. Where the individual feels the two are fair in
relation to what other people's inputs and outputs are,
there is satisfaction.

What, then, happens when there is a discrepancy between
the individual's effort and reward, and those of others?
According to equity theory, the employee may well put less
into his work, take extended coffee breaks, give poorer
quality production and so on. He might decide to withdraw
from the situation or he might change his expectations to
be more in line with what he is receiving. Certainly the
evidence of Lawler and O'Gara (1967), for example, is that
when underpaid, individuals behave so as to increase
outcomes but to reduce inputs. Subjects in their experiment
increased the quantity but reduced the quality of their
work in order to increase payments for less input. Lawler
and O'Gara's experiment was conducted under conditions of
piece-rate payment. Where individuals are on an hourly
payment then quantity of productivity is also reduced (see,
for example Campbell and Pritchard, 1976).

What if the individual is given a higher reward than he
feels is equitable? Equity theorists would predict that
this too would cause dissatisfaction. In reviewing the
literature on overpayment, Pritchard, Dunnette and
Jorgenson (1972) regard the evidence as at best limited. A
number of studies have failed to find any effect of over-
reward, although one of Pritchard *et al.'s* studies did
suggest that over-reward led to dissatisfaction. Campbell
and Pritchard (1976) note that there are a number of
methodological problems in studying the effects of
overpayment. For one thing, manipulating variables to make
individuals feel overpaid is often accompanied by threats
to the individual's self esteem, for example by telling

subjects that they are not qualified to do the task. Other problems involve the kind of set that is often induced in equity experiments to increase quality at the expense of quantity in some experiments, and job security is threatened by emphasising lack of qualifications. This factor, rather than feelings of inequity, may induce higher productivity.

In any case, as Pritchard (1969) points out, when individuals are overpaid, it is likely that they will develop 'coping mechanisms' so that they can accept excessive payments without too many qualms. Pritchard (1969) argues that in industrial situations, where there is over-payment, individuals will feel that others are underpaid and that it is the fault of the system. Certainly it seems intuitively likely that it is easier to live with a situation in which one is overpaid compared with one in which one is underpaid.

The evidence on equity theory is clearly not straight-forward. It appears able to account for some aspects of satisfaction and motivation but not others. It is also not clear how individuals come to evaluate their inputs in terms of education and skill level, for example, nor is it clear how individuals play off one set of rewards, such as job satisfaction against others such as money. Locke (1976) argues that the problem with equity theory is not so much that it has been shown to be wrong but that it is so loose that it is able to account for anything. (For an 'easy to read' review of findings on equity theory, see Carrell and Dittrich, 1978).

REFERENCE GROUP THEORY

As noted above, an essential aspect of equity theory is that the individual compares his inputs and outputs from a job with those of others, such as his friends, his work-mates, people in his industry and so on, before deciding whether or not he is equitably treated. Many theorists, such as Hulin and Blood (1968), have argued that an understanding of the group to which the individual relates (reference group) is therefore of critical importance in understanding job satisfaction.

A study of Klein and Maher (1966) suggests the importance of reference groups. They found that college-educated managers were less satisfied with their pay than non-college-educated managers. It is suggested that part of the explanation is that college-educated managers have higher expectations of pay because of their education and that they related their salary to a different reference

group, namely a highly educated and highly paid group,
compared with those of non-college-educated managers who
compared their salaries with other non-college-educated
and lower paid individuals.

As Korman (1977) points out, however, reference group
theory leaves many questions unanswered. How, for example,
do individuals choose which reference group to relate to?
Why do reference groups have the expectations they do? What
constitutes a reference group? Clearly, individuals differ
in the reference group they choose because of their own
individual personalities. Newcomb (1958), for example, in
his famous study of attitude change amongst girls from
conservative backgrounds entering a liberal American
college, found that whilst many girls took on the liberal
views in vogue in the college, a number of girls took their
parents as reference points and remained conservative in
outlook. Such girls often appeared isolated and unable to
relate to other students, and it may be that they were
basically insecure individuals. On the other hand, Korman
suggests that those most influenced by their reference
groups are those with low self-esteem. Those with high
self-esteem can afford to ignore the reference group to a
larger extend and 'do their own thing'. At present the only
certainty is that reference group theory is at best a
partial explanation of how individuals regard the inputs
and rewards of the job as equitable. It is clear, therefore,
that expectations based on reference groups must be
supplemented by a knowledge of personality factors and of
individual needs and values in any assessment of what the
individual considers equitable.

EXPECTANCY THEORIES OF MOTIVATION

Expectations also play a major role in expectancy theories
of motivation. Whilst there are a number of variations of
expectancy theory, the main characteristic of all is that
individuals are thought to be motivated to work to the
extent that they see a relationship between their efforts
and the rewards which they value, which come from
performing their work. Thus individuals will be motivated
to work to the extent that they expect a relationship
between job performance and rewards (instrumentality). In
some situations for example, where working in groups, it
might well be that the individual's efforts will count for
little in determining overall performance if other members
of the group are unwilling to work or where they are
incompetent. No matter how competent a goal scorer in a

football team is, if his colleagues are too incompetent to give him the ball in a goal-scoring position, his efforts will usually be wasted. In other situations, even where there is a relationship between effort and performance, it might not motivate the individual to work, if performance does not result in the rewards which are valued. If, for example, the individual values financial rewards, but he is paid no more providing twenty units than five units, it is unlikely that he will work hard to produce the extra amount.

In deciding how hard to work, therefore, the individual will assess three aspects; whether his effort will lead to performance, whether performance will lead to rewards, and the value (valence) of the offered rewards to him. One essential aspect of expectancy theory which will be discussed later is that rewards, when valued and achieved, give rise to satisfaction, so that satisfaction is perceived to flow from performance and not to cause performance. To some extent, however, this account of the causal relationship between performance and satisfaction is an oversimplification since the experience of satisfaction is likely to feed back to affect future performance. Thus if one has satisfaction from previous performance, this is likely to increase the chances of performing the job again to obtain further satisfaction. Of course, expectations are not the only factor which affect performance. Ability is an important factor, and this depends both on individual factors such as intelligence and special aptitudes, and on adequate training.

Because rewards lead to satisfaction and satisfaction feeds back to affect future performance, factors which affect satisfaction are also important in motivating performance, according to expectancy theory. Two aspects of satisfaction are incorporated in most models; equity of rewards, and satisfaction of needs and values. Equity theory is thus incorporated into expectancy theory rather than being a competing theory.

Lawler and Porter (1969), in their account of expectancy theory, make a distinction between intrinsic and extrinsic rewards. They argue that the relationship between intrinsic rewards and performance is likely to be closer than that between extrinsic rewards and performance, because intrinsic rewards (such as satisfaction with the job itself) flow directly from job performance, whereas extrinsic rewards (such as pay) are given some time after performance. There are at least two flaws with this argument, however. First, in high-level jobs, in particular, intrinsic reward in the form of achievement of goals may

only come a considerable time after performance, for
example, in breeding prize dogs, setting out an advertising
campaign and so on. Second, it does seem reasonable to
suppose that it is not so much the immediacy of rewards,
but their importance, which will affect effort and
performance.

There has been a considerable literature which has
reported tests of expectancy theory, and a number of reviews
of the literature have recently been published (for example
Campbell and Pritchard, 1976; Heneman and Schwab, 1972).
Campbell and Pritchard note that various aspects of the
theory are fairly well supported by empirical evidence. For
example, in terms of methods of wage payments, hourly-paid
individuals are likely to perceive a low relationship
between performance and reward compared to incentive-paid
individuals so that, other things being equal, one would
expect incentive schemes to lead to higher productivity. As
will be seen in Chapter 4, such an assumption is largely
borne out.

Campbell and Pritchard also note evidence that the
relationship between effort and performance is also affected
by expectancies. Arvey (1972) varied expectancies between
effort and performance and found that those with low
expectancies performed less well than those with high
expectancies although, as Campbell and Pritchard note, the
evidence in this area is somewhat thin.

As far as the relationship between valence (attractiveness
of outcome) and behaviour is concerned, Campbell and
Pritchard note that the results are mixed and that no
definite conclusion can be drawn on the predictive utility
of the valence function of the model. To some extent this
problem overlaps that of a failure to find a relationship
between performance and satisfaction which will be
considered presently.

There are, unfortunately, a number of difficulties with
expectancy theory. In particular, the theory assumes a
rational assessment of probabilities of expectancy,
instrumentality and valence, and that the individual will
choose between different alternatives. However, there is
ample evidence that individuals do not make exhaustive
evaluations of alternatives, but often choose the first
alternative which gives an adequate outcome. It may be, of
course, that the extent to which individuals will take the
trouble to make assessments of outcomes depends on how
important these outcomes are to the individuals.

Campbell and Pritchard in fact note a large number of
factors which present difficulties for the theory, including

problems of measuring such factors as effort, problems of
the reliability of findings, problems of low levels of
magnitude of effects, and problems of showing the effects of
particular variables in some situations only. Given the
complexity of the theory, however, it is not surprising that
it has some difficulties; what is perhaps more important is
that the theory has led to a considerable amount of useful
work, and has identified some important problems. In
particular, it has shown that understanding work behaviour
and the relationships between variables depends on a large
number of factors, so that any expectations of finding
simple answers to problems can be seen as unrealistic.

THE RELATIONSHIP BETWEEN PRODUCTIVITY AND JOB SATISFACTION

One major focus of theoretical interest to expectancy and
indeed other theorists is the relationship between
productivity and rewards or satisfaction. In their review
of the field, Schwab and Cummings (1970) argue that the
hypothesised relationship between performance and satisfaction has generated the greatest amount of research and
theoretical interest in organisational behaviour. Whatever
the exact nature of the relationship between satisfaction
and productivity, most theoretical formulations support the
notion of a causal relationship. The human relations school,
for example, has been attributed with the view that satisfaction leads to improved performance so that increasing
satisfaction will result in better performance. From this
it follows that not only is improved satisfaction of value
in its own right, it has beneficial economic implications.
As Schwab and Cummings point out, however, this view of the
human relations position is somewhat overstated, and
Roethlisberger (1941) was certainly aware of limitations in
any assumption regarding a direct causal link between
satisfaction and productivity. Nevertheless, it is certainly
a generally held view that the human relations philosophy
involved assertions about the causal link between
satisfaction and productivity.
  Herzberg's two-factor theory is unambiguous about a causal
link between satisfaction and productivity, arguing that
performance comes from satisfying the motivators such as
'challenging jobs', 'recognition' and so on, and that only
where the individual is internally motivated will this lead
to improved productivity over the long term.
  A radically different view of the relationship between
satisfaction and performance is taken by expectancy

theorists such as Lawler and Porter (1969) who see performance causing satisfaction rather than the other way around.
Thus performance leads to rewards from which the individual
will derive satisfaction. What makes individuals perform is
the anticipated satisfaction from performance, provided they
see a relationship between effort and performance and
performance and desired rewards. At the point at which the
individual performs, therefore, he is not necessarily
satisfied, but merely anticipating satisfaction. An example
might be of an individual who values promotion and
recognition, and realises that this will only come about by
successfully completing a boring job. Whilst undertaking
this job he anticipates the rewards of performance, but the
state he is in is not one of satisfaction; that comes only
once he has performed and been rewarded with recognition.
Expectancy theory is in part complicated because satisfaction
from rewards is thought to feed back to give the individual
a greater desire to perform again, in other words, to
obtain further rewards.

Whilst the causal link between performance and satisfaction
has a reasonably clear underpinning in terms of performance
leading to rewards because anticipation of rewards will
lead to performance, it is often claimed that the rationale
for a causal relationship - that satisfaction leads to
performance - is not clear. There are, however, at least
two reasons to suppose that such a causal relationship is
reasonable. In the first place, as Organ (1977) points out,
studies based on equity theory would lead one to suppose
that where individuals feel they are inequitably treated,
they will reduce productivity, especially under hourly-paid
systems. Feeling dissatisfied before starting to perform,
therefore, may affect willingness to perform and the nature
of performance. In expectancy theory terms, the anticipation
of inadequate reward may cause dissatisfaction before
performance and this results in a 'satisfaction causes
performance' relationship. On the other hand, where
individuals feel equitably treated, they will feel obliged
to perform well in order to reciprocate the good treatment
they have received. A second reason for supposing that
satisfaction may affect performance is that there is a
reasonably established relationship between satisfaction
and job involvement. Where one is satisfied with a job, it
may result in greater involvement with the job and identification with the goals of the organisation (see Chapter 3).
All other things being equal, the more involved in the job,
the more time the individual is likely to spend on the job
and the more there will be a tendency to produce.

Despite these very good theoretical reasons why a

relationship between satisfaction and performance should
exist, the evidence for a relationship of any kind has been
singularly unsatisfactory. In their famous review on the
topic, Brayfield and Crockett (1955) concluded that

> 'there is little evidence that employee attitudes of
> the type usually measured in morale surveys bear any
> simple - or for that matter appreciable - relationship
> to performance on the job'.

Their review of some fifty studies, and Vroom's (1964)
review of twenty three studies in which he found the same
lack of relationship clearly needs an explanation.

One suggestion for the failure to find a relationship
between satisfaction and productivity is given by Herzberg.
He argues that only motivators are contributors to productivity, but that most measures of satisfaction include
measures of both motivators and hygienes. Apart from the
fact that Herzberg's theory has been noted to be speculative,
and that the distinction between motivators and hygienes is
somewhat difficult to sustain, there is another major reason
to suspect Herzberg's explanation. It has been clearly shown
that by no means all individuals wish to have higher-order
satisfactions at work and that, at least in the short term,
extrinsic rewards provide satisfaction as a result of
performance. Arguing that only motivators should be involved
in the performance-satisfaction relationship therefore seems
unreasonable.

More reasonable accounts of a failure to find a relationship between satisfaction and performance are given by
expectancy theorists. In the first place, satisfaction
depends on obtaining valued rewards, and these do not
necessarily come from the performance of a job. Indeed,
social rewards such as the enjoyment of social interaction
with friends may be positively counter-productive, as in the
case of the extended tea break or excessive talking. To the
extent that measures of overall job satisfaction include
satisfaction with those job aspects unrelated to productivity,
one would expect any relationship between performance and
satisfaction to be limited.

More important than even this possibility, according to
expectancy theory, is that satisfaction will not arise from
performance unless performance results in valued rewards.
In the case of performance depending on a machine rather
than on individual effort, for example, the individual's
satisfaction is irrelevant to performance. This would also
be the case where the individual's efforts did not lead

directly to performance, as in the case of some kinds of
group task, where the efforts of any individual are submerged
by the efforts of others. In such a case, even were
satisfaction to increase effort, it would not affect
performance.

There are still more factors which are likely to mask any
underlying relationship between satisfaction and performance.
Even if the relationships between effort and performance and
between performance and rewards are positive, and the value
of rewards high, the individual may not have the ability to
attain high performance. The budding concert pianist, for
example, may treasure his own performance but may not be
a good piano player.

Another factor which negates any underlying relationship
between performance and satisfaction occurs where it is not
clear what performance leads to rewards, and where the
relationship between performance and rewards, although
positive, is not made clear to the individuals concerned.
There is at least one reported case of a failure in an
incentive payments scheme because the employees were not
made aware of the relationship between performance and
rewards. (Cammann and Lawler, 1973).

Yet another reason for a failure to find a relationship
between performance and satisfaction is that performance
often takes place because of pressure from supervisors, fear
of losing one's job or fear of poor references if one wishes
to leave for other employment. Indeed the more one is
dissatisfied and wishes to leave an organisation, the more
one may try to perform well to impress other potential
employers.

Finally, performance-satisfaction relationships may fail
to appear because the rewards offered by the organisation
are not the rewards wanted by the employees. Where, for
example, individuals are economically oriented but where the
rewards are purely in terms of the intrinsic nature of the
job itself, one would not necessarily expect satisfaction
to be related to productivity. (See e.g. Locke *et al.*, 1976).

For all the reasons outlined above, it seems reasonable
to conclude that few studies are fair tests of whether there
is an underlying relationship between satisfaction and
productivity, although the large number of studies failing
to find a substantial relationship do show that factors
other than satisfaction are usually of greater importance
in determining performance in an organisation.

Whilst the relationship between satisfaction and productivity is unclear, it should not be concluded that job
satisfaction of the employees is of no economic signifi-

cance. Gruneberg (1979), for example, notes that studies
have consistently found satisfaction to be related to staff
turnover, a factor of economic significance and there is at
least the possibility that in some situations absence and
counter-productive behaviour are related to job satisfaction.
Writers such as Steers (1977) also note that a satisfied
workforce might have some intangible economic benefits, such
as a willingness to co-operate more with management in
negotiations, in the introduction of new ideas and so on,
and various writers have reported that strike behaviour is
most commonly attributed to dissatisfaction with pay. These
factors will be considered further in Chapter 4.

3 The Job itself and Productivity

INTRODUCTION

In the last chapter it was noted that many writers, such as Herzberg (1966), regard the key to motivating individuals to work to be in making the job itself more worthwhile. Where the individual sees the job as being worthwhile he will become motivated from within, rather than requiring increased external rewards such as money. Whilst the importance of extrinsic rewards will be considered in Chapter 4, this chapter will look at these aspects of the job itself which have been shown to be important in relation to productivity. The topics considered in this chapter are success, achievement and goal-setting, recognition, feedback, the application of skill and job involvement.

SUCCESS, ACHIEVEMENT AND GOAL SETTING

One of the factors considered by many writers such as Herzberg (1966) to be essential in motivating individuals is success and achievement on the job. In other words, the achievement of goals, and the recognition by others that goals have been achieved, is an important part of job performance. The importance of achieving goals has been particularly emphasised by Locke (1968) who, in a series of laboratory studies, demonstrated that being set specific goals led to higher productivity than being set non-specific goals, and that being set hard goals led to higher performance than being set easy goals. These findings are considered below.

Specific v general goals

In reviewing the literature on goal-setting and performance, Latham and Yukl (1975) note a number of studies which have shown, in an organisational setting, the advantages of setting specific goals as far as productivity is concerned. Studies such as those of Latham and Baldes (1975) have consistently found that productivity is higher were specific targets are set, rather than the individual being told to

'do his best' or not being told anything about expected
productivity. The study of Latham and Baldes demonstrated
the effect of production improvements in a most dramatic way
in terms of financial savings. Lorry drivers, who were set
a specific, hard goal, improved performance to such an
extent that there was a saving in expenditure on trucks
alone of quarter of a million dollars, compared with the
expenditure which would have been needed to reach the level
of production attained without goal-setting. In their
review, Latham and Yukl note than ten out of eleven field
studies have shown improvements in performance as a result
of setting specific goals.

Apart from the fact that specific goal-setting *per se*
appears to have a considerable effect on production, a
number of other variables also appear to affect the
relationship between goal-setting and productivity. Amongst
the most important of these appears to be goal difficulty,
where the evidence suggests that setting hard goals leads
to greater productivity than setting easier goals. Latham
and Yukl review a number of studies which support the view
that harder goals lead to high productivity, and a recent
study by Becker (1978) illustrates nicely the effect of
setting hard goals on performance. One group of families
were asked to save 20 per cent of their electricity
consumption, a control group were asked to save only 2 per
cent. The two groups were each subdivided so that one
sub-group with a 20 per cent target received frequent feedback on how well it was getting on, whilst the other 20 per
cent group received no feedback; similarly for the 2 per
cent saving group. Only in the 20 per cent group with feedback was there significant saving, indicating not only the
importance of setting difficult goals, but the importance
of feedback on the progress being made. (The question of
feedback is considered later).

Goal acceptance
A number of qualifications have to be made, however, to the
generalisation that setting hard goals leads to higher
productivity than setting easy goals or no goals at all.
One major problem is that goals have to be accepted as
worthwhile and reasonable by the individual before goal-
setting is effective, and a number of studies have shown
that individual factors are important in determining whether
or not goals are likely to be accepted. Yukl and Latham
(1978), for example, found that those with a high need for
achievement set higher goals and that participation in
goal-setting for such individuals resulted in higher

acceptance of goals. They also found that whether or not
goals were accepted depended on whether individuals thought
that the achievement of goals led to outcomes they thought
desirable. Clearly, setting individuals goals which, when
achieved do not give any rewards, is unlikely to motivate
high performance. This is also true where the goals which
are achieved do not give rewards which are considered
equitable in relation to effort. Nor obviously, are goals
likely to be accepted which are perceived of as beyond the
skills or abilities of individuals (that is, where goals
are unreasonable in themselves).

Another factor which has been shown to affect whether or
not an individual is likely to accept a hard goal is
previous success on the task. Zander and Newcomb (1967),
for example, note that groups which had previously been
successful in attaining goals were more likely to regard
new goals as more important and more reasonable than groups
which have failed previously. In other words, success on
previous tasks increases the level of aspiration of
individuals. From a practical point of view, therefore,
setting goals that are difficult must be tempered by taking
account of what is reasonable to expect, if there is not to
be a risk of failure affecting future goal-setting. Indeed
if goals set are too difficult, this may be rejected as
unrealistic. On the other hand, success and failure need
not be all or nothing with respect to goal-setting. In
Becker's (1978) study, for example, when one set of
families were set the goal of saving 20 per cent of their
current electricity consumption, savings were in the region
of 13-15 per cent. They were, therefore, still highly
successful in relation to previous consumption and in
relation to other groups not set such difficult targets.

There is evidence that goal acceptance, if it is to
continue, has to be sustained by various means. Ronan et al.
(1973), for example, found that only where a supervisor was
present to supervise goals closely was there a continued
acceptance of goals, and several studies, for example
Ivancevich (1977), found the effects of goal-setting to
dissipate over time. Presumably the original goal becomes
less salient with time in the absence of reinforcement.

Assigned versus participate goal-setting
One way which has been advocated for increasing goal
acceptance is allowing individuals to participate in
decision-making concerning goal-setting. In their review
of participation, however, Latham and Yukl (1975) note that
while a number of studies have shown that participation

does have an effect, the findings are not entirely convincing. However, a later study of scientists and engineers by
Latham *et al*. (1978) found that participation in goal-
setting affected performance and that those participating
in goal-setting set higher goals. The findings on participation in goal-setting tend to suggest that fears concerning
individuals setting low and easily attained goals if left
to themselves are not well founded. On the basis of their
results Latham *et al*. conclude that participation in
goal-setting is likely to lead to higher set goals and that
this in turn leads to greater effort in attempting to
achieve these goals. One interesting finding in their study
was that even though those participating in goal setting
did in fact set higher goals than those not participating,
they did not perceive the goals they helped to set as
harder.

It must be said, however, that a number of studies (for
example, Ivancevich, 1977) have failed to find any
difference between assigned and participative goal-setting.
Thus it might be that where goals are set by someone
respected as an expert, success may be more important when
achieved than goals set by an individual who has no means
of knowing whether goal achievement is significant. In any
case, whether goals are set by participation or assignment,
many studies have found goal-setting superior to no
goal-setting at all, for example Ivancevich (1977).

Goal-setting associated incentives
One issue raised in the study of goal-setting is whether
feedback has a motivational effect on performance, over and
above affecting the goals which individuals accept. It is
of course the case that feedback can give information which
enables the individual to correct errors (see p. 36). Whilst
some authors have suggested that feedback and monetary
incentives have their effects through influencing
goal-setting, and various studies have failed to find any
effect of feedback *per se* (for example Latham *et al*., 1978),
the studies of Kim and Hamner (1976) and Becker (1978) both
suggest that performance feedback is a factor which
operates together with goal-setting to motivate performance.
As noted earlier, in the Becker experiment only the group
with difficult goals and with regular feedback improved
its performance. Of course, it may be the case that feedback can also affect goal-setting, and Yukl and Latham
(1978) found that when secretaries/typists in their study
were given feedback about their previous performance, it
significantly affected the level at which subsequent goals

were set.

As with feedback, Locke (1968) suggests that monetary
incentives affect performance through goal-setting, but
again the evidence would suggest that monetary incentives
and goal-setting effects are independent (for example,
Terborg and Miller, 1978). Indeed in their study, Terborg
and Miller caution that 'goal-setting procedures should not
replace financial incentives as a means of increasing
performance'.

Berlew and Hall (1966) place the findings on goal-setting
within the context of role theory. They argue that the
goals set by an organisation give the individual a set of
expectations concerning his role behaviour. In particular,
for a young manager, the expectations of the company
constitute an important class of role forces impinging on
him. In their study Berlew and Hall showed that what the
company initially expected of new recruits, and subsequent
performance and success were significantly and positively
correlated. The practical implication is of course
identical to that of goal-setting studies.

A study by White *et al.* (1977) indicates that incentives
other than goal-setting and achievement might be operating
in most goal-setting situations. White *et al.* note that in
most goal-setting situations, there is increased evaluation
of performance by others and the increased apprehension
caused by this might be an additional source of motivation.
They did find evidence for their hypotheses, and suggested
that this evaluation process is an additional motivator in
goal-setting situations, rather than an explanation of
goal-setting phenomena.

Problems with goal-setting
There is little doubt that goal-setting has been demonstrated
to be effective, in both the laboratory and in the field,
in improving productivity. The findings clearly indicate
that specific, hard but attainable goals which are accepted
by individuals as their own, lead to increased performance
compared with situations in which individuals are merely
instructed to 'do their best'. Steers and Porter (1974), in
considering how goal-setting operates, place the various
findings within an expectancy theory framework, indicating
that expectancy theory is at least compatible with other
theories of motivation. For example, they account for the
advantages of specific as opposed to general, vague goals
in terms of allowing the individual to see more clearly the
relationship between his effort and performance. Latham *et
al.* (1978) suggest that specificity might work by enabling
the individual to translate effort into performance by

choosing more appropriate action plans.

As far as participation in decision-making is concerned, Steers and Porter suggest that this may affect ego involvement and place a higher value on goal attainment. However, participation may also operate by taking account of the individual's particular needs and values in relation to a goal, and also more realistically relate skills, abilities and levels of aspiration to the goals set.

As far as the difference between performance on easy and difficult but accepted goals is concerned, it does seem possible that where easy goals are seen in terms of implications for self-esteem, they are not thought particularly desirable when attained. Again it may be the case that once an easy goal is achieved there is a reluctance to go on and 'overachieve'. For example, when writing a chapter in a book, it is our experience that if a particular section is finished before a self-imposed deadline, no further work on the book is undertaken for the day.

Setting goals which are too easy may therefore have detrimental effects on productivity, as may setting goals too difficult, which are then not accepted. Latham and Yukl (1975) note a number of other problems with goal-setting. In particular, a great deal of work has been carried out in tasks which are easy to specify and measure. With complex tasks, such as management, it is clearly a much more complex matter to set out realistic goals. Furthermore, in attempting to do this for complex tasks, those aspects of the job which can easily be specified are attended to, but with possible detrimental consequences for the aspects of the job not goal-centred. Job interdependence, too, may make goal-setting difficult, in that the actual performance of one individual may not be determined by that individual's efforts. Finally, individual differences have been shown to affect the likelihood of accepting difficult goals, and these must be borne in mind when considering goal-setting procedures. The systematic use of goal-setting in organisations, (management by objectives (MBO)) is considered in Chapter 8.

RECOGNITION

In the last section, the question of achievement and success was considered in relation to goals often set by the individual himself. As Gruneberg (1979) has noted, however, achievement for many individuals requires sooner or later external validation if it is to be sustained. This can take the form of verbal praise from a superior, the passing of

some external criterion such as an examination, or in
organisations, promotion. Promotion does not, of course,
necessarily signal external recognition of past achievements.
On the one hand, some individuals are promoted because of
seniority, on the other, individuals are promoted because
they are perceived of as having high potential in a higher-
grade job, rather than excellence in their present position.
In a great many cases, however, promotion for individuals
is a consequence of achievement in their present positions,
in the hope that it is predictive of superior performance
in a higher position.

There are, however, a considerable number of problems in
the fair handling of promotion procedures, involving for
the most part those problems discussed under performance
assessment. Promotions, for example, usually depend on the
assessment of superiors, and to the extent that such
assessment is based on subjective criteria, it is open to
doubt and challenge. Interpersonal relationships, for
example, may colour judgements or at least may be perceived
to colour judgements, leading to feelings of hostility in
those not promoted. Again even 'objective' criteria are
problematic in situations where the skills required at a
higher level are not those best suited to lower levels. A
highly competent nurse, for example, might be less suited
to an increased administrative load in a promoted post
compared to a 'less good' nurse in a technical sense.
Hackman and Suttle (1977) note that other aspects of the
promotion decision process can lead to problems. They note,
for example, that where committees make decisions in secret,
this lack of accountability may make for less adequate
decision-making. There may, for example, be less energy in
making the decision, and personal prejudices have less
chance of coming to light.

Whilst it is argued here that promotion is an integral
part of the individual's assessment of his own achievement
and is therefore an intrinsic aspect of the job, it is
equally possible to argue that promotion is an extrinsic
reward like money, held out by the organisation as an
incentive for good job performance. Obviously, one problem
with promotion as an incentive is that in times of
organisational contraction or indeed stability, the
possibilities of promotion are likely to be severely
limited. Holding out possibilities of career advancement
only to fail to meet expectations through no fault of the
individual is clearly a major problem for such organisations.
As Porter, Lawler and Hackman (1975) note, an organisation
that retains its employees only by giving extensive

extrinsic rewards can end up with a group of apathetic
uninvolved people. This is especially true where expectations
regarding rewards are not fulfilled. In such a situation one
would expect those who can, to leave the organisation, and
Porter and Steers (1973) note that failed expectations
regarding promotion are a determinant of turnover. Furthermore, the least satisfied are likely to be those who have
put most into their work, and are likely to be those,
therefore, who are most attractive to other organisations.
In other words, the effect of not giving promotions will be
to lose the most able individuals, whilst retaining those
who have put least into the organisation and are therefore
less likely to find other jobs. To the extent that the least
productive individuals are likely to be retained when there
is limited scope for promotion, the operation of an adequate
promotions procedure can be seen to have important
implications for productivity.

As to the question of whether the prospect of promotion
makes people more productive, there seems little doubt that
career advancement is a goal of a large number of
individuals. Not only is it an external validation of
achievement, promotion normally carries with it financial
reward and increased status. Furthermore, as the evidence
on goal-setting indicates, where individuals take on a goal,
there is little doubt that productivity is greater than
where no goal exists. Again the findings show that goals, to
be effective, should be attainable and preferably they should
be clearly specified. Clearly, therefore, where promotion
is used as an incentive these factors should be borne in
mind.

As noted above, recognition need not involve formal
recognition in the form of promotion. Praise from peers and
superiors is also an external validation of achievement.
Locke (1976), for example, notes that all individuals value
praise from colleagues and superiors. As far as implications
for productivity are concerned, the study of Meyer *et al.*
(1965) indicated that positive social reinforcement at an
appraisal interview had positive effects on future
productivity. On the other hand, where individuals were
criticised, they tended to become defensive about their
jobs and productivity did not subsequently improve.

Feedback

As noted earlier, praise from one's superior has the effect
of providing feedback to the individual that the goals he
has reached are considered significant in relation to the
task, and such praise is likely to increase the individual's

self-esteem. Feedback on job performance is considered by
many investigators, for example Hackman and Lawler (1971),
as a critical aspect of improving job performance. Hackman
and Lawler, in fact, consider feedback to be one of the
four core aspects of a job, and found the degree of feedback
given related to job satisfaction.

Feedback on performance has two potential effects. As
noted when considering goal-setting, it may affect the
individual's motivation so that he will, under positive
feedback, work harder (motivational feedback), or it may
affect the way the individual carries out a task (informational feedback). For example, being told that shells are
landing 200 yards too far behind enemy lines is likely to
lead to a readjustment of gun sights to take account of the
new information. Informational feedback may also convey to
the individual how much more effort is needed to reach a
goal.

A number of studies have shown the positive effects of
feedback on subsequent performance. Gibbs and Brown (1955)
for example, found that their subjects, set a boring task
but allowed to see the progress they were making, produced
at a significantly higher rate than a group not given
feedback on their performance and similar results were
obtained by Hundal (1969) in a group of Indian workers. In
a recent study by Runnion, Johnson, and McWhorter (1978)
the introduction of feedback was responsible for reducing
the turnaround time of trucks delivering to a textile
company from sixty-seven to thirty-eight minutes, even
though feedback was subsequently reduced. Savings in
electricity through feedback were demonstrated in the
studies of Becker (1978), and Seligman and Darley (1977),
where feedback of electricity consumption resulted in a 10
per cent saving in later consumption. Whilst some studies
(for example, Locke and Bryan, 1969) have failed to find
any effects of knowledge of results alone, the basic
argument is not so much about the value of knowledge of
results (feedback) but how the feedback operates. As noted
previously, for example, feedback affects the goals which
individuals are willing to accept, and it may well be that
where individuals receive feedback on how they are doing,
they will set themselves higher goals which are challenging
yet possible to meet. In other words, feedback is necessary
to effect a change in level of aspiration.

Praise

There is evidence that feedback has motivational effects
over and above that of goal-setting, perhaps of letting

the individual see the progress he is making towards the
goal (Becker, 1978). Again, positive social feedback in the
form of praise from a superior or colleague is likely to
improve or at least maintain self-esteem and hence motivation. On the other hand, as noted earlier, the study by
Meyer *et al.* (1965) shows the effects of negative feedback
on performance. Subordinates who had independent performance
appraisal interviews with their managers and who received
an above average number of criticisms on their performance
appraisal in general showed less goal achievement some
10-12 weeks after the interview. Meyer *et al.* conclude that
frequent criticism constitutes so strong a threat to
self-esteem that it disrupts, rather than improves
subsequent performance. Again, as a consequence of criticism,
subordinates often appeared defensive rather than
cooperative in undertaking goal-setting.

   In reviewing the literature on feedback, Meister (1976)
concludes that feedback has been shown to have a positive
effect on productivity, and that any feedback is better
than none, provided the feedback is relevant. Feedback
tends to be more effective the more specific it is, provided
the specificity is task relevant.

   Not all feedback represents feedback of the individual's
performance; in many cases only group feedback is available.
Meister notes, however, that even group feedback is more
effective than no feedback at all, and he argues that
post-performance feedback is especially effective in
improving team performance in highly complex tasks. Meister
notes the important distinction between intrinsic feedback,
that is feedback arising directly from the performance of
the job itself, such as the ball going wide from a shot at
goal, and extrinsic feedback, the manager indicating why
the ball was incorrectly struck so that it went wide. As
Meister notes, in a learning situation there is likely to
be greater reliance on extrinsic feedback; as one becomes
more skilled, intrinsic feedback plays a greater role. It
is therefore important to design jobs so that as far as
possible, intrinsic as well as extrinsic feedback is
possible. One application of this principle is to allow
operatives to take a more active part in quality control.
Where the individual is allowed to be his own quality
controller, there will be more direct intrinsic feedback.
One advantage of direct intrinsic feedback is that where
it is negative it will not necessarily involve negative
criticism from a superior where the individual himself can
put the defect right. Again feedback will be more accurate
and less delayed than where quality control takes place by

another individual in another part of the organisation.
Finally, the quality and quantity of feedback is likely to
be greater where the individual undertakes his own quality
control. Of course, there are problems with this approach,
such as the incentive to pass defective work as adequate
because of extra financial rewards, the difficulties of
placing machinery and plant to take account of the needs of
quality control, and so on. Yet removing quality control
from the operator clearly also has its problems.

Despite its positive aspects, there are a number of
difficulties with feedback. Meister points out, for example,
that there are difficulties where the amount of feedback is
so great that the operator is overwhelmed with more
information than he can use. In such a case of information
overload, there may be an increase in stress and a decrease
in performance. However, where stress is already present,
there is evidence that providing feedback can reduce the
stress and thus increase efficiency (Meister, p.340).

The question of information overload, or at least too
frequent feedback, is taken up by Ilgen, Fisher and Taylor
(1979) in their review of the value of feedback. They argue
that too much feedback is offputting to the individual, who
comes to regard his behaviour as too closely controlled.
They do allow, however, that in most organisations the
problem is one of too little rather than too much feedback!

Ilgen *et al.* also make the point that the value of
feedback is not as clear-cut as some commentators have
suggested. As noted earlier, the value of feedback depends
on the individual accepting the goals of the organisation.
Otherwise he is unlikely to be motivated to change his
performance, whatever the feedback. Ilgen *et al.* argue that
feedback itself is not going to be accepted by the recipient
if it does not come from an acceptable source. Acceptable
sources include those where there is, for example, perceived
expertise, personal attraction and reliability and, presumably, mutual trust. Even where the source is acceptable,
however, Ilgen *et al.* note, as did Meyer *et al.* (1965), that
negative feedback is less likely to be accepted than positive
feedback. They also suggest that individual differences play
a part in the effects of feedback. Thus, individuals high in
need for achievement perform better as a result of feedback
than others. Presumably this reflects their greater desire
to achieve goals, and the evidence that those who express a
desire to be competent also benefit from feedback presumably
reflects this. On the other hand, where individuals gain
their satisfaction from social relationships or factors
unrelated to job performance, presumably feedback will have

little effect on improving performance.

Nevertheless, despite these various limitations on the effectiveness of feedback, there is little doubt that without it, performance improvements would not be possible for those who do want to improve performance.

THE APPLICATION OF SKILL

In considering the question of goal acceptance, it was noted that only goals which were valued by the individual would be likely to be accepted as worthwhile. Within the context of the job itself, a worthwhile job is one which normally involves the application of skill, and in relation to job satisfaction at least, a number of studies have shown the relationship between low skill level and job dissatisfaction.

One of the most influencial studies in calling attention to the motivational problems in de-skilled jobs was carried out by Walker and Guest (1952) in an automobile plant in the USA. The plant used many production methods, of which the major features were a paced assembly line, mechanical pacing, a repetitive job, limited scope of the job and limited social interaction at work.

That the jobs described by Walker and Guest had considerable problems as far as employees were concerned can be seen from this extract of men describing the repetitive nature of their job:

> I work on a small conveyor which goes round in a circle. We call it a merry-go-round. I make up zig-zag springs for front seats. Every couple of feet on the conveyor there is a form for the pieces that make up the seat springs. As that form goes by me, I clip several pieces together, using a clip gun. I then put the pieces back on the form, and it goes on around to where other men clip more pieces together. By the time the form has gone round the whole line, the pieces are ready to be set in a frame where they are made into a complete seat spring. That's further down the main seat cushion line. The only operation I do is work the clip gun. It takes just a couple of seconds to shoot six or eight clips onto the spring and I do it as I walk a few steps. Then I start right over again.

For some time psychologists have been aware that highly de-skilled jobs are frustrating for large numbers of individuals. It is part of Herzberg's (1968) argument, for example, that jobs which offer satisfaction of lower-order

needs such as pay and good supervision do little to motivate
the individual to perform. Positive motivation occurs as a
result of the fulfilment of higher-order needs of self-
autonomy and self-fulfilment. These in turn, within the
context of employment, require a job which presents challenge
and the opportunity to use real skills in order to give the
possibility of real achievement.

A similar, and highly influential approach to motivational
aspects of jobs has been proposed by Hackman and Lawler
(1971), who base their work on the earlier work of Turner
and Lawrence (1965). Hackman and Lawler talk of 'core' job
aspects. These are high autonomy, variety, identity and
feedback. The question of feedback has been discussed
previously, the other aspects will be discussed in turn.
Because the work of Hackman and Lawler has been so
influential in calling attention to the motivating aspects
of jobs, it is now considered in some detail.

Job variety
As far as job variety (the opportunity to do a number of
different things) is concerned, Hackman and Lawler confirmed
the findings of Walker and Guest in showing a relationship
between variety and job satisfaction. Indeed, when account
was taken of whether individuals had high 'higher order
needs', correlations between task variety and aspects of
satisfaction were sometimes quite high (0.55). Clearly
there is the possibility that job variety might lead to
greater productivity for the individual with higher-order
needs. This is because variety can be regarded as contributing to the meaningfulness of a job, since high variety
jobs typically involve a number of skills which may be
important to the employee. Unfortunately, the evidence from
Hackman and Lawler is that the relationship between job
variety *per se* and productivity is low, reported correlations being -0.03 for quantity, 0.17 for quality and 0.20
for overall effectiveness, and statistically insignificant
when taking the higher-order needs of individuals into
account. Certainly on the basis of the evidence presented
by Hackman and Lawler, there is no justification of
assuming a substantial relationship between job variety
and productivity.

It is interesting to speculate why the correlations
between job satisfaction and variety are high and significant whilst the correlations between productivity and
variety are low and often insignificant. It could be that
in some situations, irrespective of motivational factors,
warm-up times on a number of different tasks result in more

lost production than any loss due to boredom in undertaking
only one or a limited number of tasks. This is not to argue
that increased variety is a bad thing. On the contrary, as
noted above, Hackman and Lawler found substantial correlations between variety and satisfaction, and Walker and
Guest found that the number of operations to be performed
often distinguished the most from the least satisfied in
their study. As noted in Chapter 2, satisfaction has
important economic implications for organisations.

Job autonomy
Job autonomy is defined by Hackman and Lawler in terms of
the opportunity for independent thought and action. As with
the findings on job variety, Hackman and Lawler found a
significant relationship between job autonomy and job
satisfaction, the more so for individuals with higher-order
needs (0.43).

The findings on the relationships between autonomy and
productivity are also similar to those for job variety. In
other words the correlations are low, 0.13 for quantity,
0.16 for quality and 0.26 for overall effectiveness, for
those with higher-order strength needs. As Porter *et al.*
(1975) note, autonomy would appear to tap the degree to
which workers feel personally responsible for their output.
Autonomy is also necessary for the application of real
cognitive skill. If an individual's work is totally
determined by others, then no matter how complex it is, an
essential aspect of cognitive skill is missing – the
judgement which the individual himself puts into a task.
Few tasks, however complex, would be described as skilful,
if there were no part left for individual judgement and
responsibility. Yet as noted above, whilst such autonomy in
job performance appears to lead to greater satisfaction
with the job, the evidence on substantial effect on
productivity is undoubtedly missing. Porter *et al.* argue
that the failure to find effects on productivity is not
surprising as far as quantity is concerned. Producing
large amounts of material is unlikely to be perceived as
meaningful by individuals, especially those with higher-
order needs for fulfilment. However, it would be expected
that quality of production would be significantly affected
by autonomy for those with higher-order needs and here,
too, the correlations are low and not statistically significant. Why increased autonomy does not lead to substantially
increased quality of productivity, when it apparently leads
to increased intrinsic motivation and satisfaction, is a
matter for speculation. It may be that in some situations

the pattern of operations determined by an expert who is a
superior is a more efficient way of producing qualitatively
superior work than allowing freedom of decision-making lower
down the organisation. Again, however, it must be emphasised
that satisfaction is substantially related to autonomy, and
satisfaction is a worthwhile humane and economic goal in
itself where it does not conflict with productivity. It
should be noted in this connection that the correlations
produced by Hackman and Lawler between productivity and
autonomy are insignificant rather than negative.

Task identity

The third core job aspect investigated by Hackman and Lawler
is task identity, described as the opportunity to do a whole
job from beginning to end. As with the other core dimensions,
the relationship between satisfaction and identity is
significant although rather low. The relationships between
identity and productivity measures are even lower, however;
only the correlation between task identity and overall
effectiveness (0.11) being statistically significant. When
higher-order needs are taken into account, however, not only
is there no correlation between productivity and identity
for those with higher-order needs, there are significant
correlations for those with lower-order needs. In other
words for task identity, the greater the reported identity
for those with lower-order needs, the greater the productivity! Task identity is supposed to work through giving
the individual a more meaningful task and hence increase
his intrinsic motivation. Clearly this would be expected to
work more for those with higher-order needs.

Hackman and Lawler account for these unexpected results
in terms of the kind of jobs in which their subjects were
engaged. Their subjects were telephone operators, for
whom the whole task is a small one, repeated again and
again. Those with strong higher-order needs are therefore
likely to become bored very quickly with the task. Whilst
this explanation may account for a failure to find a
relationship between productivity and identity for those
with higher-order needs, it is difficult to see why at the
same time there should be a significant correlation between
job satisfaction and identity for this group.

Productivity and the four core dimensions

There can be little doubt that the relationship between
measures of productivity and the core job aspects analysed
by Hackman and Lawler are consistently low and often
statistically insignificant. In no way could they reasonably

be used to support any theory of motivating jobs, at least
in terms of objective measure of job productivity. At best
the core aspects individually give some slight support for
the view that jobs, when they are high on core dimensions,
are minimally related to increased productivity. Hackman and
Lawler did, however, seek to examine the effects of adding
the core aspects together in order to assess whether jobs
high in all core aspects would show significant differences
from those low in all core aspects. Their results showed,
that for quality and overall rated effectiveness, there
were significant differences between low, medium and high
rated jobs. However, the basis upon which jobs were categorised into high and low score categories appears to be
arbitrary and the size and significance of the difference
between the groups was of a low order for both quality and
overall effectiveness. The strongest relationship appears
to be with quality rather than quantity of production, as
Porter, Lawler and Hackman (1975) readily acknowledge.
However, the important point to note is that even the
relationship with quality is of a very low magnitude. Again,
there was no significant effect of higher-order need strength
on any of the measures of performance. The findings,
therefore, of Hackman and Lawler on the relationship between
core dimensions, either taken separately or together, are of
so low an order that other evidence is needed before any
convincing conclusions can be said to be established. As
Hackman and Lawler themselves note, however, such evidence
is almost wholly lacking, except in the form of reports on
job enrichment studies, which will be seen in Chapter 8 to
be almost invariably suspect in scientific terms, and are
in any case not normally designed to test the contribution
of core aspects separately.

Apart from that provided by Hackman and Lawler, other
evidence, for example, Hall and Lawler (1970), often fails
to find a relationship between productivity and measures
of meaningfulness and variety, or find relationships of a
very low order. Nevertheless the work of Hackman and Lawler
(1971) has been extended by Hackman and Oldham (1976) into
a comprehensive theory in which the motivational potential
score (MPS) is given by the equation

$$\text{MPS} = \frac{\text{autonomy} \times \text{feedback} \times}{(\text{skill variety} + \text{task identity} + \text{task significance})}$$

They acknowledge however, that growth needs moderate this

relationship and must be taken into account in arriving at
an MPS. As Umstot, Bell and Mitchell (1976) note, the
empirical evidence for the MPS-productivity relationship is
very weak, taking both the original Hackman and Lawler
(1971) and the later Hackman and Oldham (1976) study into
account. In their own experimental study Umstot *et al.* once
again failed to find support for the enrichment-productivity
relationship. Wall, Clegg and Jackson (1978) also examined
Hackman and Oldham's model, and they too found only relatively small correlations between productivity and core job
aspects, although the correlation between task variety and
performance (0.40) was statistically significant.

In sum therefore, the studies of Hackman and Lawler and
Hackman and Oldham do not convincingly establish a
relationship between core job aspects and measures of
productivity. However, a failure to find any relationship
between core aspects of jobs and productivity in these
studies does not prove that core aspects are unimportant
in productivity. It was noted, using an expectancy model of
the motivation-performance relationship, that effort would
not lead to increased productivity where there was no
relationship between effort and productivity where, for
example, the nature of the job precluded any relationship.
It might be that in some jobs, for example increased variety
involves increased learning times for different operations
which, while improving satisfaction and effort, decreases
the amount produced. Again it may be that the nature of the
job high on core aspects precludes a direct relationship
between individual effort and performance, as when group
performance is involved, for example, or where skill rather
than effort is a major determinant of performance. There
appears to be little evidence in most published studies on
what the relative relationships are between effort and
performance for jobs low and high on core job aspects.

Again it must be emphasised that the deficiency of
evidence is in the area of the relationship between core
aspects and measures of productivity. Hackman and Lawler
have, for example, shown reasonably large correlations
between core job aspects, satisfaction, and job involvement.
Such relationships are undoubtedly of importance to the
efficient functioning of the organisation.

JOB INVOLVEMENT

If increases in the core aspects of jobs do lead to
increased productivity (and as noted previously, this is in
doubt), then the mechanism for this might be job involvement,

where increased psychological identification with the job
(job involvement) has sometimes been shown to be related to
increased productivity (for example, Vroom, 1962).

In their study of the core aspects of jobs, Hackman and
Lawler (1971) found significant relationships between job
involvement and all four core job aspects. Whilst the correlations were not particularly high, their findings do
indicate that job involvement might be increased with greater
job variety, autonomy, meaningfulness and feedback.

Nevertheless, Rabinowitz and Hall (1977) claim in their
review of job involvement, that the relationship between job
involvement and productivity is complex and confusing. Whilst
studies such as those of Vroom (1962) do show a relationship
between job involvement and productivity, other studies such
as those of Lodahl and Kejner (1965), Goodman, Rose and
Fircon (1970) and Siegal and Ruh (1973) failed to find any
such relationship. In the Goodman *et al.* study, for example,
no relationship was found between the level of job
involvement and the number of papers and publications of
scientists and engineers in a government research
establishment.

It does seem intuitively likely, however, that despite
these studies, job involvement and increased productivity
should go together. The manager who wants his firm to be
successful is going to try harder than the man who doesn't
care. The scientist who is interested in his work and who
spends his evenings in the laboratory is likely to be more
productive than the individual who prefers to paint his
house. The question arises, therefore, as to why some studies
have failed to show any relationship. One possible answer is
that in many studies the wrong productivity measures are
being used. Lawler (1970), for example, argues that when
individuals are job involved, it is quality of production
which is improved rather than quantity. Again in research
institutions, the number of publications which one produces
may be only one of several ways of contributing to research.
For any research establishment to function smoothly,
efficient administration is also important, for example, so
that involvement leading to higher productivity may not be
measured by looking at the individual's quantitative output
in terms of publication. In other words, before the question
of the relationship between job involvement and productivity
can be established, one must answer the question, involvement
in what?

The study of Goodman *et al.* reveals a number of difficulties in trying to relate job involvement to productivity.
Measures of productivity in their study involved papers

produced in the previous five years, for which involvement
up to eight years previously would be required. However,
involvement was measured only considerably after productivity
occurred, a methodological aspect present in the Siegal and
Ruh (1973) study also. Again in the Goodman *et al.* study,
neither age nor ability were examined in assessing the
effects of involvement, yet it is self-evident that no matter
how willing a person is, if he is incompetent he will not be
able to publish research papers in large numbers. As to some
extent competence at paper writing and research is likely to
increase with age, this variable too must be examined. Age
is also an important variable as, with increasing age,
individuals may come to take a greater interest in
administration of research institutions.

Whilst, of course, studies such as those of Goodman *et al.*
do not show whether there is a relationship or not between
involvement and productivity, studies which show the relationship between job involvement and performance to be low
or non-existent do indicate that other factors are important
in performance. As noted before, ability, for example, is
likely to be an important factor in high skill jobs. Again
no amount of job involvement will affect performance if the
task does not allow for increases in performance as a result
of increased effort. Furthermore, individuals may perform at
a high level, not because they are job involved, but because
they want to impress potential future employers with their
abilities. The ambitious executive who is keen on moving to
a more progressive firm may try harder because he wants to
get away from his present employer. It is also likely to be
the case that in some situations too much job involvement
will be detrimental to performance where it results in a
failure to be objective as, for example, when a doctor
treats his own family.

Nevertheless, the failure of a number of studies to find
a relationship between job involvement and performance is
at first sight puzzling and counter-intuitive. Yet it is
clear that many studies which fail to find a relationship
are totally inadequate as tests of the relationship. One
cannot, therefore, say that because two studies have shown
a relationship and three have not, the relationship is
unclear. The relationship is unclear, not because a number
of studies have failed to find a relationship, but because
few of the reported studies have been conducted in such a
way as to test the relationship. Studies must be conducted
in situations in which a relationship is likely to be
found, for example, in skilled occupations where the
individual's efforts are likely to make a difference to

productivity, where the individual has some discretion in
the amount of effort he can put into the job, where performance can be adequately measured in terms of quality as well
as quantity, and where job involvement and performance can
be related in terms of time at which they occur.

Given that quantitive measures of performance are often
inadequate in relation to job involvement, a more realistic
measure of the value of job involvement might be considered
in terms of its relationship to absenteeism and turnover. A
number of studies have in fact shown a relationship between
both absence and turnover, and job involvement. Patchen
(1965), for example, found quite high correlations, (0.43)
and (0.53), between measures of job involvement and absenteeism in work units for the Tennessee Valley Authority,
although other studies have failed to show such a relationship. Given the generally inconsistent measures of
absenteeism from study to study (see Chapter 7), such
inconsistencies in results are perhaps not too surprising.
On the other hand, a number of studies have shown a relationship between turnover and job involvement. This, of
course, is not surprising. If one is not involved with one's
present job, the temptation to move to another job more in
line with one's interests is likely to be greater than
for the individual who sees his goals being fulfilled by
his present job.

Whilst the evidence on the effects of job involvement on
productivity are somewhat inadequately investigated, the
findings of studies on withdrawal behaviour do make it
reasonable to conclude that job involvement does have implications of economic significance for the organisation.
Furthermore, as Rabinowitz and Hall note, there does seem
to be a relationship between job involvement and job
satisfaction, which again points to the value of increasing
job involvement in organisation. The question therefore
arises as to how job involvement can be increased and how
individuals can be identified who are likely to become job
involved.

Psychologists have taken two distinct approaches to the
question of the 'nature' of job involvement. Some, such as
Lodahl (1964) regard job involvement as a basic characteristic of the individual. In other words, whether an
individual is going to become involved with a job or not
will depend on the individual, almost irrespective of the
kind of job he is faced with. The goals of individuals not
involved in their jobs, in such a view, are not capable of
being achieved by fulfilment at work. For middle-class
individuals, job involvement will often involve applying

the Protestant work ethic, which involves a belief that work
is a good thing in itself. Whether or not an individual is
job involved, argues Lodahl (1964), depends on early socialisation, through parents, friends and the general sub-culture
in which one lives. Hulin and Blood (1968), for example,
found that the sub-culture of the workers they studied
affected their job attitudes.

In their study of blue-collar urban workers, they noted
that many had no desire for intrinsic satisfaction from the
job, but regarded their jobs as a means to satisfy 'off-the-
job' goals. Such individuals were regarded by Hulin and
Blood as alientated from the middle-class norm of the value
of work as a goal in itself. Of course, the findings of
Hulin and Blood do not demonstrate that working conditions
are unimportant in influencing the individual's attitude to
job involvement. The reason why the blue-collar workers in
their study were alientated may well be because the kind of
job they were normally required to do was dull and routine
and gave no real opportunity for growth. Furthermore, where
there is a feeling of alienation among workers, attempts at
improving the situation on the part of management may well
be treated with scepticism. Obviously, if such feelings
exist in a community as a whole, the children will take on
hostile attitudes to work before they enter employment. Only
in this sense would it be the case that job involvement lies
in the individual rather than the job.

As opposed to the view that job involvement or its absence
is a characteristic of the individual, is the view that job
involvement is a function of the situation. Theorists such
as Argyris (1964) regard the organisational environment as
one which frequently blocks major individual growth and ego
needs. In particular, the lack of possibility for the individual to exercise responsibility and control, and to
involve himself in more complex behaviour than organisations
normally allow, is seen to be frustrating. Argyris's thesis
is that when such development is not possible, employees
will respond by having less ego involvement in the job.

As with most aspects of behaviour, it is likely that job
involvement involves characteristics both of the individual
and of the situation, and both individual and situational
characteristics have been shown in some studies to be
related to job involvement. As far as individual characteristics are concerned, Rabinowitz and Hall (1977), in
their review, find relationships between sex, age, education, length of service, status and job involvement,
although findings from some of the studies are contradic-
tory. One reason for this is that the relationship between

many of these variables and job involvement is likely to be
complex. For example, the older the individual, the likelier
it will be that he has had an opportunity to find a job with
which he can become involved. On the other hand, the older
the individual, the more failure he is likely to have
experienced, and the more likely he is to settle for his
present job because of extrinsic rewards. It should be
pointed out, however, that a number of studies do show a
positive relationship between age and job involvement, that
is, the older the individual, the greater his job involvement (for example, Jones *et al.*, 1975), whilst none of the
studies reviewed found a negative relationship. It does
seem at least possible that age is positively related to
job involvement.

One major individual characteristic related to job
involvement is the strength of higher-order needs. Hackman
and Lawler (1971) in their study, for example, found a
correlation of (0.45) between job involvement and core
aspects of the job for those with higher-order needs,
compared with (0.28) for those without higher-order needs,
and Rabinowitz (1975) also found a significant relationship
between strength of higher-order needs and job involvement
in a sample of Canadian public employees. The results do
not seem surprising; those wishing higher-order need satisfaction are presumably more likely to identify with jobs
offering higher-order need satisfaction, whereas it is
difficult to see how those with only lower-order need satisfactions are going to identify with a job at all. Nevertheless, the findings of higher-order needs, and to a lesser
extent age, do indicate that individual factors can be a
determinant of job involvement, prior to arriving at the
job.

As far as situational factors in job involvement are
concerned, Rabinowitz and Hall review a number of factors
which seem to be important. Of particular significance are
the findings on participation in decision-making. Rabinowitz
and Hall note a number of studies which find a correlation
of about 0.5 between job involvement and participation in
decision-making. This is a reasonably high correlation and
suggests a relationship between the two factors. It does
not, of course, suggest what the relationship is. It may be
that those who are more job involved are more likely to
participate in decision-making within the organisation. On
the other hand, it might be that participating in decision-
making leads to greater identification with organisation
goals and hence greater job involvement.

Apart from participation in decision-making, adequate

social relationships have been shown to be related to job
involvement in the study of Lodahl and Kejner (1965). They
found that job involvement was significantly correlated with
the number of people contacted per day on the job, and the
degree to which it was necessary to work closely with others.
One reason why social factors may facilitate job involvement,
apart from increasing the probability of satisfaction at
work, is that social interaction on the job has the potential
for increasing orientation towards the job through dis-
cussions with others, and for increasing feelings of being
part of a team with a common goal.

A major job factor considered by Rabinowitz and Hall in
relation to job involvement concerns the nature of the job
itself. As noted earlier, Hackman and Lawler found a
significant relationship between job involvement and the
core job aspects of autonomy, variety, meaningfulness and
feedback. Patchen (1965) demonstrated a relationship between
job interest and various intrinsic aspects of the job, such
as job difficulty and feedback. He found, for example, that
jobs with high difficulty, but where the individual had
control over the means of executing the job, led to higher
job interest. This of course relates to the importance of
autonomy, found in Hackman and Lawler's study.

A final job factor related to job involvement is noted by
Rabinowitz and Hall as being success on the job. They note
a number of studies in which prior success led to later
increased job involvement. Bray *et al.* (1974), for example,
found that successful managers showed increased job
involvement over time, and other studies have shown similar
results. There is, of course, every reason why success
should lead to greater job involvement. Success results in
rewards; where these are desired it is likely that the
individual will seek further success and come to take a
greater interest in the means by which success is achieved.

Clearly both situational and personality factors have a
role to play in job involvement, with results of job factor
studies showing the more consistent relationship. In
interpreting the results, however, a major problem deserves
comment. Almost all of the studies deal with people once
they have chosen an occupation and may therefore have some
intrinsic job involvement to begin with. How one stimulates
an interest in a job in the first place cannot necessarily
be deduced from such studies, although of course studies
showing the effects of success in increasing subsequent
job involvement are helpful. Furthermore, the self-selecting
mechanism of job choice does operate for most individuals,
so the major problem in job involvement may be in exploiting

the potential involvement already present rather than
stimulating an interest which was previously absent. Nevertheless, the conclusion of Rabinowitz and Hall seems well worth
bearing in mind,

> Since most of our work has been static research, we know
> very little about the process of becoming involved in a
> job. Future longitudinal research should do more than
> correlate changes in predicator variables with changes
> in involvement. Methods are needed that will reveal the
> sequence of events and processes that take place as a
> person becomes 'turned on' to his or her work.

Given that job involvement is a matter of economic
importance, and given that both situational and personality
factors are involved, how can the employer increase the job
involvement of his employees? From the point of view of
selection, various factors such as age (possibly), strong
growth needs and a belief in the Protestant work ethic seem
useful factors. It also seems reasonable to determine whether
the individual has a history of job involvement, as previous
behaviour is often a reasonable predictor of future
behaviour. From the point of view of the job, those jobs
having the potential for intrinsic satisfaction (that is,
being high in autonomy, variety, task identity and feedback),
which allow for participation in decision-making and which
give the potential for successful achievement, appear more
likely to induce job involvement, provided they are jobs
where successful achievement is valued by the individual
himself.

4 Job Context Factors and Productivity

The previous chapter dealt with the relationship between productivity and aspects of the job itself. Factors such as achievement, recognition and feedback were examined in order to assess their relevance to productivity. In contrast such factors as pay, supervision and so on have been described as context factors. Whilst much work in organisational psychology has focused on content factors, few psychologists would deny the importance of context factors in an understanding of psychological aspects of productivity. In this chapter, therefore, the main context factors will be considered. These are pay, work groups, supervision, participation in decision-making, role strain, organisational structure and climate, and hours of work.

MONEY

It is self-evident that financial reward is an important motivator of performance, at least in the sense that the vast majority of jobs would not be undertaken were there not the promise of some payment for performance. At first sight this might seem to conflict with findings which frequently show pay to be rated as of little importance in relation to job satisfaction. Lawler (1971), for example, found pay to be ranked on average third in importance in relation to job satisfaction and a number of studies report pay to be ranked lower than this. As Gruneberg (1979) points out, however, any average rank of the importance of pay is relatively meaningless as studies differ so much in the questions they ask, different groups will have different priorities and in any case many of the studies are poorly designed. For example, studies have asked job applicants to rate the importance to them of various job aspects. Clearly anyone wishing to obtain a job is not going to say that he wants the job mainly for the money, rather he will emphasise intrinsic aspects of the job in order to increase the chances of success. Nevertheless money may have less importance as a reward for some individuals than for others. Wernimont and Fitzpatrick (1972), for example, found students

to place little value on money and a study reported by Smith
and Wakely (1972) found a group of young girls to prefer
time off work to increased payment. The girls had to give
their earnings to their parents, so that extra money had
little importance to them compared with time off work.

Money, of course, means different things to different
people. Thus money can have its main significance in terms
of what it can buy, or it may be a symbol of success and
recognition. Whatever its exact value and meaning, however,
there is as noted above, little doubt that financial reward
is of considerable importance to almost all individuals.
For some individuals, of course, it might take second place
to other rewards when satisfactory levels of payment are
reached. However, as the evidence to be considered presently
will show, financial incentives undoubtedly play a major
part in the repertoire of rewards which organisations
utilise to improve productivity.

SATISFACTION WITH PAY AND PRODUCTIVITY

A number of studies have shown a relationship between
satisfaction with pay and measures of productivity. As far
as 'on the job' productivity is concerned, there is some
evidence that pay satisfaction is related to productivity,
particularly in cases where rewards are tied to productivity
(for example, Schneider and Olsen, 1970). Lawler (1971) in
his review found level of pay satisfaction to be a good
predictor of turnover and absence. Counter-productive
behaviour too, such as striking, is reported by James (1951)
to be related to satisfaction with pay. He found a significant difference between strikers and non-strikers in one
study which related strikes to pay satisfaction. Lawler in
fact reports that pay dissatisfaction is claimed by unions
to be responsible for 70-80 per cent of all strikes. Whilst
such evidence is not entirely reliable, as pay may be a
focus for a number of other dissatisfactions, it again does
lend support to the view that pay satisfaction and
dissatisfaction are likely to have considerable economic
consequences.

Factors Affecting Satisfaction With Pay
Perhaps the most influential theory regarding pay satisfaction
is equity theory, which, as noted in Chapter 2, argues that
satisfaction with pay is not determined by the absolute
amount of pay one receives, but rather with the amount of
pay one receives in relation to others. This comparison
with others involves taking account of inputs such as education, skill, effort, danger and so on, and relating that to

outputs such as financial rewards compared with others. Where the individual feels that the ratio of input to output in relation to others is fair, then there is satisfaction. Equity theory argues that both under-reward and over-reward are likely to lead to dissatisfaction. As noted earlier, in the case of perceived under-reward, there will be less effort, low morale and efforts to bring payments into line with equitable perceptions by such means as striking. The findings on over-reward appear to be less clear-cut although studies have been reported in which 'overpayment' led to a reduction in the quantity produced in a piecework situation. Adams and Jacobsen (1964), for example, found that subjects 'overpaid' reduced the quantity but increased the quality of their work. On the other hand, as Pritchard (1969) has noted, in an industrial situation, overpayment is likely to be perceived of in terms of the 'fault of the system' in underpaying others, rather than in overpaying the individual concerned. It does seem intuitively likely that adjusting to overpayment is easier than adjusting to underpayment.

Of course, pay satisfaction is unlikely to be determined solely by the relative level of payment. However fairly one might perceive one's payment in relation to others, individuals might well be dissatisfied because such payments do not allow for an adequate perceived standard of living. As Warr and Wall (1975) point out, for example, as people get older, they have an expectation of an increased standard of living, whatever the social comparison involved.

Payment Systems

A basic distinction in payments systems is that between payment related to and payment unrelated to performance. On the face of it, payment related to performance should increase productivity, as the greater is productivity, the greater will be the reward. There is, in fact, little doubt that payment incentive schemes can work. Locke *et al.* (1980), for example, reviewed ten studies which compared individual piece rates and hourly pay and found a median performance improvement of 30 per cent as a result of the introduction of a piece-rate payment plan. They also found that all ten studies showed some gain.

There are, however, a number of problems with individual incentive schemes which must be borne in mind when considering the best method of rewarding effort. In his study of incentive schemes for example, Hickson (1961) found that in spite of an incentive scheme, workers restricted their output. One of the most important reasons for this was that the workers feared an increase in productivity in response to the incentive system would result in management

redefining the amount to be produced for a given payment.
Clearly, if an incentive scheme is to work, trust must exist
between employer and employee.

Hickson also suggests that incentive schemes may be
problematic because they lead to the disruption of healthy
social relationships. Thus when the individual tries to
maximise his own productivity, he may do so at the expense
of his workmates, or may fail to help and co-operate with
others in difficulty. Related to this problem is the finding
that, under incentive schemes, individuals often concentrate
on those aspects which 'pay off', to the detriment of other
important aspects of the job. Quality, for example, might
suffer in the attempt to produce more (for example, Rice,
1953). Hickson also suggests that workers can derive positive
satisfaction from the social aspects of output restriction,
and may also restrict output where there is a fear of
unemployment. In situations where increased productivity is
perceived as a threat to the group, sanctions are likely to
be placed on individuals who are 'rate busters', the famous
'bank wiring-room' experiment in the Hawthorne studies being
an example of this.

A further problem with payment by results is that performance is often difficult to evaluate. This is likely to be
true, for example, in complex tasks involving co-operation
with others, where the role of any one individual is
difficult to evaluate. Again, as noted in the discussion of
performance appraisal, productivity is difficult to assess
where the end product is subjective or intangible and depends
on a superior's subjective judgement rather than objective
reality.

Some incentive schemes fail, not because employees are
uninterested in monetary rewards or do not trust management,
but because there is no obvious link between effort and
performance or reward. Camman and Lawler (1973), for example,
found that one incentive scheme failed because the employees
were unsure what the relationship between performance and
reward was, in other words, the incentive scheme was not
clear to employees.

Even where incentive schemes do 'work' in the sense of
increasing productivity, the gains sometimes have to be set
against loss elsewhere. Marriott (1957), for example, notes
that incentive schemes often involve increased clerical
costs, disregard of safety regulations and increased health
risks through overworking.

One factor which must be considered in deciding whether or
not to introduce an individual incentive plan is how close
current productivity is to the practical limit. There is a
limit to the amount of effort that an individual can sustain

for any length of time, clearly the nearer the individual
is operating to that limit, the less the possibility of
improvement.

If individual incentive schemes are to be successful,
they must overcome the problems outlined above. They are
likely to work best, therefore, where productivity can be
objectively measured, where trust is high, where there is
job security, where the individual is not dependent on others
or on unreliable equipment, where high productivity is not
against the norms of the group, and where the basis of payment is clear to the individual concerned. In addition,
incentive payments will not be effective unless there is
the possibility of variability in performance according to
the effort of the individual and where the rewards reflect
directly on performance and not on measures such as 'profits'
which are beyond the control of the individual.

Marriott (1957) points out that where incentive payments
systems are introduced, they should cover the maximum number
of workers possible in order to prevent dissention from those
not benefiting. Many studies have shown that job improvements
have come to grief, not because they fail in themselves, but
because they do not take account of effects on other parts
of the system not directly involved. Again Marriot notes
the importance of an adequate grievance procedure, given
that any system is likely to involve problems not envisaged
when the system is set up.

Group Incentive Schemes
Perhaps the main difference between group schemes, which
reward individuals on the basis of total group performance,
and individual incentive schemes, which reward employees
on the basis of their own performance, is that the relationship between effort and reward is seen to be less direct in
the case of group incentive schemes. Individuals working in
group schemes may come to feel that as their rewards are
dependent as much on the efforts of others as on their own
efforts, they need not put so much effort into their own
work in order to obtain rewards. In many circumstances,
however, group incentive schemes have advantages which outweigh their disadvantages. For relatively small groups,
individual effort can be related to reward to some extent,
and group schemes do overcome the difficulties of disruptive
competition inherent in individual schemes. Indeed in group
incentive schemes, co-operation between members is likely
to be encouraged where it leads to higher total productivity.
Furthermore, the high producer, who is a threat to the
group in an individual incentive scheme, as he might cause
redefining of minimum work output, is an asset to the group

under a group incentive scheme as his hard work will benefit
everyone.

Camman and Lawler (1973) report a study comparing a
successful and an unsuccessful group incentive scheme involving employees of a shipping group. Among the important
pre-conditions of the successful plan were that trust existed
between management and worker, that the plan was easily
understood, and that the relationship between effort and
reward was clear. The latter two conditions in particular
distinguished the successful from the unsuccessful plans.
Clearly, many of the conditions for a successful individual
scheme apply to group schemes also.

Apart from increased production as a result of incentive
payments, various studies have found that incentive plans
which reward attendance can be effective. Scheflen, Lawler
and Hackman (1971) found, for example, that a pay incentive
plan improved attendance behaviour as measured a year after
the incentive plans were introduced and Tjersland (1972)
also found rewards to affect attendance favourably, though
in this case the increased payments did not cover the savings
in improved attendance.

Where pay incentive plans do work it may not be because of
pay incentive plans *per se*. Katzell and Yankelovich (1975)
note that many job changes often accompany changes in payment
systems. Working hours and employee-employer relationships
for example, might be affected in ways which improve productivity. Of course, from a practical point of view it does not
matter too much why the scheme works, as long as it does.

Given that almost all pay plans have to surmount a large
number of difficulties (and for a fuller review of these
see Marriott,1957; Lawler, 1971), Warr and Wall suggest a
three tier pay plan, in which 75 per cent of pay is determined on an hourly basis, 20 per cent on an incentive basis,
and 5 per cent on a company-wide basis.

Finally, one problem of incentive schemes which has to be
faced is what happens if the scheme is too successful? If
productivity increases by more than the rest of the organisation can cope with? Homans (1965), for example, paints
a picture of disaster as a result of a rapid increase in
productivity, with surplus parts in abundance going onto
the conveyor belt to the embarrassment of the management.

Incentive programmes are clearly not without problems.
Yet despite the problems, there clearly are many situations
in which they are reported to work, and after all, not
providing incentive schemes also has its problems.

Pay Preferences
Whatever the actual relationship between pay and productivity,
an important question concerns what people actually want.
Opsahl and Dunnette (1966) found in a number of studies that
workers preferred payment in terms of time worked rather
than output, and it may be that for relatively low-level jobs,
stress is involved in producing consistently at levels which
are above the normal 'rhythm'. On the other hand, results
are not entirely consistent, and preference may depend on
experience and success with an incentive scheme. Dissatisfaction with schemes where the relationship between effort
and reward is poorly defined and ill-understood may well
not occur in schemes which are accepted by the group, and
where the effort-reward relationship is clear and reasonable.

For managers, as opposed to blue-collar workers, there
does seem to be a preference for merit-based rewards, although
the pay secrecy which surrounds managerial pay in many
situations makes it difficult for managers to assess the
merit-performance relationship (Lawler, 1971). Most managers
overestimate the pay of their subordinates and therefore
may be dissatisfied with the perceived inequity of their
own pay. Yet making everyone's pay public may well not be
the answer. Public knowledge about pay may give rise to
pressures to equalise pay, which may in turn give rise to
feelings of inequity in the good performers. Another problem
with the assessment of managerial performance is that it is
likely to be based on the subjective assessment of superiors
to a greater extent than is the case with low-level workers,
again leading to difficulties in perceived equitable
assessment. Clearly the satisfaction of managerial pay
aspirations, no less than that of blue-collar workers, is
a complex problem.

WORK GROUPS AND PRODUCTIVITY

Work groups, small groups of individuals working for a
common productive goal, are well known as an important
influence on the productivity of individuals. One of the
most famous examples of this comes from the bank wiring-
room experiment of the Hawthorne study, in which it was
found that social disapproval was brought to bear on
individuals who produced 'too much'. The 'too much' was in
relation to what the group regarded as a reasonable output
for the job.

That group influences can be an influence for higher
productivity has also been shown. In the classic study of
Coch and French (1948), increased productivity was attributed to individuals accepting group goals of higher

productivity as their own, and various studies have shown
that public commitment to group goals increases the probability of the individual achieving the group goal.

Why then, do groups have an influence on the productivity
of the individual? In general terms, groups give rewards and
punishments for conforming to the accepted patterns of group
behaviour, and where the group establishes accepted patterns
for productivity, group members will tend to conform to the
appropriate productivity level.

There are a number of aspects of the group which lead to
rewards. Thus groups satisfy a basic human need for social
interaction and friendship. A number of studies have shown
that where social interaction is reduced by technological
factors, job satisfaction can suffer (Trist and Bamforth, 1951)

Of course, it is not social interaction *per se* which causes
satisfaction. Many individuals have retreated to their 'local'
pubs to reduce the interaction with their nagging spouses!
What is satisfying is interaction with individuals who enable
the person to achieve important goals. Amongst these,
being accepted socially as someone of value is of significance,
as it has implications for increased self-esteem.

The group also can have a social significance for the
individual in giving social support in times of stress.
Hackman (1976), for example, notes that groups of friends
have the effect of reducing arousal in times of stress. It
is common experience that having friends to talk to in a
crisis reduces the individual's level of anxiety.

Apart from social satisfaction, the group can be an important source of task relevant information. Particularly
for a new recruit to a group, information is usually supplied
on the 'real' relationship between effort and reward, on which
ways of performing the job are most effective in the particular
group situation (know-how), and in general terms the group
will supply the individual with information concerning the
job. For individuals having task-orientated goals, such information makes group membership attractive. It must not be
thought, however, that social interaction is always sought.
Too much social interaction can interfere with the individual's
own goals on some occasions, as when studying for examinations.

As Lott and Lott (1965) in their review of the literature
note, exactly how attractive a group will be to the individual depends on a number of factors. Physical closeness, for
example, is normally a prerequisite of social interaction. It
is difficult to interact socially with someone not easily
contactable. In the Trist and Bamforth study, increased
physical distance after job reorganisation was a major

source of dissatisfaction. Frequency of interaction also affects group attractiveness, particularly when the inter-action involves co-operation with others. Group prestige and group size also affects the attractiveness of the group. In the case of group size, when the group becomes too big, interaction amongst all the members becomes difficult.

Stability, too, is important, in that where group member-ship is continually changing, social relationship will tend not to develop or will be disrupted. Individuals having a common goal, common interests and abilities are also likely to lead to greater group attraction. Van Zelst (1952), for example, found that where work groups were constituted on the basis of personal choice, satisfaction and indeed productivity increased. This may have been because indivi-duals chose those with whom they knew they could work best, as well as those with whom they were friendly. Cross and Warr (1971) also found that groups matched in ability were more satisfied and produced more. Individuals were able to interact at their own natural 'pace' in such matched groups. Smith and Wakely (1972) suggest that matching individuals in terms of sex, age, and other background variables is likely to increase the attractiveness of the group as interpersonal and values conflicts will probably be reduced.

Perhaps the most important aspect of a group is whether the group is successful in achieving for the individual the goals he seeks, whether of a social or a task-oriented nature. Where an industrial organisation, for example, is unsuccessful, then an ambitious and able executive is unlikely to join them, whatever the social interaction rewards. And, of course, task success and failure can affect social interaction. In unsuccessful groups, for example, interaction can become unfriendly with individuals blaming each other for failure.

To the extent that the group is attractive to its individual members, they will identify with it and tend to 'stick' together, a characteristic known as cohesiveness. Groups which are cohesive have often been shown to produce greater adherence to group norms. This of course is not surprising, since the more attractive the group is, the more likely it is that individuals will hope for group success. As Napier and Gershenfeld (1973) point out, the function of the group norms is to regulate the performance of groups as an organised unit, and keep it on the course of its objectives. Individuals who deviate from accepted group behaviour (group norms) are therefore potentially threatening both the group objectives and the internal relationships within the group, by increasing the possibility of conflict.

Cohesive groups are able to control individuals to the
extent that there are rewards for being a group member, and
there is the threat of punishment, in the form of exclusion,
should norms not be adhered to. The more attractive the group,
the more is the reward and the greater is this threat of
punishment to the individual.

Group Cohesion and Productivity
As Hackman (1976) points out, there is no overall relationship
between how cohesive a group is and subsequent productivity.
This is because where group norms in cohesive groups are for
high productivity, there will tend to be high productivity.
On the other hand, in many situations the group norm will
be for low productivity, in which case the more cohesive
the group, the less likely are individuals to deviate from
the norm of low productivity. Berkowitz (1954), for example,
found that highly cohesive groups with norms of low
productivity had members who stuck more closely to the norms
of low productivity than a non-cohesive group with low
productivity. A similar finding was reported in relation to
norms for high output.

There are a number of reasons why cohesive groups should
develop low output norms. In the first place, individual
satisfaction with the group may well arise because of the
satisfaction of social needs - friendly interaction. Where
the main source of satisfaction is through such social needs,
then productivity will suffer if the satisfaction of social
needs conflicts with task requirements. In one of the
Hawthorne experiments, for example, two girls had to be
dismissed for talking too much, and it is common experience
that social aspects of work provide satisfactions which
interfere with productivity - the extended tea-break being
an example of this. Again a concentration on friendly social
interaction may discourage the production of fruitful new
ideas where these seem to conflict with current group
thinking.

There are, however, other important reasons why groups
might develop norms of low productivity. The study of
Hickson (1961) discussed earlier, for example, shows how
individuals will restrict output if there is a feeling of
insecurity or fear of reassessment of adequate productivity.
Again if the relationship between effort and reward is
inadequate then individuals may fall back on 'social' rewards.

That some studies have noted difficulties with cohesive
groups does not mean that group cohesion is without advantages
for productivity. As Napier and Gershenfeld note, cohesive
groups which have been established for a time will have an
increased knowledge of the resources of the group, will have

more realistic levels of aspiration and will have increased
confidence in the abilities of other group members to fulfil
their roles. There is evidence, as noted above, from the
studies of Van Zelst (1952) and Cross and Warr (1971) that
where individuals are allowed to choose others as their
workmates, and that where workmates are matched on abilities,
then productivity increases. Presumably this is to some
extent because individuals have a knowledge of and confidence
in their workmates.

Studies of group cohesion clearly show that group cohesion
can be a force for either high or low productivity. Even
where the norm is for low productivity, it would seem unwise
to break a work group up in the hope that productivity would
improve. Where, for example, the cause of low productivity
is a fear of unemployment or a fear of increased output
demands, the solution is, where possible, to increase trust
between management and the work group. Where low productivity
is due to a failure to see any relationship between effort
and reward the solution is to clarify the relationship.
Where low productivity is due to high social rewards in a
situation where no other rewards are available, the solution
is to investigate the ways in which other rewards might be
made available. Of course, as Porter, Lawler and Hackman
(1975) point out, this may not be easy in a situation where
social rewards are high and other rewards are limited. It
may be, of course, that as in the Hawthorne experiment,
changing the personnel is a necessary step, in which case,
as in the Hawthorne experiment, new individuals should be
more task-oriented than those they are replacing. There is,
however, a heavy price to pay for breaking up work groups
in terms of the job dissatisfaction which may occur and
subsequent costs of turnover and possibly absence.

Group cohesion, of course, is likely to affect the effort
that individuals put into a job. As Hackman (1976) notes
however, low group productivity might also be due to poor
strategies in performing the job, low or high levels of
arousal (under too much stress individual performance
deteriorates, under too little, effort might be affected)
and inadequate skills due to poor training with the group.

Lippitt (1961) suggests a number of steps in increasing
the productivity of groups. Among these are :

(1)   the group should have clear goals and an understanding
      of its goals;
(2)   it should be conscious of its own processes; by
      improving its interpersonal effectiveness it is likely
      that there will be increased task performance (the
      better interaction of skills);

(3)   it should become aware of the skills available to it;
(4)   there should be methods of evaluating performance so
      that methods of operation can be improved.

Clearly the group, whether cohesive or not, is highly
dependent on the skills of supervision in order to maximise
some of these objectives. The next section, therefore,
considers supervisory behaviour.

SUPERVISION AND PRODUCTIVITY

As with pay, supervision is often considered to be a factor
of considerable importance in improving productivity. As
Dubin (1965) notes, however, improving co-operation, handling
technical problems, dealing with information, quality control
and discipline, are all functions of the supervisor, so
that in some situations increasing productivity may play a
minor role. Furthermore, providing motivation for the work
group is not necessarily the only way in wich the supervisor can affect the productivity of his group. Bare (1978),
for example, examined a number of supervisory functions and
found that staffing and training were those aspects of
supervisory function which most related to supervisor
effectiveness. Nevertheless, improving the motivation of the
work group is considered by many to be a major factor in a
supervisor's effectiveness and this aspect of his function
is now considered.

Supervisory Styles
Perhaps the most commonly made distinction in dealing with
supervisors concerns the differing styles of supervision.
Weed *et al.* (1976), for example, make the distinction between
task-oriented and employee-oriented leaders. An employee-
oriented supervisor is one who establishes friendly supportive
relationships with his subordinates, takes account of their
interests and goals and pays regard to their problems. The
employee-oriented leader is thus considerate, pleasant and
in so far as he allows his employees a say in decisions
affecting their jobs, he is democratic. The task-oriented
leader, on the other hand, regards his group as instrumental
in achieving production targets set by employers, and is more
concerned with this than the welfare of the individuals in
the group. To the extent that he does not consider the
problems of individuals in meeting employers' goals, he will
be autocratic in behaviour.
    A number of studies have reported employee-oriented style
leaders to be more productive and to have more satisfied
subordinates (see, for example, Korman, 1966). As Korman,

however, points out, almost all studies are correlational, so that it is just as possible that in these studies high productivity leads to friendly supervision. After all, supervisors have their goals to attain, and to the extent that the group is co-operative in attaining set goals, it is likely that the supervisor will become more friendly to his subordinates. Indeed, a number of experiments have shown that subordinates affect the supervisory style of their leaders. Farris and Lim (1969), for example, found that a knowledge of previous good performance of a group increased the leader's use of 'friendly' supervision, and Barrow (1976) found that supportive or autocratic leadership was influenced by how well the workers performed. Improved performance led to greater consideration, decreasing performance to the use of punitive behaviour and autocratic leadership style.

However, that performance can be shown to affect supervision does not rule out the possibility that leadership style can influence group performance. Weed *et al.* (1976) conducted a study in which leaders were trained to be high either in employee or in task orientation. One finding was that for subordinates low on a 'dogmatism' personality scale, employee oriented supervisors got greater productivity from their group than supervisors high on task orientation. On the other hand, for those subordinates high on 'dogmatism' the reverse was the case. It does appear, therefore, that for certain kinds of personality, supervisors high on employee orientation can increase the productivity of the group. On the other hand, a study by Kahn (1956) found that groups given either high employee or high task-oriented supervisors increased productivity. In other words employee-centred supervision may not be the only supervisory style to increase productivity. Dubin (1965), in commenting on the Kahn study, suggests that productivity can either be forced or encouraged with about the same outcomes with respect to output (although employee-centred supervision was related to greater satisfaction).

To some extent the distinction between employee-oriented and task-oriented leaders is an artificial one, as it is quite possible to be interested in the group members, to consider their problems and yet be oriented towards fulfilling production targets. As Warr and Wall (1975) point out, however, it is likely that a supervisor very high on task orientation will not be considerate, and will tend not to take the views of his subordinates into account. The evidence certainly suggests that the ideal supervisor combines both the 'employee-oriented' and 'task-oriented' approach. The study by Weed *et al.*, for example, showed that the highest production was achieved by groups where the supervisor was high on both task and employee orientation. Again a study by Misshawk (1971) indicates that individuals regard as important qualities in a supervisor, someone who has both technical and administrative skills, as well as 'human relations' skills.

The studies reviewed above strongly suggest that no simple relationship exists between employee-oriented supervision and productivity. One major reason for this, apart from the moderating influence of personality traits, is that effective supervisory style is likely to vary from situation to situation. Dubin (1965), for example, highlights the importance of technological factors in effective supervision. In highly technical supervision, much of the supervisor's time is likely to be involved solving technical problems, making plans and dealing with safety as opposed to situations in which there is little technology, where social interactions are likely to be more important. Variations in supervisory style are likely to be important, therefore, in unit or small-batch production situations, where motivation is likely to affect productivity, and to be less important in process and mass production organisations, where productivity is less under the control of individual supervisors.

Production stress in industrial organisations is another situational feature which has its influence on productivity and supervisory style. Likert (1955) presents some evidence that the greater the pressure from the foreman to produce, the greater is productivity, although the evidence suggests that production declines if the pressure is excessive. There is also some suggestion that under pressure supervisors will become less considerate in their behaviour to subordinates, which would certainly fit in with common experience of behaviour under stress.

Not only does leadership effectiveness vary with the situation and with the personality of subordinates, Vroom (1976) suggests that for the same individuals and the same groups, different leadership styles will be appropriate for different types of tasks. For example, for relatively unimportant decisions such as the colour of stationery, it is likely to be acceptable for the leader to make decisions without consulting the group. Again, consultation is likely to be necessary where the supervisor has insufficient information to make a decision, but may not be so necessary where all the information is available. Where the group as a whole is likely to accept the supervisor's decision, clearly consultation will not be as necessary as where a decision is likely to lead to controversy, and so on.

The findings on supervision and productivity would seem to

indicate that there is no one best supervisory style for
every situation, but that supervisors high in both task and
employee orientation are often reported as successful in
terms of both productivity and satisfaction. Homans (1965),
however, questions the importance of supervisory style as
far as productivity is concerned. He suggests, on the basis
of a survey of the literature, that any difference in
productivity in workgroups resulting from contrasting methods
of supervision is usually small and usually not larger than
15 per cent of total output. Homans argues that 15 per cent
is not a really big difference, and yet supervision is a focus
of much interest in organisational psychology. Homans goes
on to argue that the reason for the relatively low effect
of supervisors is that they do not have the power to
distribute rewards and punishments which would materially
affect group behaviour. Pay and payment systems, for example,
are often determined externally, as are hiring and firing.
What rewards he can give are 'small-change', such as praise,
taking an interest in men and giving autonomy of action within
limits. Furthermore, as was noted earlier, even his capacity
to give these rewards is to some extent limited by technology
and the pressures exerted upon him. Where the job is
mechanically paced, and where there is pressure to meet
deadlines and schedules, the supervisor's ability to reward
with consideration and autonomy might be severely limited.
  It is important to emphasise the difficulties facing
supervisors in industrial settings. Even if they are sent
on programmes to increase considerate behaviour, there is
little that they can do to implement their knowledge if the
technological and organisational pressures, particularly
from superiors, are against a participative style. Furthermore, pressures against change may come from below, where
subordinates may feel unhappy about the amount of new
responsibility they are given, especially if there is no
financial reward for their new status. There is often a
feeling that the appropriate behaviour of a supervisor
involves decision making, and subordinates feel uncomfortable
when he is not seen to make decisions.
  In discussing their difficulties, Miller (1965) notes
that supervisors characteristically take on a number of roles,
all with attendant difficulties for production. Supervisors,
for example, may come to identify strongly with their subordinates, and take their part against management, as well
as becoming indulgent about production targets. Alternatively
they may become management and task-oriented and may 'lose'
their subordinates to informal leaders, who will define
production goals. Supervisors aware of these difficulties
may become trapped in the dilemma of dual loyalty. This

approach involves double talk and gamesmanship, and if
discovered can lead to a lack of confidence on both sides.

In summary, what emerges clearly from a review of the
literature is that effective supervision is a complex problem,
determined by situation, technology and personality factors.
Appropriate supervisory style is also likely to change from
time to time within the same organisation. Nevertheless there
is some evidence that increasing considerate leadership,
where this is at a low level, can improve productivity, as
can increasing task orientation where this is at a low level
and where considerate supervision is already present. Whilst
Homans argues that supervisory style does not matter all
that much in terms of its implication for productivity, the
evidence indicates that under some circumstances supervisory
style can influence productivity substantially. After all,
a 15 per cent increase in productive capacity could make an
enormous difference to an organisation, where, for example,
quality was a problem and more time could be spent on quality
control. For effective supervision to be implemented, however,
it is not enough to send individual supervisors on training
courses. The situation under which changed supervision occurs
must be favourable, and the organisational climate must be
supportive of supervisory practices.

PARTICIPATION

One major aspect of considerate leadership style is that it
involves the participation of the group in decision-making,
at least to the extent that the views of group members are
sought before decisions are made. As Wall and Lischeron
(1977) point out, however, considerate leadership involves
more than participation in decision-making. Dimensions such
as trust, openness, warmth and concern for the needs of the
individual are also involved. It may therefore be that it
is these aspects of considerate leadership, rather than
participation *per se* which affects productivity. In this
section, therefore, the effects of participation on decision-
making are considered in greater detail.

Warr and Wall (1975) make the useful distinction between
immediate participation which involves one's own immediate
work group, and distant participation, which involves
participation in wider company policies. Of course, the two
are not always easy to distinguish, as participation with
more senior management in questions of general policy might
well result in changes affecting the immediate work situation. The introduction of new machinery, for example, may
materially affect the way the individual's job is performed.

The distinction between immediate and distant participation

highlights the fundamental question when discussing
participation - participation in what and how? Participation
in decisions on goal-setting, on work schedules and on work-
sharing, say, is not likely to have the same implications
for the running of an organisation or for the individual,
as participation in investment plans, or on the colour of
toilet paper to be used in the loo. Clarke *et al.* (1972)
report management far less favourably inclined to allow
participation in financial and investment decisions than in
work scheduling.

A further problem with the term 'participation' is that
there is often a failure to distinguish situations where
group members are consulted but have no say in what decision
the supervisor takes, and situations in which group members
determine the decisions by their votes, in other words,
where the leader devolves power. In many cases, 'democratic'
leadership involves the first alternative.

Immediate Participation
On the face of it, participating in decision-making concerning one's immediate job should improve the efficiency
of organisations and increase productivity for at least
three reasons. First, participating in decision-making
increases the amount of communication between the supervisor
and the group, so that the supervisor should have more task-
relevant information on which to base decisions, and the
group should have a greater appreciation of the problems
involved in arriving at a particular decision. Second, there
is evidence (eg Coch and French, 1948) that where individuals
participate in decision-making, they have a greater commitment to seeing that the goals which have been set are
achieved. There is, as it were, an identification of the
individual with the group decision. Third, participating of
itself involves greater job variety, autonomy, responsibility
and feedback, those 'core' job aspects regarded by Hackman
and Lawler (1971) as critical to increased job satisfaction
and performance. It must be remembered, however, that with
the exception of feedback, there is little evidence of an
association between core job aspects and productivity (see
Chapter 3).

The argument for participation improving productivity
presumes, of course, that work groups wish to take part in
decision-making. The evidence is that many individuals do.
Hespe and Wall (1976), for example, found 60-70 per cent
of industrial workers in their study desired more participation in decision-making. On the other hand, by no means
everyone sees it as appropriate to participate in decision-
making. Vroom (1959) suggests that those with authoritarian

personalities are unaffected by the opportunity to participate in making decisions, and Weed *et al.* (1976) found
authoritarian individuals to prefer authoritarian leaders.
Nevertheless, individuals with needs of autonomy are likely
to desire to play a part in decision-making.

What then, is the evidence on participation and productivity?
A number of correlational studies have shown a significant
relationship between the two factors, but, as has been
previously noted, it is difficult to know whether participation causes increased productivity or whether high levels
of productivity incline a supervisor to more democratic
behaviour. A number of field studies have, however, shown
the effects of participation on productivity. One of the
classic studies was undertaken by Lewin, Lippitt and White
(1939). The study involved supervising boys under three
different leadership conditions, authoritarian, democratic
and a *laissez-faire* leader who took little part in decision-
making at all, and because of this, effectively blocked
efficient decision-making through lack of organisation.

Productivity was superficially greater under the autocratic
condition, but productivity continued when the democratic
leader left the room, whereas it stopped when the autocratic
leader left. Productivity was worse for the *laissez-faire*
leader.

A study by Morse and Reimer (1956) also indicates the value
of participative leadership, although productivity also rose
under autocratic leadership in their study.

Another famous study of participation and productivity was
carried out by Coch and French (1948). They found that groups of
employees in a pyjama-manufacturing company who participated
in decisions concerning new production techniques produced
at a higher rate than a group not allowed to participate.
A further group had two representatives participate in
decision-making, and whilst this group produced at a higher
level than the non-participating group, it produced below
the level of the 'full participation' group.

One of the most successful studies of participation is
reported by Bragg and Andrews (1973). They found that the
introduction of participative decision-making in a hospital
laundry setting resulted in savings of about $1000 per
employee per year. In addition, absence rates were reduced
and job attitudes improved. As Locke *et al.* (1980) note,
however, much of the improved productivity may have come
from the many ideas for work improvement originated by
employees, rather than improvement in work effort *per se.*
A study by Rice (1953) of autonomous work groups also showed
the effects of participation on increased productivity.
Dubin (1965) however, points out that improved productivity

in Rice's study could have resulted, not from the fact of participation in decision-making, but from the fact that any kind of organised decision-making would improve the very low level of productivity due to a chaotic existing work organisation. This, too, is the implication of Morse and Reimer's finding, not that participative leadership is ineffective, but that any organised attack on a problem, whether participative or structured, may well lead to productivity improvements.

A further problem of generalising from the positive results of studies such as Coch and French is the fact that a number of studies, noted by Vroom (1976), have failed to find an effect of participation on productivity, and Locke *et al.* (1980) in a recent review found that in many of the studies they considered, there was no improvement in productivity as a result of increased participation. Negative findings do not, of course, show that participation is ineffective in improving productivity; they do suggest that there are circumstances which limit its effectiveness.

One factor limiting the effectiveness of participation is, as noted above, the individual's willingness to take part in decision-making. Not only may individuals be against participation due to personality disposition, the expectations of individuals in particular organisations may be violated. In an otherwise authoritarian organisation, for example, individuals may hold beliefs that participation is inappropriate - 'it's his job to make the decisions - that's what he's paid for'. On the other hand, in institutions such as universities, individuals may have expectations that they should participate.

Of critical importance, too, is the question of participation in what. To participate in decisions which are perceived as trivial and to be excluded from decision-making in matters of perceived importance may be more frustrating than no participation at all. Only where decision-making is in matters of perceived importance is there much chance of the individual identifying with the organisation's goals. Again, as Campbell *et al.* (1970) point out, what is important to the supervisor may not be important to the group. Whether decisions can be important depends to some extent on the technology involved. In highly structured jobs, there may be relatively little of importance that a workgroup can decide. In research departments, on the other hand, a highly skilled scientist may well have an important contribution to make to group decisions.

How the group perceives their leader's influence in relation to his superiors is also noted by Sutermeister (1976) as being of importance. Where supervisors are not

perceived of as having influence in the organisation, then
participation in decision-making is likely to be perceived
of as of little importance, as it will have only limited
effects.

Trust between the group and the supervisor is a further
critical element in the efficient use of participation. If
one of the main goals of participation is to increase
communication so that more information is available upon
which decisions can be made, then a lack of trust between
supervisor and his group will nullify this possibility.

Campbell *et al*. (1970) note a number of problems with
participation. One major problem is that participants may
become absorbed in needs satisfaction and respond to problems
in terms of what would satisfy them most, rather than what
is best for the organisation. Even the participation process
itself may, of course, be used to satisfy social needs,
rather than to promote efficient problem-solving. Nor is it
at all clear that group wisdom is greater in problem-solving
than the wisdom of the most able member of the group. Indeed
Vroom (1976) suggests that managers are often defective in
the 'motivation' aspect of management rather than in terms
of the quality of their decisions.

A further problem pointed out by Campbell *et al*. in
relation to participation, is that divergent views may be
ignored in situations where a group has to come to a con-
sensus on a particular point. To this extent the needs and
values of the individual may become less important rather
than more important. Clearly it is important to make a
distinction between group and individual participation in
decision-making.

All of the factors outlined above indicate that the
relationship between participation and productivity depends
on the situation and the individuals involved. In some
situations participation is likely to be of value, in others
it is questionable.

Again, in areas where it is successful it is not clear
what the mechanisms for success are. It may be, for example,
that only where participation leads to goal-setting on
matters related to productivity is it effective. Furthermore,
in a number of studies on participation, financial reward
occurs as a result of any improvement in productivity, as
for example in the Scanlon Plan (see Chapter 8). It may be
that increased financial reward for achieving goals is
therefore the main mechanisms for increased productivity.

Vroom and Yetton (1973) make the point that appropriate
supervisory style not only varies between individuals, but
that the same individual will have to act in different ways
at different times. For example, the appropriate behaviour

for a supervisor faced with a simple, non-controversial decision is probably 'non consultative'. On the other hand, where information is lacking, where acceptance by the group is essential but in doubt, and where the issue is of importance, participation is likely to be appropriate.

Apart from these questions, other factors are important in deciding whether participation is important. One of these is the time factor. Participation takes time, and it may be that where time is a critical factor, participation may be inappropriate. In that case, however, reasons for a particular decision might be given.

Clearly the question of participation in decision-making is not a straightforward one, and there are a number of difficulties involved which may outweigh the advantages of greater involvement and communication. As Herzberg once said, too much communication can be undesirable - do you tell your wife everything? Yet the problems do not preclude the possibility that in many circumstances participation is useful. Vroom's work would seem to indicate that flexibility and skill on the part of the supervisor, rather than the adoption of any one style, is the most efficient approach to immediate participation.

Distant Participation
One of the major reasons for employees participating in the policy-making of organisations is the assumption that this will lead to greater involvement and hence more identification with the goals of the organisation.

Distant participation is in some cases a consequence of political decisions exerted from outside, although a number of organisations have developed their own participation schemes. Distant participation can vary from worker control of the organisation at one extreme to consultative committees restricted to an advisory role.

As with immediate participation, there is not too much evidence concerning how much individuals desire distant participation, although Hespe and Wall (1976) did show some desire for medium and distant participation, particularly after some experience of it. Startup and Gruneberg (1973) also found a desire for distant participation in their study of university teachers. It may be, of course, that desire for distant participation increases with the educational level of the organisation. In many routine jobs, there may well be a limit on what distant participation is perceived as being capable of achieving. However, Startup and Gruneberg found it was not so much that individuals themselves wanted to participate in distant decision-making, but rather they wanted more representation from individuals of their level

in the organisation, perhaps as a defence against their
interests not being safeguarded. For job-involved individuals
distant participation might be regarded as a nuisance if it
takes time away from activities such as research and teaching,
which are central to their interests.

Distant participation has been tried out in a number of
countries, with varying success. Thus Wall and Lischeron
(1977) report that in Israel there are doubts that worker
representatives at higher management levels really represent
the rank and file. In Norway, too, it appears that distant
participation schemes fail to some extent because of the
increasing distance between representatives and those they
represent, and in Yugoslavia, which has developed employee
participation to a greater extent than most, top and middle
management nevertheless exert the greatest influence.

Miller (1978), in discussing participation in Yugoslavia,
notes that a major difficulty is that workers who are elected
as representatives are easily influenced by management and
come to take on management attitudes. He too, emphasises
that representatives often become remote from those they
represent and fail to communicate adequately with them. The
rank and file, therefore, find it difficult to identify
with the organisation through this kind of participation.

Participation has been encouraged in some organisations
through bonus schemes in which shares are given to employees.
As Clarke *et al.* (1972) point out, however, it is unlikely
that organisations will build up organisational involvement
by the distribution of a few shares, many of which are almost
immediately disposed of.

One major problem with distant participation is that, where
it involves general policy, management is clearly hostile
(Clarke *et al.* 1972). One reason for this may be that general
policy decisions may have to be taken for the good of the
organisation which are not necessarily good for some of the
individuals in the organisation, for example, the introduction
of advanced machinery.

As with immediate participation, the fact that there are
problems with distant participation should not mean that it
should be abandoned. Many schemes may have failed because
they were imposed from outside. They may have been set up
in order to overcome industrial relations difficulties, as
an instrument to solve problems, when perhaps they should
be set up once trust is established in order to sustain
good relationships.

Finally, participation in decision-making is an integral
part of such job redesign programmes as the Scanlon Plan,
management by objectives, job enrichment and socio-technical
systems design, all of which report improvements in

productivity under certain circumstances. These are discussed separately in Chapter 8.

ROLE STRAIN AND PRODUCTIVITY

Supervisors in work groups are, of course, responsible for
the allocation of work roles of group members. To the extent
that he fails to make clear the nature of the individual's
role, the supervisor will create role ambiguity. To the
extent that the role the individual is given is in conflict
with other duties which he has to perform, role conflict
will result. Of course the supervisor is not the only source
of role ambiguity and conflict. Poor communication in the
organisation, in general, or lack of adequate organisational
structure can obviously be sources of conflict and ambiguity.
    Many writers (for example Kahn *et al.*, 1964, Rizzo *et al.*,
1970) have suggested that role conflict and ambiguity can
lead to a lowering of morale. Rizzo *et al.*, for example,
note that a number of studies have found that individuals
who are subject to a variety of sources of authority tend
to be dissatisfied and also experience stress. Role conflict
is often reported in the foreman, who is often caught between
the demands of management and his subordinates. As Miller
(1965) notes, the foreman might try to identify with both
groups, but be seen as unreliable by both, leading to his
becoming less effective in his supervisory role.
    Role conflict need not only involve conflict between
performance of different aspects of the job. One area of
role conflict is between the role which the individual is
required to perform and the role which he desires to perform.
Graen *et al.* (1973) found that in a group where role orientation was high and where the individual regarded the job as
relevant to his future career, satisfaction was high, as was
the evaluation of performance by superiors, compared with a
group where role orientation was low. Furthermore, after
ten months only 25 per cent of the high orientation group
had resigned compared with 59 per cent of the low orientation group.
    Role conflict can also involve conflict between the
requirements of the job on the one hand and the family on
the other. Ross and Zander (1957), for example, found this
type of conflict to be directly related to turnover.
    As far as role ambiguity is concerned, Kahn *et al.* (1964)
found high role ambiguity to be associated with increased
stress and lower productivity, and Rizzo *et al.* note a
number of studies which point in the same direction. In one
study, for example, by Smith (1977), it was found that role
ambiguity led to increased hostility among group members

involved in a problem-solving task, but the removal of ambiguity at a later stage did not completely remove the hostility which had been established. In their own study, Rizzo *et al.* examined the effects of role conflict and ambiguity in a group of managerial, technical, foreman level and clerical personnel. Their findings support previous research in showing a relationship between role conflict and ambiguity and turnover. However, the relationship was found to be weak and suggests that the relationship between role ambiguity, conflict and behaviour is complex.

In fact, a number of studies suggest that various factors moderate the relationship between role conflict and ambiguity and performance. Beehr (1976), for example, found that autonomy in decision-making removed the effects of role ambiguity on performance. One difficulty, therefore, with role ambiguity is in situations where the individual has no clear goals but in addition has little possibility of setting his own. Schuler (1977) also suggests that the effects of role ambiguity are moderated by ability. In other words, those with ability can to some extent solve their own problems of role ambiguity. Clearly it is likely that a number of factors can affect the importance of role conflict and ambiguity in relation to productivity.

Nevertheless, despite limitations, the work on goal-setting discussed in the previous chapter clearly indicates that providing individuals with clear goals has a considerable effect on performance, and the work of Smith (1977) shows that role ambiguity can have lasting effects even after ambiguity is removed. Clearly ambiguity and conflict can have serious practical implications, and that one important supervisory function, therefore, is to reduce them as much as possible. One must, of course, distinguish between defining an individual's goals and the paths to these goals, as too close a definition of the latter removes autonomy and responsibility.

One technique for reducing role ambiguity has been described earlier when discussing the value of giving new recruits a realistic job preview. The work of Ilgen and Seely (1974), for example, shows that giving realistic job previews can reduce subsequent turnover. One possible reason for this is that the new recruit has a clearer view of his job role from the start.

One further aspect of role strain deserves to be mentioned, namely role overload. Role overload occurs where the task requirements are too great for the individual to cope with. Role overload is not, of course, necessarily something imposed by a superior, it is quite possible for the individual to take too much upon himself. One major effect of role overload, however it arises, is physiological stress. Russek

and Zohman (1958), for example reported that one of the
main distinguishing features of young coronary patients and
a healthy control group was in terms of prolonged stress
associated with job responsibility. This occurred in 91 per
cent of the coronary group compared with 20 per cent of the
control group. Again, evidence of role overload in terms of
hours worked per week is related to heart disease. Buell
and Breslow (1960) found that those people in their study
who worked for more than 48 hours per week had twice the
death risk of 'light' workers. Of critical importance in
role overload is whether the individual has the latitude
to make decisions. Karasek (1979) found that where people
have a large amount of discretion in decision-making, then
they can handle increased job demands without increased
stress. (The whole question of physical and mental health in
relation to jobs will be considered in greater depth in
Chapter 7.)

ORGANISATIONAL STRUCTURE AND CLIMATE

As with small groups, whole organisations can be described
in terms of whether they are basically democratic or autocratic in nature. Thus organisations may have decision-
making power basically at the top of the organisation – in
other words have centralised decision-making. They may be
highly task-oriented at the expense of individual needs,
such that jobs are de-skilled and routine, and individuals
can be moved from job to job without taking account of social
relationships and social satisfactions in the job situation.
    Organisations which are authoritarian in nature, having
highly centralised decision-making, are known as bureaucracies. They are hierarchical in nature, such that there is a
progression in skill level, occupational status and power
as one moves from the bottom levels to the top. Bureaucracies
are often pyramid shaped, with large numbers of individuals
at the bottom, and relatively few at the top making major
decisions. A number of individuals are normally responsible
to one supervisor. A number of supervisors in turn, of a
given level, are responsible to their superiors, thus giving
rise to a pyramid structure. The larger the number of
individuals in a group responsible to one superior, the
greater is the 'span of control' of the supervisor. Again,
the smaller this span of control, the greater will be the
number of levels in the organisation. Organisations with a
large number of levels between top and bottom are known as
'tall' structures, those with relatively few levels are
known as 'flat' structures.
    A number of writers have examined the relationship between

various aspects of organisational structure and organisational functioning (for example, Porter, Lawler and Hackman,
1975). They note that organisational shape, that is whether
tall or flat, is often related to the technology of the
organisation. For example, span of control is greater in
large-batch and mass production than in small batch and
process units such as chemical plants. The size of span of
control can vary, however, within technology and one of the
major findings of Woodward (1965) was that the most successful companies were those which were typical in terms of span
of control, for their kind of industry. In many cases, as
noted above, jobs at the bottom are as de-skilled as possible,
in the belief that this leads to high efficiency. Thus with
minimal training, those who join the organisation can
contribute to the productive process, and those already in
the organisation can be moved to other jobs where they are
needed with relative ease. Because jobs are so de-skilled
and power rests with progressively higher levels in the
organisation, there is often little opportunity for participation in decision-making. Such low-level de-skilled jobs,
therefore, are likely to be low in variety, autonomy and
meaningfulness, core aspects of jobs found by Hackman and
Lawler (1971) to be related to job satisfaction if not
productivity.

The nature of the product is important, of course, in that
it can determine the most appropriate technology, in, say,
manufacturing chemicals as opposed to mass production of
cars and specialist instruments. Organisational structure,
too, can vary with the development of the organisation.
Where an organisation is in a stable period, producing for
a mass market in a highly predictable way, then bureaucratic
organisation, with relatively little participation, may be
more appropriate than when an organisation is at a developing,
innovative stage, where new procedures have to be rapidly
adopted and new ideas are important.

Harvey (1968) did in fact find that organisations with
less changing technologies did show higher levels of
organisational structuring. There is, however, evidence that
flat organisations can be more productive in some situations.
Ivancevich and Donnelly (1975) found salesmen to be more
satisfied and to be more productive under flat rather than
hierarchical organisation.

Porter, Lawler and Hackman (1975), in reviewing the literature on organisational structure and behaviour, conclude
that highly structured organisations are most effective
when individuals are relatively inexperienced and unskilled,
have strong needs for security, the environment is calm and
stable and where the technology is stable and involves

standardised materials and programmable tasks.

Steers (1977) has looked at various aspects of organisational structure as they affect organisational efficiency. As far as decentralisation of power down the hierarchy is concerned, a number of studies were found to have shown positive benefits, in, for example, reducing turnover. On the other hand, the effect on productivity is unclear, with at least one study, that of Lawrence and Lorsch (1967), finding detrimental effects of decentralisation in production departments, but improved performance in research departments.

Another major aspect of organisation structure is organisational size. Steers (1977) concludes that increased organisational size appears to be positively related to increased efficiency, due to such factors as reduced labour costs, and orderly managerial succession. However, Steer's conclusion that increasing size is associated with increasing turnover is not supported by Ingham (1970). In his study, Ingham failed to find any relationship between organisational size and turnover, although there was a relationship between size and absence; the larger the organisation, the greater the absence.

Ingham notes some of the differing characteristics of small and large firms. In small firms there is a greater variety of work tasks, greater opportunity for social interaction, but small firms give less good wages. Ingham argues, therefore, that different kinds of individuals will be attracted to small and large firms. Those who seek satisfaction in the work itself or in social relationships rather than financial returns will seek small organisations. Those more interested in financial rewards will seek larger organisations. Certainly Goldthorpe *et al.* (1968) found workers in car assembly plants in their study to be instrumentally oriented, and not particularly concerned with on-the-job rewards. The reason given by Ingham for a failure to find any difference in turnover in his study of organisation size, was that the needs of individuals in both large and small organisations were congruent with organisational rewards. And whilst there were significant differences in absence rates, these were of a small magnitude, and might reflect differences in felt moral obligation to attend when feeling ill.

Porter, Lawler and Hackman (1975) note some of the difficulties in interpreting studies relating organisational size to behaviour. In the first place, what is organisational size? Is it one plant in an organisation which is geographically dispersed or is it the whole organisation? Furthermore, large organisations may contain larger subunits, and it may be the size of subunits, such as departments or primary

work groups that are the critical factors relating size to
behaviour.

Porter and Lawler (1965), in reviewing the evidence on
subunit size and behaviour, conclude that 'when blue-collar
workers are considered small size subunits are characterised
by high job satisfaction, lower absence rates, lower turnover
rates and fewer labour disputes'. This conclusion is supported
by the study of Gill and Warner (1979) as far as industrial
conflict is concerned. They found that in the chemical
industry in the UK there was a relationship between organisational size and industrial conflict. For organisations
employing up to 1000 employees, the larger the organisation
the greater the incidence of strikes. For organisations
larger than this the relationship did not hold.

Porter and Lawler point out that most individuals are
members of a number of different subunits, so that an
unequivocal interpretation of why there is a relationship
between subunit size and behaviour is difficult. They suggest
that as subunit size increases, it becomes more difficult
to have good internal communications. A further factor which
might be important is the tendency for larger workgroups to
involve more task specialisation, with consequent effects
on job satisfaction.

As far as productivity and subunit size is concerned, the
evidence seems to be equivocal, with some studies, such as
that of Marriot (1949), indicating the smaller the group
the greater is productivity, whilst other studies such as
that of Argyle *et al.* (1958) show the reverse. Obviously
with so many different factors involved in different studies,
such as different technologies, no firm conclusions can be
drawn.

In summary, structural aspects of organisations are clearly
related to aspects of organisational efficiency. Whilst there
is no one best organisational structure for all situations,
factors such as optimum span of control have been shown to
be related to organisational success, and factors such as
subunit size have been shown to relate to absence, turnover
and to the number of labour disputes (Clelland, 1955). As
these structural aspects are in some cases within the
control of the organisation, they are important aspects of
the relationship between the organisation and the individual.

Organisational Climate and Productivity

Organisational climate can perhaps best be regarded as the
'personality' of the organisation, particularly as perceived
by its employees. It involves a number of dimensions such
as warmth, support, degree of risk-taking and so on, all
of which are affected by the underlying structure of the

organisation. As noted previously, organisational structure is in turn determined to some extent by technology, management decisions and the nature of the relationship between the organisation and the environment.

A number of studies have found a relationship between organisational climate and factors such as job satisfaction and productivity. Steers (1977), for example, cites a number of studies which show that organisations with climates high in authority structure have low productivity and job satisfaction, whereas climates which stress good employee relationships have high job satisfaction but again low productivity. Only the achievement-oriented climate which placed emphasis on goal achievement led to high productivity and high job satisfaction. Steers concludes, 'one way for managers to facilitate effectiveness is to bring about a climate that stresses the importance of goal attainment while at the same time encouraging mutual support, co-operation and participation in the activities that contribute to goal attainment.'

It is clear that the conclusions based on research into organisational climate differ little from those based on research into leadership style, workgroup behaviour and participation in decision-making. Clearly, too, the limitations in terms of general statements that are made of these aspects of organisational functioning must be made of organisational climate. In particular, a number of studies, such as those of Pritchard and Karasek (1973) and Schneider and Snyder (1975) have shown how different groups and different individuals react differently to the same organisational climate. (For a detailed discussion of organisational structure and climate see Payne and Pugh (1976).)

HOURS OF WORK: SHIFT WORK

As Shipley (1980) notes, a significant number of the workforce (20 per cent) work shifts in European countries, where the majority of those involved are male manual workers in manufacturing industries. Such shift work is thought desirable because it allows for the greater utilisation of expensive plant and equipment. A number of recent reviews, however, have noted some undesirable side-effects of shift working (Shipley, 1980, Dunham, 1978, Wilkinson, 1978). In particular it has been noted that shift work can have effects on physical health, on social relationships, and on productive efficiency.

Physical Health
As far as the effects of shift work on physical health are

concerned, Dunham (1977) notes a study in which 27 per cent
of shift workers felt that shift work adversely affected
their health. Among the health problems which are reported
to occur are disturbances of appetite and digestion. As
Shipley (1980) notes, the diet of shift workers tends to be
less nutritious than that of ordinary workers, and problems
of elimination are reported frequently, as are problems of
a gastro-intestinal nature. One reason for the increased
incidence of physical disorders may be the lack of adequate
sleep, and it is frequently reported that sleep patterns of
shift workers are badly disrupted. Thus sleep during the day
is qualitatively different from sleep at night, the rapid
eye movement stage of sleep being earlier during day sleep
(Shipley, 1980).

Nevertheless, despite the reported effects of shift work
in some studies, the effects of night work on physical
health over the longer term are probably not a major problem
for at least two reasons. First, there is evidence of large
individual differences in the ability to adapt to shift work,
and for those who do adapt the health effect does not seem
to be a major problem (Dunham, 1978). Those who fail to
adapt physically will presumably give up before any real
harm results. Second, as Wilkinson (1978) points out, a
number of studies have failed to find any effects of ill
health. It may be therefore, that where physical effects
are reported, they are not due to shift work *per se*, but to
other factors associated with shift work in a particular
situation. It may be, for example, that only in relatively
high stress jobs is the additional stress of shift work
likely to be detrimental to physical health.

Social Relationships
There seems little doubt that working shifts can have
damaging effects on the individual's social life and marriage.
Dunham, for example, reports on a study which found that
64 per cent of shift workers had unfavourable family relationships and there were reports of a higher incidence of
sexual problems and a higher divorce rate. Dunham also notes
higher reported difficulties in child-parent relationships.
Friendships, too, are reported to be adversely affected and
shift workers report less visits to friends and less activity
in the community at large. Dunham notes that the shift
worker is out of phase with the family, which in turn is out
of phase with the community at large. Clearly the problem
of social relationships is a real one and presents major
problems to some individuals. However, the causal relationship between shift work and social problems is not entirely
clear. It may be that in some cases people choose night work

to get away from an unhappy home life. In any case, as
Wilkinson notes, problems of permanent shift work are
probably less than might appear. One reason for this is that
those individuals who do select themselves for shift work
are likely to have at least satisfactory sleep arrangements.
Indeed, in communities where shift working is prevalent, the
social problems are considerably less, as the community as
a whole has adjusted to the system. Furthermore, as Dunham
notes, there is no firm evidence that job dissatisfaction
results from shift work. On the contrary, where social and
physical problems are overcome, shift work is popular because
average earnings are some 20 per cent more than for non-
shift workers.

Productivity
There can be little doubt that shift working can result
in lower individual productivity. Dunham, for example, cites
two studies which indicate that shift workers make more
errors and produce less, although he argues that this is
likely to be due to individuals being out of rhythm. When
the individual adapts, in 4-14 days, errors are reduced.
The evidence is not entirely clear, however, and researchers
such as Wilkinson claim that workers only adapt partially.
Wilkinson points out that this lack of adaptation involves
sleep disruption and this is likely to affect efficiency.
Thus various studies have shown the effects of sleep disruption on performance, especially on tasks involving
vigilance. This lack of alertness is likely to be more
serious in a sleep-deprived individual who works in a mono-
tonous environment.
   In summary, it is clear that shift work can materially
affect the social and physical well-being of individuals
and can result in lower productivity. People differ, however,
in their ability to adapt to shift work and one aim of
management must therefore be to identify those who are likely
to adapt best. Obviously a suitable, supportive home background is a prerequisite. Shipley also considers the
possibility of identifying suitable individuals in terms of
personality. There is some evidence to suggest that evening
'owls' are more suited to shift work. There is some evidence
also that those who are natural 'short' sleepers have
different temperature rhythms from 'long' sleepers. One
major factor which will aid the adjustment to shift work,
whatever the personality, is permanent night shift arrangements rather than rotating shifts, as this allows the body
to adjust its rhythms to night working (Wilkinson).

5 Ergonomic Aspects of Productivity

INTRODUCTION

Whatever social and motivational aspects are important for maintaining a high enough rate of work output, it is a fact of life that the operator on the shop floor cannot be fully efficient if the equipment provided and the working environment are inadequate. Despite some of the paradoxical findings of the Hawthorne experiment (see Chapter 1), a worker is unlikely to do a job effectively if too little light is available to see (or, indeed, if too much light is present); similarly, ambient noise levels which are too high are likely to lead to missed warning signals, and very cold environmental temperatures may well cause reductions in manual dexterity. In the same way the quality of the equipment which is to be used can also affect performance: controls which are placed too high to be reached; displays which are unreadable; written instructions which are ambiguous can all lead to increased fatigue and reduced efficiency.

The debilitating effects of all of these aspects at work, and many more, are gradually being considered and understood through the field of ergonomics (and its American sister discipline of human factors). Both of these fields consider the interaction between the operator and the environment at work to 'fit the job to the man' (Rodger and Cavanagh, 1962), rather than the normal industrial approach of selecting and training operators to suit the job in hand (that is, 'fitting the man to the job').

Being a multi-disciplinary field of study, ergonomics crosses the boundaries between many scientific and professional disciplines and draws on the data, findings and principles of each. Present day ergonomics is an amalgam of physiology, anatomy and medicine as one branch; physiological and experimental psychology as another; and physics and engineering as a third. These separate fields of interest provide information about the structure of the body and the functioning of the brain and the nervous system, about the basic ways in which the body is used in work behaviour, and about the physical capabilities of the machine and the

environment with which the operator has to contend. From
these three areas an ergonomist takes and integrates data
to maximise the operator's safety, efficiency and reliability
of performance, to make his task easier to learn and to
increase his feelings of comfort and ease. This chapter will
consider briefly some of these aspects.

COMMUNICATION AT WORK

When considering how an operator interacts with his environment, the underlying concepts are those of communication
and information - no work can be done without them. Worse
still, faulty work (perhaps leading to accidents) is likely
to result from incomplete information or inefficient
communication. Both the quality of information, then, and
the quality of the information transmission (communication)
play a fundamental role in everyday living and working.
When considering these aspects, however, it is important to
realise that the concepts of both information and information
transmission need to be taken in their widest context, and
not simply in terms of the written or spoken word. At work,
for example, an operator is likely to need information about
how a machine works, how to operate it safely, what to do
when it breaks down and so on. Much of this he will obviously
receive from his colleagues, from his supervisor or from a
manual. However, information is also passed to him from the
machine itself via its display, telling him, for example,
how hot it is, how fast it is moving, etc. In addition the
operator imparts information to the machine via his own
controls, 'telling' it what he wishes it to do - to go up,
to go down, to turn left, or to increase speed.
    Information, then, is passed from one component in the
system (the transmitter) to another (the receiver). Only if
the receiver interprets the message in the way that the
transmitter intended can communication be said to take place.
It is one of the roles of the applied psychologist in
industry to make these communication channels act in their
most efficient manner by abolishing, or at least reducing,
the barriers between the two components.

Environment-Man Communication: Displays
Perhaps the first communication link with which an operator
has to contend at work is that in which the environment
(usually the machine) acts as the transmitter and the
operator as the receiver. The quality of the information
displayed can set the scene for the efficiency of the
operator's future actions. Since the operator is only able
to make an appropriate response on the basis of the infor-

mation which he receives, this aspect of the system needs
to receive careful consideration, and thus the display should
be designed with both the worker and the work in mind.

At this point it is important to remember that the concept
of a display does not end simply in terms of a piece of
hardware such as a dial or a counter or even a warning
klaxon. A display is any aspect of the environment which
enables information to be presented to the operator. Using
this extended concept, therefore, a window or windscreen
can be considered to be a display since information passes
through it to the operator. In many respects, too, a control
becomes a display if it is designed to present the operator
with relevant information. For example, the fact that a
switch is in the 'down' position normally displays the
information that the machine is 'on' (in some countries,
however, 'up' is 'on'. Problems such as these will be
discussed later).

Since they pass information from the environment to the
operator, displays can act only by stimulating one or more
of man's five senses: sight, hearing, touch, taste or smell.
In practice, however, only the first three of these senses
are normally used, and only the first two used extensively.
Before discussing visual and auditory displays in more
detail, it is useful to compare the two types and to consider the situations in which they are more usefully employed.
In general, *visual* displays are more appropriate when:

(a)   the information is presented in a noisy environment.
       Under such conditions the auditory displays may not be
       perceived;
(b)   the message is long and complex. Compare, for example,
       a written sentence from a teleprinter (visual) and the
       same information presented from a tape-recorder
       (auditory). Because the eyes are able to scan the visual
       material more than once, the memory capacities are not
       overloaded. Unless the taped message is translated into
       written material, the words which are decoded somehow
       have to be stored in memory whilst other words in the
       message are being decoded;
(c)   the message needs to be referred to later. Visual
       information can be used to produce a permanent record;
       unless auditory recording equipment is used, acoustic
       information is stored only in memory;
(d)   the auditory system is overburdened - perhaps because
       of too many auditory displays or (as in (a) above) in
       a noisy environment;
(e)   the message does not require an immediate response.

Visual displays are appropriate, therefore, for providing continuous information to the operator. On the other hand, *auditory* displays are more appropriate when:

(a) the message requires an immediate response. It is for this reason that warning messages are normally presented in the form of a klaxon or bell. They are more attention-getting;

(b) the visual system is overburdened - perhaps because of too many visual displays or in conditions having too high a level of ambient lighting;

(c) the information needs to be presented irrespective of the position of the operator's head. The drawback of visual displays lies in the fact that the operator needs to be looking at them before they are able to communicate the information. Auditory displays, however, do not have such restrictions. It is for this reason, too, that they make such acceptable warning indicators;

(d) vision is limited - for example in darkness, at night, or when it is likely that the operator will not have had time to adapt to the light or dark conditions.

Types of display Visual and auditory displays can be categorised as being one of two forms - either digital or analogue. Digital displays present the information to the operator in direct numerical form, for example a digital clock, a counter, or a voice reading numbers. With an analogue display, on the other hand, the operator needs to interpret the information from some aspect of the display - perhaps the position of a pointer on a dial, whether or not a light is illuminated, whether a bell is sounding or is quiet, the position or inclination of a shape on a screen, or from some other indication which is analogous to the real state of the machine.

In many respects the use to which a display is to be put determines which type of display (digital or analogue) is chosen. The traditional classification is made in terms of the nature of the information to be received. Thus displays may be used:

(a) to make quantitative readings (that is, to read the state of the machine in numerical terms - the temperature in degrees centigrade, the height in feet, the speed in mph, etc.),

(b) to make qualitative readings (that is, to infer the 'quality' of the machine state - whether it is 'safe' or 'unsafe'; 'hot', 'warm' or 'cold'; moving 'quickly' or 'slowly', etc. (rather than the precise temperature

or speed),
(c)   in combination with controls to set the machine or to
       track (maintain) a particular machine state, and
(d)   to warn the operator of danger or that a specific
       machine state has been reached.

Displays for Making Quantitative Readings Numerical information is normally presented visually and in this case it is
extremely important to make the correct choice of display
type - digital or analogue. Both have their advantages and
disadvantages. If the display is to present information
which is relatively slow-changing, then a direct digital
representation is clearly most appropriate. No interpretation of the meaning of the display (which could incur
errors) needs to be made. This aspect was clearly demonstrated by Grether (1949) who used photographs of different
forms of altimeters bound into booklets, to compare the
readings errors produced by trained pilots and by college
students. Each photograph showed a different height on one
of either eight analogue displays or on a counter. Using the
digital display, the subjects were able to read the 'height'
immediately, whereas they took nearly two seconds when
using a dial with a single pointer. A similar difference
was also seen in terms of their error rate. Murrell and
Kingston (1966) also describe results from an experiment
which they carried out on skilled journeymen using a
graduated (analogue) and a digital micrometer. Whereas
about 3 per cent of the readings were in error using a
graduated micrometer, the same men made only 0.C5 per cent
errors when they used a digital micrometer.
   Digital displays do have their drawbacks, however, and
these lie in three areas. Firstly, if the counters are
mechanical and are operated by a revolving drum, situations
may arise in which only parts of a number are displayed as
the drum revolves, perhaps the bottom part of 'eight' and the
top of 'nine'. This is clearly likely to make the operator's
task more difficult leading to increased reading time and,
possibly, to increased errors.
   Secondly, if the information is changing quickly the
numbers may appear blurred. This can have serious consequences if the numbers have to be read with some precision
- as anyone who has tried to read the fast-changing times
produced by a digital clock at a sports meeting will know.
   Finally, digital displays make prediction difficult. It
is very rare that an operator will simply read the values
indicated on a display. As Kelly (1968) has pointed out,
information from displays in general is required not to
tell the observer the conditions of a system at present,

but what action is needed in the future; how things will be
if no action is taken. The display is used, therefore, in a
predictive manner. For example, on seeing a road sign indicating a 30 mph speed zone, a car driver is likely to check
the reading displayed by his speedometer. His subsequent
control action (perhaps to brake) is a direct response to
his prediction of the future state (speed)of the vehicle.

Although the information required to make such predictions
is provided by digital displays, it is not necessarily given
in a form which makes it easy for the operator to use. The
position of a pointer on an analogue display, however, does
give this information in a more accessible form. For example,
compare the conventional (analogue) with a digital clock
face. If the minute and hour hands are pointing to eight
and four respectively (that is, twenty minutes to four),
the position of the minute hand provides spatial cues to
enable the reader to predict quickly that one third of the
hour (twenty minutes) is left. This same information is
also contained in a digital display indicating '3:40', but
the reader needs to carry out fast numerical computations
(with all of their attendant problems) to achieve the same
result.

The increased predictive efficiency of analogue over
digital displays has been demonstrated by Simons and Roscoe
(1956). Using information displayed either digitally or as
an analogue, their subjects were asked to predict the future
state of a machine. Whereas the subjects took an average of
seventy-five seconds to complete various predictions using
a digital display (and made 7 per cent errors), when they
used a vertical analogue display (that is, the pointer moved
vertically rather than around a dial) they took only fifty-
six seconds and made far fewer (3 per cent) errors.

In summary, therefore, it would appear that for recording
quantitative information, digital displays make the task
easier for the operator (faster reading time and fewer
errors) than do analogue displays. The superiority of digital
displays is reduced, however, if the display is mechanical,
if the values change quickly, or if the operator needs to
predict the future 'conditions' of the machine.

Displays for Making Qualitative Readings Both visual and
auditory displays are used for this purpose and, since the
purpose of making the reading does not include recording
numerical values, digital displays can have no advantages
at all over analogue displays. One problem which does arise
when considering the use of analogue displays, however, is
how to ensure that the aspects of the display which indicate
the different machine states are discriminable from each

other. This is normally carried out using some type of coding technique which, in the case of visual displays, usually takes the form of colour coding different areas of the display face. Naturally other coding systems are available, such as using shapes, pictures or letters to indicate the various areas on the dial, but colour has been demonstrated many times to be a superior coding system (for example, Hitt, 1961; Christ, 1975).

One specific function for which a qualitative display is often used is to check either whether a specific machine state has been reached, for example whether the amount of fuel in the tanks is dangerously low, or whether a group of components in the system are operating within normal limits (for example the temperature, pressure and speed of a process are safe). An interesting design for a check-reading dial face was proposed by Kurke (1956), who suggested one which was so arranged that when the indicator is pointing to, say, a 'danger' reading, there appears on the dial face a high contrast wedge-shaped 'flag' which was not present under 'safe and normal' conditions. Using this display, therefore, the operator's task would simply be to perceive the presence or absence of the wedge, rather than to have to perceive the position of the pointer. In an experiment carried out to test this type of display, Kurke's subjects reduced their error rate by 94 per cent and increased their detection time by 79 per cent over simply a colour-coded display.

To ensure that all systems are operating normally, of course, a set of dials could be arranged, each of which incorporates the 'wedge' display. However, a more appropriate system might be incorporated which uses the existing dials, each of which are rotated so that, under normal conditions, all pointers are pointing in one direction, say to the right. Any deviating pointer can then be perceived as a 'break' in the line of pointers. Again, then, the checker's task is reduced to one of noticing a change in the state of the dial(s) rather than having to make a series of readings.

The use of patterns such as these was taken one step further by Dashevsky (1964) who extended the lines made by pointers under 'normal' conditions on to the console. Comparing these extension lines with the open (no line) arrangement, he produced an 85 per cent reduction in error rate.

Displays for Setting and Tracking Little work has been carried out to find the optimum type of display to use when settings have to be made. It may be suggested, however, that as long as the display and control movements are compatible

(a concept which will be discussed later), the precise
design of the display for this function is not too critical.

Comparing the merits of analogue and digital displays for
this type of task it would appear that, on balance, analogue
displays cause less strain for the operator to use than do
digital displays. For example, Benson *et al.* (1965) demonstrated that, although subjects' tracking performance using
the two types of display was not significantly different,
their heart, sweat and respiration rate, and their muscle
activity all increased when the digital display alone was
used. Furthermore, their performance on other tasks which
had to be carried out at the same time as the tracking task
was also reduced when using the digital display. It would
appear, therefore, that analogue displays demand less
attention from the operator.

The use of the auditory modality to aid tracking performance has been rather restricted in the past, with most
information being presented in the visual mode. However,
some evidence exists to suggest that such a strategy is not
always the most appropriate. Hoffman and Heimstra (1972),for
example, report an auditory tracking system which proved to
be superior to a visual display. In this case the subject
was required to maintain a particular random course using
a hand wheel, in which he heard no noise if he was on target
but a noise signal in the respective ear if he deviated to
the right or left. More time was spent on target when using
this system than with the visual display. As McCormick
(1976) points out, however, auditory tracking displays should
be used with some caution in an otherwise noisy environment
- a point made earlier when discussing the relative merits
of visual and auditory displays.

Displays for Warning Warning displays are used to make the
operator aware of some action which he has to take with
respect to the environment. As such, their overriding
requirement is that they should attract the operator's
attention immediately. In this case, therefore, visual
indicators will normally be at a disadvantage since they
need to be looked at before their presence can be registered.

Man-Environment Communication: Controls
When considering the environment-man-environment communication
system, the return link concerns the way in which the operator passes his information to the environment. Controls,
then, are important components in the system - they are the
operator's own displays for the machine. As such they are
the complement of the environment's displays and need careful consideration when designed in a working system.

As an example of the need to design a control system effectively to fit the user, Singleton (1960) discusses a study in which he compared the efficiency of an 'old' and a redesigned speed control for an industrial sewing machine. The new design incorporated relatively simple changes in the machine-control dynamics. Records taken over one month's operation showed a potential improvement in production rate of between 10 per cent and 15 per cent. Although translating the improvements into economic terms proved difficult, Singleton estimated that by dividing the gains equally between the management and the operators, earnings would increase by 5 per cent and the capital cost of the new control units would be recovered in about three years.

Whatever type of control is used in the system, whether it be a finger push-button, a wheel, a lever or a pedal, a number of principles are important in determining the effectiveness of their use. These include the degree and type of feedback incorporated into the control, and its size and weight.

Like the social feedback discussed in Chapter 4, the feedback from a control informs the operator about his performance with the control. Again, like social feedback, this information may be intrinsic or extrinsic.

Intrinsic feedback arises from the operator's own muscles. Specific receptors in the muscles, which form a sensory system known as the proprioceptive system, enable the operator to know the position of his limb in space without him having to use his eyes. For example, if the arm is lifted above the head, whilst looking straight ahead, one 'knows' roughly where the hand is, what the fingers are doing etc. because of the stretch sensations arising from the muscles. Similarly, then, when rotating a control one 'knows' by how much the control has been rotated (that is, one receives feedback) by the degree of stretch of the finger and wrist muscles.

Extrinsic feedback occurs mainly from the control itself in terms of both the control 'feel' (that is, its resistance to movement) and any texture which may be incorporated on the control surface. Possibly the main feedback cue during operation, however, arises from the control's resistance to movement. In the majority of cases, particularly when continuous settings are to be made, some inbuilt resistance is desirable since it allows the operator to make his settings with some degree of precision. In addition, resistance will often help to guard against the accidental operation of the control. If too much resistance is incorporated into the control, however, or resistance of the wrong type, performance may be reduced and the operator experience fatigue.

Understanding the nature of different types of resistance,
therefore, is important. Discussion of these is outside
the scope of this book,but they are considered in detail by
authors such as McCormick(1976).

The control texture performs two functions. First, naturally
it helps to prevent slipping when gripping the control.
Secondly, as suggested above, it provides some feedback to
the operator in terms of coding. Thus the operator learns
to associate a knurled knob as, say, the speed control, or
a hexagonal knob with, say, the height control. Control
coding may take a number of forms, although the two primary
techniques, as these examples suggest, are in terms of the
surface texture and control shape. Bradley (1967) and Moore
(1976) have both produced sets of non-confusable control
textures and shapes for coding purposes.

The optimum size and weight of a control depends entirely
on the limb or part of the limb which is to operate it. As
such, these two variables will be related to the anthropometric dimensions of the respective limbs. Thus the diameter
of a push-button should be at least that of the fingertip
(approximately 0.6 in.); the size of a knob on a lever equal
to the breadth of grip (1.92 in.). Garrett (1971) provides
a set of these various dimensions for the human hand, but it
should be remembered that these dimensions will be altered,
sometimes considerably, if the operator is wearing gloves.

Having chosen or designed an appropriate control for the
system, the next problem confronting the applied psychologist in industry is where to site it 'in front of' the
operator. This decision is quite crucial to the efficient
working of the system, particularly when the problem of the
placement of the respective display is also realised. Thus,
just as a single display or control may severly interrupt
the communication process in one direction or another, the
system's overall efficiency is at stake if the display and
control are not arranged appropriately.

This problem, then, takes two forms; firstly to place the
components in their most relevant positions on the console,
and then to ensure that they are compatible with one another.
When determining how controls and displays should be arranged
in front of the operator, the overriding consideration is
to ensure that they can be used quickly and accurately. A
number of principles have gradually evolved to aid these
decisions and are called the 'sequence', 'frequency' and 'importance' principles respectively.

As the name suggests, the sequence principle implies that
if displays and controls are used sequentially then they
should be arranged in this order. For example, if an operation involves switching the machine on, altering the height

of a bit, increasing its speed, etc., then the controls and displays should be arranged in this order - say from left to right on the console. Similarly, the frequency of usage principle is self-describing. Thus the more frequently used controls and displays ought to be placed in more accessible positions, and these are normally directly in front of the operator. Overriding the frequency principle, however, is that of importance. Emergency controls, for example, are used (hopefully) very infrequently; however, when they are used they need to be operated extremely quickly and should thus be positioned where the operator can easily see and use them.

Unfortunately, little data exists with which one is able to evaluate these guidelines. However, an experiment carried out by Fowler *et al.* (1968) (discussed by McCormick, 1976) indicates that when controls and displays are arranged on the operator's console according to one of these principles, the average time taken to carry out a task was lowest for the sequentially arranged components. The 'importance' and 'frequency' arrangements respectively took progressively longer.

Finally, Haines and Gilliland (1973) have produced guides for designers to help them to place controls and displays in the most appropriate positions on the consoles. These guides take the form of equal speed-of-response boundaries in the visual field, and the authors suggest that by superimposing the contours over a scaled-down model the positions for various displays may be pinpointed.

The problem of (in)compatibility between displays and controls can take two forms: position and movement. A control and display are said to be position-compatible if the position of one suggests to the operator that of the other. This can possibly best be exemplified by a simple experiment carried out by Crossman (1956) (described by Welford, 1976). Crossman presented his subjects with up to eight stimulus lights, to any one of which they had to respond as quickly as possible by pressing the appropriate numbered key. In the highly-compatible condition each button was located directly below its light, whereas in the low-compatible condition they were placed in random order. Crossman's subjects took significantly longer to make a correct response when the lights (displays) and keys (controls) were incompatible than when they were compatible.

As the name suggests, movement compatibility concerns some aspect of the movement of the display and control. Again, however, the extended concept of a 'display' should be emphasised. In the case of a car driver, for example, it is clear what is meant by the movement of a control such as a steering wheel. The associated display, however, may not be so clear. It is, in fact, what the driver perceives through his windscreen - the movement of the vehicle relative to the road.

As an example of the importance of these movement relationships, Murrell (1970) describes the case of a press which was wrecked because the movements of the control (a lever on the side of the press) and display (the press itself) were incompatible. In this case, an upward movement of the lever caused a downward movement of the press and vice versa. The operator was able to learn this relationship and carry out the operations effectively under 'normal' conditions. When an emergency arose, however, and he wished to raise the press quickly, his 'natural' reaction was to lift the lever, so exacerbating the situation.

For most types of control and display, general movement is 'up or clockwise' for an increased or right moving reading, and 'down or anti-clockwise' for a left or reduced reading. In addition, to make the operator's task easier, it has often been suggested that strip displays are associated with linear controls and dial displays with rotary controls. Loveless (1962) has reviewed a number of studies which have investigated different relationships between different types of display and control and in different planes on the console.

In addition to an increased speed of response which is likely to result from using compatible displays and controls, Murrell (1970) suggests two further advantages of compatibility Firstly the time taken to learn how to operate the equipment with compatible displays and controls will be much shorter than if the controls are incompatible. Having an arrangement which is not what one otherwise would have expected means that the incompatible display/control relationship will need to be realised before the learning process can take place. Secondly, under stress conditions (perhaps an emergency) the compatible controls are more likely to be operated correctly than those which are incompatible (as Murrell's example illustrates).

ENVIRONMENTAL EFFECTS ON PERFORMANCE

The discussion so far has centred around the simple communication channels which are set up, in the operator's immediate vicinity, between himself and his particular 'machine'. This communication, however, can be affected, sometimes considerably, by the physical environment in which the operator and his 'machine' are situated. Thus the remainder of this chapter will consider the effects of environmental parameters such as noise, vibration, temperature and illumination. Each of these aspects can affect the operator

in one or more of three ways. Firstly, at extremes it can
seriously damage   health, to the point of death; secondly,
at lower levels, it can disrupt performance; and thirdly it
can interfere with feelings of ease and well-being. The
remainder of this chapter will discuss mainly the performance
effects.

Environmental Noise

Noise is conveniently and frequently defined as 'unwanted
sound', a definition which in its looseness allows a sound
source to be considered as 'noise' or 'not noise' solely on
the basis of the listener's reaction to it. To any one person,
then, the same Beethoven Sonata can be 'music' on one occasion
perhaps when he wishes to rest, and 'noise' on another,
perhaps when he does not wish to be distracted from an
intricate task.

The health effects of noise are important not only from
the point of view of the operator but also insofar as they
affect his performance. In this respect Kryter (1970) has
suggested that noise-induced deafness is a significant
health problem in most modern countries. It is an insidious
complaint since an operator whose hearing is being damaged
is unlikely to demonstrate any decrease in performance as
a result of the deafness when he is in a noisy environment
- as will be discussed later the noise masks all other
auditory stimuli so, effectively, making all operators
temporarily 'deaf'. It is only when he moves into quieter
environmental conditions that his reduced hearing ability
may manifest itself in missed acoustic signals and thus
reduced efficiency and increased errors.

There is no doubt that continuous intense noise can cause
a gradual reduction in the operator's ability to perceive
sounds. This has been demonstrated on numerous occasions
and the fact has been incorporated into industrial codes of
practice in a number of countries (see, for example, Kryter,
1970). Nixon and Glorig (1961), for example, have demonstrated
that workers in industries which have an average noise level
greater than 94 db were liable to hearing damage. The
incidence of hearing loss was less, however, in other
industries with lower noise levels.

At levels lower than those which cause damage, noise can
have a definite and measurable effect on performance. This
can arise in two ways: first as an interfering effect with
auditory communication channels through masking, whether
these channels be with another operator (through speech) or
with a machine (through auditory displays). Secondly, some
evidence exists which suggests that noise interferes with
cognitive performance, but this evidence is contentious as

will be discussed later.

Auditory masking effects are wellknown, and the ability to perceive a signal in noise has probably been experienced by everyone. The importance of this effect at work is obvious - auditory warning signals or instructions may be missed, or perhaps more importantly, misinterpreted. A number of factors affect the ability of a signal to be masked and these include the intensity, frequency and phase relationships of the signal and masker (noise).

Perhaps the most obvious factor is the masker intensity - as the intensity of the environmental noise increases, its ability to mask also increases. Indeed this relationship was demonstrated as early as 1924 by Wegel and Lane, and the investigation continued by experimenters such as Fletcher and Munson (1937), who showed that the level of masking increases fairly linearly with increases in the masker intensity.

Possibly less immediately obvious are the effects of the frequency relationships between signal and masker: the extent to which a signal can be masked increases as the frequencies in the masking noise approach those in the signal (again demonstrated by Wegel and Lane in 1924). This has direct implications for hearing signals in noise since it suggests that the masking effect can be reduced providing the noise frequencies and the signal frequencies are different. Thus taking speech as an example of a signal which often needs to be heard: male speech is characterised as being composed of a broad band of frequencies which spread from about 100 to 5000 Hz (Dunn and White, 1940); the majority of the frequencies are compressed within a band between 200 and about 1000 Hz. If the predominant frequencies of the environmental noise lie outside this band, significant masking effects will not occur. Similar principles will also hold for the perception of pure-tone, auditory warning signals.

The effects of the phase relationships between signal and masker are less easy to understand. A pure tone is produced by the action of an earphone diaphragm vibrating sinusoidally. If a second diaphragm (B) is made to vibrate with the same frequency but, when A is at its peak position B is at its lowest position, then the two diaphragms are said to be out of phase. They are in phase when both move in the same direction at the same time. Different phase relationships occur between these two extremes of 0 degrees (in phase) to 180 degrees (out of phase).

During the Second World War, workers at the Harvard Psychoacoustic Laboratory, in particular Licklider (1948), conducted many experiments on masking - particularly the masking of speech by noise. Their interesting results

demonstrated that if either the signal or the noise is made
to be out of phase between the two ears, then masking was
reduced.

These three aspects of masking, therefore, point to practical measures which can be taken to reduce its effect:
first to increase the level of the signal relative to the
masker; second to ensure that the signal frequencies are
different from the main frequencies of the environmental
noise; and third, if earphones are worn, to (electronically)
arrange for the signal to be presented out of phase at the
two ears.

The position regarding the effects of noise on cognitive
performance is by no means as clear-cut as its effects on
hearing ability. Indeed Teichener *et al.* (1963) conclude
that the literature reveals three conflicting effects:
performance is benefited by noise; performance is reduced
by noise; and noise has no effect on performance. They suggest
that many reasons explain why these discrepant results arise,
including the type and level of noise and the type of task
used. To this short list should, perhaps, also be added the
variable of the type of subject used in the experiment since
evidence exists to suggest that introverts react differently
from extroverts to noise (for example, Hockey, 1972; Elliot,
1971).

The studies which show a decrease in performance in noise
use one of two types of task – either a vigilance task or a
memory task. The type of vigilance task used can best be
exemplified by a study carried out by Broadbent (1954) who
asked subjects to monitor twenty gauges for $1\frac{1}{2}$ hours. If
they saw any of the pointers reading above a danger mark
they were required to turn a knob below the gauge to bring
the pointer back to the mark. This was carried out under
two conditions, 'noise' (100 db) and 'quiet'(70 db), and
Broadbent's results indicated that the subject's performance
was impaired in the noisy relative to the quiet conditions.

In a review of such studies, Poulton (1977) lists thirty-
two experiments which have demonstrated similar results.
However, he questions the validity of the findings by suggest-
ing that many of these effects can be placed at the door of
equipment deficiencies. For example, the equipment used by
Broadbent contained microswitches mounted directly behind
the knob which recorded the subject's response. Poulton
argues that auditory feedback could have helped the subjects
enough in the quiet conditions to enable them to produce a
faster and a more accurate response than had they not been
present. The 'noise' conditions, however, probably masked
these cues.

Whether or not these criticisms are fully valid is still

an open question which will be resolved only when further experiments have been carried out in the light of Poulton's criticisms. McCormick (1976) concludes, however, 'although we probably can reject the notion that noise generally brings about degredation in performance, there are accumulating indications from experimental studies that certain types of noise may adversely affect performance on certain types of task' (p.368).

The position as far as memory is concerned is no less equivocal. Thus reviewing many of the experiments, Jones (1979) again provides examples of the three possible performance outcomes described above, both in terms of the initial input of the information to be remembered and at the retrieval stage. These discrepancies he ascribes to the differing arousal properties of the varying noises, subjects and tasks, a view also strongly argued by Poulton (1978).

A hypothetical performance-arousal relationship has been under discussion in the psychological literature for a number of years and suggests that the two variables are related according to an inverted-U function. Thus when body arousal is very low (perhaps because the individual is nearly asleep), performance is also low. Performance increases, however, with increasing arousal, but only up to an optimum level. If arousal is increased after this point (perhaps because of anxiety or fear) then performance begins to fall again. Using this 'arousal hypothesis', it can be suggested that the different tasks, noises and types of subjects differentially affect the individuals' arousal level, so that sometimes they are taken past the optimum noise level, whereas in other cases their arousal is raised so producing increased performance.

The practical application of the arousal hypothesis is perhaps illustrated by those studies which demonstrate an increase in performance in the presence of auditory stimulation. It should be noted that the term 'stimulation' is used rather than 'noise' since these studies are concerned with the effects of background music on productivity - the music may not be unwanted and, strictly speaking therefore, is not 'noise'.

Fox (1971) has argued that music might aid performance by alleviating the boredom and fatigue which occurs with repetitive work - the level of operator arousal can be increased and, indeed, many studies appear to support his contention. For example, Stevenson *et al.* (1959) (reported in Roberts, 1959) have indicated that the number of cheques ruined by mistakes in the accounts department of a large organisation dropped from 9 per cent to less than 5½ per cent after music was introduced. Similarly Fox's review

indicated studies showing increased output and production
quality, and reductions in poor time-keeping, staff turnover
and accidents in the presence of background music.

When considering the type of music to be played in the
background, Fox insists that it should not be continuous
throughout the day - otherwise it loses its stimulating
effect. Equally important is that it should be timed to
counteract the peaks of fatigue during the day. Broadbent
(1957), for example, reports a study in which music (the
type not reported) was played to workers carrying out a
'light manual task' at different periods. Whereas output
did not increase significantly when the music was played
between either 9.30 and 10.00 or between 11.00 and 11.45,
increases were obtained with music between 10.00 and 11.15
and between 8.45-9.15, 9.45-10.15, 10.45-11.15 and 11.45-
12.15.

With regard to the effect of the type of music, a study
by Fox and Embrey (1972) suggests that the workers themselves
should choose their music. Using a laboratory detection task,
although an increase in detection occured with 'a commercially
prepared lively programme', the increase was greater when the
subjects were allowed to select a programme.

Before concluding this discussion of the effects of background music, it is important to emphasise that other
influencers of performance might be present in addition to
the music. Thus the music may influence not only attention
and vigilance but also feelings of well-being and ease, and
these effects could be reflected by drops in absenteeism,
bad time-keeping and labour turnover. It is for this reason
that controversy surrounds the claims for background music.
At a pragmatic level, however, although the point is debat-
able, an increase in performance remains an increase in
performance.

Environmental Vibration
At high enough intensities, and over long periods of time,
vibration can be detrimental to health. Damage to the
neurovascular structures in the fingers from prolonged use
of machines such as chain saws (Guignard and King, 1972)
and increasing spinal complaints of tractor drivers who
drive over deep ploughed furrows (Rosseger and Rosseger,
1960) are just two examples. Unless the damage to health
becomes debilitating, however, no direct performance effects
will arise from these problems. Of more importance to the
present discussion is the degradation in motor control caused
by the body parts vibrating in sympathy with the vibrating
machinery. In this case two types of control are important;
first, control of the eyeballs, resulting in a reduction of

visual performance due to blurred images, and secondly the
direct control of limbs such as the arms or legs.

As far as visual performance is concerned, any reduction
in ability due to vibration can be related directly to the
degree of blurring of the image on the moving retina. In
this case three situations can cause a moving image to appear
on the retina: first if the object alone is vibrating, with
the observer stationary; secondly if the observer is being
vibrated whilst the object is stationary; and finally if
both the object and the observer are being vibrated.

As far as vibrating the object alone is concerned, Griffin
and Lewis (1978) point out that the problem of blurring
becomes apparent only when the eye is unable to track the
vibrating object. At low enough frequencies (less than 1 Hz)
the eyes are able to compensate for the movement by tracking
the object and are thus able to produce relatively stable
images on the retina (over time, of course, this is likely
to lead to fatigue in the eye muscles). As the frequency of
the object increases, however, there comes a point when this
pursuit tracking is carried out less effectively.
The precise critical frequency at which this occurs is
uncertain, but various authors have suggested between 3-4 Hz.

With regard to the vibration intensity, the evidence suggests
that within reason this becomes an important variable only in
otherwise unfavourable conditions. For example, Griffin and
Lewis (1978) report a series of experiments carried out by
Crook *et al.* who demonstrated no significant change in either
reading errors or in reading time when vibrating the objects
at different intensities. When the room lighting was poor,
however, the performance decreased as the amplitude of the
object increased.

The visual effects produced when the observer is vibrated
are similar to those resulting from vibrating the object
along - a blurred image which, in this case, is due to the
movement of the eyeball itself relative to the object. With
observer vibration, however, further problems may occur due
to resonance effects of the eyeball and head.

When vibration passes through any physical structure, its
level may be affected in one of three ways. Firstly it may
be reduced, as for example, with a soft cushion. Secondly
it may not be affected in any way and so is transmitted in
a 1:1 relationship. Finally, the body may increase the
vibration as it passes through. This last effect occurs only
if the body is vibrated at specific frequencies - known as
the resonant frequencies of the body.

Since every structure has a different resonant frequency,
it can readily be seen that the human body and the eyes
which are attached to the body may react differently to

different frequency vibration stimuli.

If the frequency of the vibration which is experienced by
the body is outside the resonant frequency of the head/eye
complex, then the eyes will vibrate at the same frequency
and amplitude as the rest of the body, and any visual blurring
effects will be similar to those experienced when the object
alone is vibrating. At the resonant frequencies of the head/
eye complex, however, the eyes will begin to vibrate at
higher intensities and out of phase with the remainder of
the body, thus causing increased blurring. In this respect
transmission studies of the various body structures (for
example, Thomas, 1965; Lee and King, 1971) suggest that the
eyeball will begin to accentuate the input vibration if the
vibration frequency is above about 20-25 Hz. At lower
frequencies, between about 8-10 Hz, the head and neck resonance is also likely to cause the eyes to move at higher
intensities than those which enter the body.

If the problems when either the object or observer are
vibrating alone are complex, when they are vibrating together
(as occurs in many situations at work, for example in transport), they are increased infinitely. Because of different
resonant characteristics of the man and parts of his machine
there are differences in both the amplitude, phase and
possibly direction of the observer and object motions which
cause complications. For these reasons very few well-controlle
studies have been carried out to investigate this aspect of
visual performance under vibration, but the few studies which
are available have been reviewed by Griffin and Lewis (1978).

Whereas the operator can usually compensate for small
amounts of vibration when carrying out a visual task, decrements in motor performance are less easily overcome. Because
the vibration tends physically to move the operator's limbs,
possibly out of phase with the rest of his body, any compen-
sating will be done by tensing different muscles to steady
the limb (in the same way that the seated body seeks stability
Even if the operator is able to compensate for the motion,
therefore, it is likely to cause fatigue.

For vibration stimuli below 20 Hz, there appears to be
fairly good agreement that any decrease in performance is
related to the amount of vibration which is transmitted
through the body. For example Buckhout (1964) has shown that,
for vertical vibration at 5, 7 and 11 Hz, tracking error
was highly and positively correlated with the amount of
vibration which was transmitted to the sternum. This observation is particularly important since it implies that, when
in vibrating conditions, the presence of a backrest or arm-
rests may reduce, rather than increase, body stability.
Vibrations transmitted through the seatback to the shoulder

and chest areas are likely to play a part in reducing an operator's performance on a motor-tracking task. This effect will be accentuated if the operator is using a safety harness or seat belt, which tends to force the body back into the seat and into the backrest (see, for example, Lovesey, 1975).

Finally, with regard to cognitive performance, a number of studies have been carried out, most of which have investigated the operator's speed of reaction (reaction time), or his ability to do some complex reasoning task. Most studies, however, have demonstrated either no effect at all or no consistent effect as a result of the vibration (Grether, 1971). Any reduction in performance which might occur was shown by Shoenberger (1974) to be due to difficulties in perceiving the stimulus due to visual interference by the vibration.

Environmental Temperature
As has been seen, the effects of the environmental noise and vibration on an operator's performance in a system are extremely complex. However, if the intensities alone of these parameters are considered, the problem is simplified slightly – thus performance decrease can be related directly to an increase in either the noise or the vibration intensity. Any reductions in the intensity, therefore, will probably lead to reductions in the interference with the performance.

For both temperature and illumination, however, the position is slightly different. In both cases there is a narrow range of intensities under which a worker can, and should, operate. Departure from this optimum range, either by increasing or by reducing the intensity, is likely to affect the operator's performance. For example a man's ability to see fine detail is impaired in both dark and extremely bright conditions; his ability to perform complex mental operations can be affected in conditions of both extreme cold and extreme heat.

The relationship between experimental temperature and behaviour is made even more complex by the actions of a number of variables which influence the overall sensation of 'temperature'. These include the temperature *per se* (as measured by a mercury thermometer), the amount of radiant heat present, the air humidity and velocity (draughts), and the subject's activity and type of clothing. Naturally the interactive effects of all of these variables are too complex to be considered here. All of these factors act to affect the body's natural thermal balancing system. Provided this system works effectively, performance remains relatively systematic, but as the body becomes gradually unable to cope with the additional stress posed by either too hot or too cold

conditions (by producing heat or by dilating the blood
vessels respectively), the operator's ability to sustain
performance also falls. For this reason, and after conducting
extensive tests using many different tasks (weight lifting,
vigilance, complex reasoning, etc.), Mackworth (1950) proposed
the concept of a critical temperature region for performance
'above which most acclimatised men dressed in shorts will not
work effectively indoors. This region lies between 90 and
95^0 F ($32-35^0$ C) when the air movement is 100 ft/min.'

A number of studies subsequent to those of Mackworth have
been carried out and demonstrate similar trends for a variety
of tasks (for example grip strength, Clarke *et al.*, 1958;
manual dexterity, Winer and Hutchinson, 1945; a tracking task,
Azer *et al.*, 1972; and cognitive tasks, Pepler, 1958). Further
more Wing (1965) has combined the data from some of these
studies in an attempt to indicate, in terms of the duration
of exposure, the temperature levels able to be endured before
cognitive performance decrements become apparent.

After reviewing much of the work of the effects of environmental cold on human performance, Fox (1967) concluded that
cold can affect performance in five areas: (a) tactile
sensitivity, (b) manual performance, (c) tracking, (d)
reaction time, and (e) 'complex behaviours'. These five
behaviours, however, can be further sub-divided into two
main categories: motor performance and cognitive performance.

As far as motor performance is concerned, two factors appear
to be important; first the temperature of the limb which is
being used, and secondly the rate of cooling.

The limb temperature, rather than the overall body temperature, affects motor ability by interfering with muscular
control. It causes a loss of cutaneous sensitivity, changes
in the characteristics of synovial fluid in the joints, and
a loss of muscular strength.

It is, perhaps, obvious to point out that the important
consideration in relation to limb sensitivity is not the
level of environmental temperature *per se* but, ultimately,
the temperature of the limb itself. As Fox (1967) suggests,
therefore, it is more appropriate to consider the effects
of factors such as hand skin, or finger skin temperatures.
In this respect Morton and Provins (1960) have demonstrated
a significant reduction in dexterity whenever the skin
temperature falls below $20-25^0$ C ($68-97^0$ F), although there
is large individual variability.

Because the main factor affecting manual performance in
the cold is related to the skin temperature of the affected
limb, when gloves are unable to be worn it would appear
sensible to attempt some means of locally warming the skin.
Lockhart and Keiss (1971), for example, showed that for most

tasks, impaired manual performance could be greatly aleviated by applying radiant heat to the hands only (raising the temperature of the little finger from 12 to 19.5^0 C (from 54^0 to 67^{0}F).

Artificially raising the temperature of the affected limb, however, cannot fully overcome the effects of the cold if the rest of the body is not similarly heated. For example, Lockhart (1968) maintained the temperature of his subject's hands at the 'normal' temperature, whilst cooling the body from 25.5 to 19^{0}C (78 to 66^{0}F). His results suggest that cooling the whole body affects the operator's ability to carry out some manual tasks even though the hands were kept 'warm'. The tasks affected involved fine dexterity and Lockhart suggests that part of the reason for the performance reduction was shivering.

The effects of cold on manual performance, therefore, appear to be two-fold. First, if the cold is applied locally to the operating limb, it can have a direct effect on the muscular control of that limb, reducing such abilities as dexterity and strength. This may be overcome somewhat by locally warming the limb. Cold applied to the whole body, however, can reduce performance due to shivering. If the body can be stabilised during this shivering, generalised cold would appear not to affect manual performance to any great extent.

As far as cognitive performance is concerned, the experimental work which has been carried out does not lead to any firm conclusions. As an example of the conflicting results, Bowen (1968) investigated the effects of cold (7^0 C (45^0 F) for up to thirty minutes), on both manual tasks (for example, tactile sensitivity, grip strength, dexterity) and cognitive tasks (for example, mental arithmetic, complex coding tasks). On all tasks Bowen's results indicated an impairment in performance in the cold compared with the ability in 'normal' temperature (22^0 C; 72^0 F) water.

Bowen's conclusions, however, have not been substantiated by other experimenters. For example, Baddeley *et al.* (1975) asked their divers to perform different cognitive tasks (vigilance, memory, reasoning) in colder water and for longer than usually accepted (40^0 F for fifty minutes). However, a reduction in performance was not demonstrated on either the reasoning test (judging a series of statements as being either 'true' or 'false') or the vigilance test (detecting the occasional onset of a dim light mounted in their helmet). On the basis of their experiments, therefore, Baddeley *et al.* conclude that cognitive efficiency may be surprisingly resistant to the effects of cold, given good conditions and well-motivated subjects.

The results of these different studies, therefore, are
inconclusive. Both were well controlled but each seems to
lead to contrary conclusions. However, if the 'riders'
introduced by both authors are noted, some conclusions may
be drawn. Thus Bowen suggests that only the very complex
tasks will be affected by the cold. Certainly the vigilance
and reasoning tasks used by Baddeley *et al.* were not as
complex as Bowen's complex reasoning task. Secondly Baddeley
et al. suggest that the cold will not affect the cognitive
efficiency of well-motivated subjects since the cold 'tends
to reduce his motivation by making him uncomfortable, and
his discomfort may in turn distract him from the task in
hand'. This is less likely to happen to a well-motivated
subject.

Environmental Illumination
Before we can see any object we need to be able to separate
its image from its background or surroundings, otherwise it
becomes 'camouflaged'. The quality of an individual's visual
performance, therefore, can be related simply to the extent
to which the viewed object stands out from other stimuli in
the observer's visual field. Three factors affect the degree
to which an object stands out and is able to be perceived:
first the overall illumination, secondly its size, and thirdly
the contrast between its luminance and that of the surround.
These three factors were amongst others extensively investigated by Gilbert and Hopkinson (1949).

   To investigate the effects of illumination level Gilbert
and Hopkinson asked subjects to read various letters on the
chart used by opticians as an aid to assess eye deficiencies
(the Snellen chart - the authors suggest that this constitutes a simple test for assessing visual acuity). The charts
were lit with different levels of illumination ranging from
0.1 to 100 lumen/ft^2.

   Their results showed that the visual performance of subjects
with 'normal' vision increased with increasing illumination,
although this increasing advantage tended to level out above
about 10 lumen/ft^2. Children with 'subnormal' vision, however,
did not demonstrate the levelling off, even up to an illumination level of 100 lumen/ft^2. Hopkinson and Collins (1970)
suggest that these data confirm the generally held opinion
that people with poor eyesight benefit from increased levels
of lighting more than do people with normal sight.

   Regarding the size of the object being viewed, Gilbert
and Hopkinson's data confirmed the widely-held belief that
as the objects (letters on the Snellen chart) became smaller,
more light was required for them to be read accurately. Any

suggestions for appropriate lighting levels in various
situations, therefore, need to take account of the type of
detail required in the task.

In its code for interior lighting, the Illuminating
Engineering Society suggests illumination levels for many
different types of work interiors, which are related to the
type of work carried out. Overall, seven illumination levels
are suggested, as shown below. For any type of work, however,
the code suggests that if the contrast is low or if errors
have serious consequences then the next higher level of
illumination should be used.

Type of work	Recommended Illumination level (L/sq ft)
Storage area with no continuous work	150
Rough work (rough machining and assembly)	300
Routine work (office, control rooms, etc.)	500
Demanding work (drawing offices, inspection)	750
Fine work (colour discrimination, fine machinery)	1000
Very fine work (hand engraving)	1500
Minute work (inspection of very fine assembly)	3000

Finally, contrast effects provide vivid examples of the
need for the object to stand out from its surroundings
before it can be perceived. Without contrast an object cannot
be seen, however large it is, and this applies equally to
such stimuli as words on the printed page, to a large machine
in a dimly lit room, or to a well-camouflaged insect.

As an example of the importance of contrast to efficient
visual performance, in the illumination study Gilbert and
Hopkinson asked their subjects to read the letters on a
Snellen chart under different illumination levels, using
different contrast ratios between the letters and the background. Their results indicated strongly that as the contrast
was increased the subject's ability to read the letters
accurately also increased. The effect was particularly marked
at the lower levels of overall illumination, whereas the
performance increase was not so marked when the overall

illumination was reasonably high.

Although a high contrast is clearly important in ensuring that the object is perceived accurately, it is also important that the direction of the contrast effect is considered. Thus if the surround is brighter than its object, it will be likely to reduce the visibility of the object due to glare.

Glare is caused whenever one part of the visual field is brighter than the level to which the eye has become accustomed. This definition, therefore, is much like that given for noise (unwanted sound) since it defines glare in terms of the circumstances prevailing at the time at which the 'bright' stimulus occurred. Just as the same acoustic stimulus may be acceptable at one time but 'noise' at another, therefore, a particularly bright light may produce no adverse effect during, for example, the day but may cause glare at night.

Glare is commonly described as being one of two types. If there is direct interference with visual performance, the condition is referred to as disability glare. However, if performance is not directly affected, but the bright stimulus still causes discomfort, annoyance or distraction, the condition is called discomfort glare. The effects of both types of glare, however, may eventually be to cause distraction and reduced performance and to draw the eyes away from the visual task.

Both types of glare can be caused by two sources. First, direct glare occurs when the excessive light appears directly from the light source itself, such as a car headlight at night or from the sun during the day. Second, and perhaps more insidious, reflected or specular glare is caused by reflections of high brightness from polished or glossy surfaces that are reflected towards the observer. These effects can be more problematic since they may occur under various, and often unpredictable, circumstances, for example, when the object is placed at a certain angle to the light or when a number of lights are brought together in a particular way. Only then will the objects be unable to be seen adequately.

6 Individual Differences and Productivity

INTRODUCTION

One of the arguments often brought against theories in organisational psychology is that they take little account of individual differences. Not everyone, for example, wants fulfilment from his job, and what is wanted by one group of individuals is not necessarily wanted by another. In this chapter, some of the major differences between individuals in relation to productivity will be examined, including age, sex, personality, abilities and racial and cultural differences.

AGE AND PRODUCTIVITY

As with the relationship between other variables previously considered and productivity, it is impossible to give an unqualified account of the relationship between age and productivity. It is common knowledge, for example, that athletes reach a peak in their twenties and then rapidly decline, whereas historians tend to improve with age as their judgement and experience increase. Whether age is going to improve or retard performance, therefore depends on the kind of task involved.

In general terms, ageing results in a decline in certain kinds of ability, particularly sensory and motor abilities. (see, for example, Miner and Brewer, 1976). This involves speed of movement, manual dexterity, co-ordination, physical strength, visual and auditory sensitivity and perceptual speed. There is evidence, too, that various aspects of memory decline with age (Miller, 1979). That failings in these factors have serious consequences for performance can be seen in accident figures, where for example, a third of all serious home accidents occur in the over sixty-fives. There is also evidence that those over sixty have more motor accidents (Kay, 1978).

A number of studies have, in fact, shown that productivity in certain occupations declines with age. McFarland (1956),

for example, in a study of truck drivers, found that drivers
between the ages of 50 and 55 years had encountered difficulties in driving at night and in lifting heavy cargoes,
and Miner and Brewer note that in manual jobs there is a
falling off in performance with age. In particular, as
Bromley (1968) notes, speed of performance is adversely
affected, so that machine-paced jobs are particularly
unsuited to the older worker.

Whilst a decline in capacities with age may well affect
performance, a number of writers, for example, Murrell and
Humphries (1978), have pointed out that experience can often
compensate for any decrement caused by age. Murrell and
Humphries, for example, found that age resulted in decrements
in performance of inexperienced but not of experienced
translators. As Murrell and Humphries point out, testing
individuals in real life situations may produce quite different results from findings in laboratories, where the
individual's experience cannot compensate for his
deficiencies due to age. Laboratory studies may therefore
overestimate the importance of age decrements in the
performance of 'real-life' jobs.

Not only may experience compensate for certain age-related
deterioration in performance, certain skills may, as noted
above, increase with age, at least until late on in the
individual's career. Winston Churchill was after all, at
the age of normal retirement when he was called upon to
lead the United Kingdom against Germany in the Second World
War. Intellectual capacities in the area of verbal ability,
too, have been reported to rise with age. Furthermore, as
Miner and Brewer note, other cognitive skills such as memory
often decline slowly, especially for people who start out
with above average skills.

Not only may older workers manage to perform as well as
younger workers in many tasks, they are often seen by
managers as having a number of advantages. Bromley (1966),
for example, notes that managers often regard older workers
as needing less supervision, having a greater sense of
responsibility, reliability and greater interest in the job.
Rabinowitz and Hall (1977), in their review of job involvement, regard older workers as being more job involved,
although the evidence is far from clear-cut. Older workers
will have had more opportunity to find the job more suited
to their needs and this might explain any greater job
involvement found. On the other hand, it is possible that
with increasing maturity, older workers will come to make
more satisfactory adjustments to their working situation,
at least from the managers' point of view. Further evidence

of the reliability of older workers can be found in the
evidence that they are less prone to leave the organisation,
and absence behaviour is sometimes reported as being less
(see, for example, Davis and Shackleton, 1975), although it
may be that the pattern of absence changes with age. For
example it may be that older individuals will be absent for
longer when they are absent; a reflection of increasing
health problems with increasing age (Taylor, 1967).

Whilst increasing age may be accompanied by greater reliability, job involvement and sense of responsibility,
Cooper (1978) points out that increasing age can also bring
its motivational problems in terms of mid-career crises.
Thus increasing age sometimes brings with it an increasing
sense of insecurity and failure. As Cooper notes, with
approaching middle age most employees find their progress
slowed or indeed stopped, with job opportunities becoming
fewer, and those job opportunities which are available often
difficult to take because of family pressures. The man in
his mid-forties, for example, who is offered promotion in
another town, has the conflict of personal advancement and
the interruption of schooling for his children. Furthermore,
as many wives now work in jobs which are increasingly
difficult to obtain, for example teaching, a promotion for
a husband could well mean a loss of job for the wife, and an
actual reduction, therefore, in the family income. Such
problems are likely to mean that many individuals become
'locked into' jobs for which their motivation is likely to
be less than optimal. There is other evidence (for example,
Saleh and Otis, 1964), that as individuals approach retirement there is a further loss of interest in the job, as if
the employee were distancing himself from the job in order
to prepare for retirement. Indeed Saleh and Otis note a
decline in job satisfaction in the pre-retirement years,
contrary to a number of other findings which tend to show
job satisfaction increasing with age (see, for example,
Gruneberg, 1979).

Whilst studies on ageing, therefore, show that increasing
age does not necessarily result in poorer performance, or
in decreased motivation and poorer attitudes to work, there
are some jobs and some situations in which work performance
and attitudes are likely to deteriorate with increasing age.
As far as performance is concerned, Miller (1979) notes that
steps can sometimes be taken to reduce the problems of
ageing by adjusting the environment. For example, keeping an
elderly person in his home surroundings, with familiar
supermarkets, is likely to result in better day-to-day
adjustment than moving him into a new social

situation with new physical surroundings. In such a situation
the older individual finds it difficult to cope with the
learning demands placed upon him. McFarland (1956) in an
occupational context notes that truck drivers in their
fifties who find night driving and lifting heavy loads beyond
them, can be helped by considerate employers who place them
on day driving only and provide machinery for lifting heavy
loads. Indeed, as Bromley points out, many employers take
account of their older workforce by moving them from one job
to another when vacancies arise. This movement often involves
a loss of pay and status, but at least allows the older
worker to continue to function in a working environment. It
is perhaps too much to hope that large-scale redesign of
equipment and jobs will take place in order to help older
workers. Indeed there is evidence that the employment
patterns of older workers is significantly different from
that of younger workers. Sobel (1970), for example, notes
that in the USA older workers are found in disproportionate
numbers in many unskilled services occupations which require
low levels of skill and training. Older workers are also
found in declining industries (although on the credit side
it should be noted that many of the professions contain a
large proportion of older men).

Given the value that older workers often have, with their
maturity of outlook, their reliability and sense of responsibility, employers should perhaps spend more time in
considering their value to the organisation. Certainly within
academic institutions, it is a common experience that mature
students add considerably to the well-being of a department
by their more mature outlook, even if their academic
attainment is not particularly high.

SEX DIFFERENCES AND PRODUCTIVITY

As with the findings on age and performance, findings on sex
differences and job behaviour have sometimes proved inconsistent. For example, a number of studies, such as
Schuler (1975), have found women to be more socially
orientated in relation to jobs, whereas males value more the
opportunity to influence important decisions and direct the
work of others. Bartol (1974) found males to be more concerned with their long-term careers and a number of other
studies have also pointed to women being more person-
oriented and males to be more job and career-oriented. Brief
and Oliver (1976), on the other hand, failed to show any sex
difference in work attitudes when controlling for occupation
and organisational level, and it may well be, therefore,

that where women are given the opportunity to have a career and job achievement, they will display similar job attitudes to males. The social orientation of females may, in other words, just reflect their concentrating on a 'hygiene' factor, because no motivator is available to them.

There are, however, a number of reasons to suppose that achievement of women in organisations and female job attitudes are determined in a more complex manner than purely in terms of an absence of 'higher order' rewards on specific jobs. Hoyenga and Hoyenga (1979), for example, point to the evidence that males and females may differ in their need for achievement, although the evidence on differences is by no means clear-cut (Hoffman, 1977). Assuming, however, that women do differ in their need for achievement, Hoyenga and Hoyenga suggest three possible reasons for this. One is that women fear failure more than men, and will thus avoid situations where there is the possibility of failure, that is in situations where there is the possibility of achievement. Another possibility is that women have a greater fear of success. Thus they will again avoid situations of achievement where success is possible. Finally, it is suggested that women are socialised in such a way as to focus on motives for affiliation and achievement. Thus women are taught to achieve through socialisation, a successful woman being one who marries a successful man and raises successful children.

As far as the evidence is concerned, Hoyenga and Hoyenga note that the evidence on differences in fear of failure are inconsistent and unlikely to explain any sex differences in achievement. On the other hand, the evidence on fear of success is far more plentiful. Horner (1972), for example, found that women had far less favourable reactions to a successful member of their sex than men. Hoffman (1976) found that women with an expressed fear of success married and had children earlier, thus removing themselves from the competitive arena. Indeed Hoffman (1977) argues that an ideal way out of the problem of a woman being successful is to become pregnant as it confirms her femininity and establishes her affiliative relation to her husband. Hoffman and others have emphasised that fear of success usually involves fear of loss of femininity. It may also be the case that for particular relationships, a female perceived by the male as being more successful may be a threat to the continuing relationship. Nevertheless, as Hoyenga and Hoyenga note, the findings on fear of success are by no means universally established and may well be confined to certain situations, and there are too few reliable sex

differences on 'fear-of-success' to allow an explanation of
sex differences in terms of need for achievement *per se*.

As for the possibility that women focus on affiliation and
achievement needs, Bardwick (1971), for example, found that
women tended to give affiliative responses to questions
such as 'what would make you happy', whilst Hoyenga and
Hoyenga report on a study where women more frequently than
men reported they were happy when they can succeed at
something 'which makes other people happy'. They also note
a number of studies in which women more than men equate
affiliation with achievement. Such studies suggest, therefore, that merely being denied jobs with 'higher order'
opportunities for self-actualisation is not the only reason
why women are more oriented towards social rewards in job
situations. It is not necessarily a deficiency in need for
achievement, *per se*, which differentiates males and females,
although there may be an element of this; it appears that
for females, achievement is in terms of different goals
than for males. Indeed the 'fear-of-success' reported in
some studies may be a reflection of the higher value put on
achieving successful social relationships by females,
especially as job success on the part of the woman can be
seen as threatening to the man's self-esteem and thus
likely to damage the relationship.

Apart from differences in orientation to achieve, there
is evidence that males and females differ in terms of
cognitive abilities, with males outperforming females in
mathematical ability (for example, Gruneberg, 1970), whilst
females are often reported as outperforming males in terms
of verbal ability (Hoyenga and Hoyenga). A reason often
given for poorer female performance in mathematics is that
this is not seen as useful or as relevant by females with
their greater orientation to social rewards. On the other
hand verbal ability is clearly advantageous socially, so
that perhaps females practice this more!

From the point of view of employers, of course, statistical differences between males and females must take second
place to an evaluation of the likely performance of the
individuals in front of them. As was already noted, Brief
and Oliver (1976) failed to find any sex difference in job
attitude when position in the organisation and occupation
were controlled for. Of course, given their different
socialisation processes and intrinsic job orientations,
males and females often choose different occupational
patterns. Gruneberg (1970), for example, found significantly
more females than males to leave school after a fifth year
of senior secondary school education in Scotland, rather

than to return for a sixth year, and to enter 'traditional' female occupations such as secretarial, nursing and auxiliary medical occupations in large numbers. Nevertheless it is important to emphasise Brief and Oliver's finding that where males and females are in the same occupation and at the same organisational level, then job attitudes are not necessarily different. (It must be pointed out, however, that this finding differs to some extent from that of Kuhlin (1963), who found that male and female teachers had different orientations to their work in terms of need for achievement.)

PERSONALITY AND PRODUCTIVITY

Any casual observation of those who are productive and those who are not in many organisations reveals that differences between the productive and unproductive are as likely, if not more likely to come about because of personality differences rather than intellectual differences. This is not to imply that intellectual factors are unimportant, but rather, given a reasonable intellectual and competence level, factors such as motivation and drive are critical in determining who is going to produce and who is not.

The most influential theory in accounting for personality differences in achievement is that proposed by Atkinson (1964), who argues that the need for achievement is an important motivator that distinguishes those who are successful from those who are not, particularly at a managerial level in organisations. Individuals with a high need for achievement are those who think in terms of accomplishing something important, advancing their career, and achieving recognition. According to Atkinson, an individual with a high need for achievement will be motivated to act when there is an expectation that his actions will lead to success and when that success involves achievement of valued goals. One assumption is that there is an inverse relationship between incentive value and probability of success for those with a high need for achievement. Thus tasks that are not very challenging, or where success will come easily, will not be highly valued. On the other hand, the individual with high achievement motivation will not take on extremely difficult tasks because he may not succeed. He is therefore likely to place his main efforts on moderately difficult tasks.

A further characteristic of the individual with a high need for achievement is that he is very concerned about feedback. Steers (1975), for example, notes a number of studies which have shown that those with a high need for

achievement require considerable feedback, presumably
because they are concerned about their performance and
constantly seek information on their progress.

A number of studies have shown a relationship between need
for achievement and performance in organisations. Cummin
(1967), for example, examined the characteristics of successful and less successful business executives, and found that
successful executive had significantly higher need for
achievement scores, and Andrews (1967) also found need for
achievement to be related to success in one of the
organisations he investigated.

There are, however, as Steers and Mowday (1977) note, a
number of qualifications to generalising too far on the
basis of studies conducted to date. In the first place many
studies have been conducted in laboratories, and studies
conducted in business organisations have to some extent
given equivocal results. For example, in the study by
Andrews, described above, only in the organisation emphasising achievement motivation was there a relationship
between success and the individuals' need for achievement.
In the organisation emphasising power striving, individuals
showing high 'need for achievement' were not successful.
Atkinson and Reitman (1956) emphasise that the motivation
to perform is the sum of all motives to act. In their study,
the relationship between achievement need and performance
disappeared when other motives such as need for affiliation
and money were also aroused. These studies do not disprove
the importance of the need for achievement as a factor in
business executive success, but they do emphasise that
other motives, such as need for power or money may also be
important determinants of action.

The need for power has, in fact, also been investigated
in relation to executive success. As with the need for
achievement, the need for power has been shown to be related
to success in business organisations, in, for example, the
study of Andrews (1967). Those with the need for power seek
to gain leadership positions and are seen by others as
forceful and outspoken, hard-headed and dominating. As with
the study of the achievement need, however, the need for
power appears to be associated with success only in the
organisation where the need for power is rewarded.

The whole question of the value of personality measures
in personnel selection has been reviewed by Guion and
Gottier (1967). After examining a large number of studies
published in the twelve years prior to their review, they
conclude, 'It cannot be said that any of the conventional
personality measures have demonstrated really general

usefulness as selection tools in employment practice' (p.
140). On the other hand, it does appear that 'custom built'
devices have shown better predictive validity on average
than conventional personality measures. As Guion and Gottier
note (p.159) 'A home-made personality or interest measure,
carefully and competently developed for specific situations,
is a better bet for prediction than is a standard personality
measure with a standard system of scoring'. Given such
findings as those of Andrews, that success depends not only
on the individual's needs but on the organisation's reward
system, such a conclusion is not perhaps surprising. Whilst
it is reasonable to conclude that organisational success
does sometimes depend on personality factors, given a
reasonable level of competence, exactly what personality
factors are important will be situationally determined.
Nevertheless, it does seem likely that in some situations,
for example, in higher managerial positions, those with a
need for achievement and power are likely to be more
successful.

ABILITIES

It is self-evident that in some situations, no matter how
hard the individual tries, and how well rewarded he is for
achievement, there is a failure to perform a job because of
lack of ability. On the other hand, a number of abilities
are related to good performance in different occupations;
from academic ability and intelligence in university
teachers, to manual dexterity in carpentry, to motor ability
in racing drivers.

There can be little dispute that individuals differ
markedly in their intellectual capacities and that such
differences are related to occupational choice. Harrell and
Harrell (1945), for example, on the basis of the army
general classification test, found considerable differences
in verbal ability between those in 'top' occupations such
as 'lawyers', 'accountants' and 'school teachers' and
'lower level' occupations such as 'truck drivers', farmhands',
and 'plumbers'.

Such differences are not hard to understand when one
considers that high scholastic aptitude is necessary for
entrance into the higher occupations and intelligence and
verbal ability tests to some extent, at least, predict
scholastic performance, although Korman (1977) argues that
mental ability tests may predict school grades and very
little else. A number of studies have, for example, found
that within occupations such as in the arts, sciences and

police work, there is very little relationship between
general mental ability and accomplishments.

To argue, however, that within an occupation mental abilities do not distinguish the successful from the less
successful, does not mean that intellectual abilities are
unnecessary for success. It may merely mean that for some
occupations, provided there is a reasonable level of
intellectual competence, other factors such as personality
and motivation become more important. It is difficult, for
example, to see how someone of only average intelligence
could make a success of a career in nuclear physics,
although, given a high level of intelligence, those with
higher drive and motivation and somewhat lower intelligence
than their colleagues may be more successful. There is,
however, evidence that even within occupations, factors
such as general intelligence are sometimes related to
performance. Dunnette (1976), for example, found a correlation of 0.32 between general intelligence and performance
for employees involved in operating and processing in the
petroleum and refining industry. On the other hand the
correlation for clerical work was only 0.17. Clearly, as
with measures of personality, the extent to which intelligence is likely to be related to performance is dependent
on the kind of job which is under consideration, and the
kinds of other skills which it is important to apply in the
situation. Social skills, for example, need not be related
to intellectual capacity.

Motor ability
One major ability which is required in a considerable number
of jobs is motor ability, that is the ability to manipulate
physical objects. Perhaps the most important conclusion
based on studies of motor abilities is that there is no
general factor of motor abilities which will distinguish
the generally good from the generally bad. As Dunnette
(1976) notes, tests designed to measure skills such as
manual dexterity, steadiness, speed of response and
eye-hand co-ordination show low correlations. Furthermore,
the acquistion of motor abilities necessary in the performance of a task involves the mastery of different skills at
different stages in the acquisition of skill. Clearly, as
Dunnette notes, the prediction of ultimate task performance
is difficult. As with tests of personality and intellectual
ability, it is necessary to design tests with specific
organisational goals and tasks in mind, rather than employ
'off the shelf' tests. Fleishman (1962), for example,
notes eleven fairly independent motor skills, each of which

could be relevant to a particular job in combination with other skills. These skills are:

(1) control precision: this involves control over fine movements;

(2) multi-limb co-ordination: as, for example, in boxing, car driving and so on;

(3) response orientation: the ability to react quickly and accurately to a stimulus, particularly in relation to discriminating correct stimuli to react to;

(4) reaction time: involves reacting quickly to a stimulus;

(5) speed of arm movement: involves speed rather than accuracy, for example, in gathering wood or coal;

(6) rate control: the ability to make motor adjustments to a continuous moving target;

(7) manual dexterity: skilful hand and arm movements in handling large objects under speeded conditions;

(8) finger dexterity: skilful movements of small objects, for example, tweezers;

(9) arm-hand steadiness: for example in threading a needle;

(10) wrist-finger speed: as in morse code;

(11) aiming: as in firing a gun.

Because of the difficulties involved in predicting motor performance on the job on the basis of ready-made tests, a number of workers, such as Anastasi (1968) have argued for tests which closely resemble the job performance to be predicted. Job and task samples as predictors of future job success have been examined by Campion (1972). He found that the best correlations with performance involving the use of tools was work sampling, which correlated 0.66 with performance, compared with 0.08 for mechanical comprehension, 0.23 for general intelligence, and 0.07 for numerical ability. As was noted earlier, tests such as those for intelligence are clearly only relevant in certain specific situations, and even tests which at first might seem relevant, such as mechanical comprehension and numerical ability, are totally inadequate in this particular study.

As Dunnette notes, however, one normal method of job sampling, giving the individual a trial period on the job, is likely to be of limited use unless the job sample is carefully constructed to test performance on relevant job dimensions. Unless this is done, judgements are often made on such factors as time-keeping, social interaction and so on; indeed once someone is in a job, it is often difficult to dismiss him for social reasons.

PRODUCTIVITY AND CULTURAL DIFFERENCES

Racial differences

As with the study of sex differences in job orientation, a number of investigations into differences between black and white employees suggest that the two groups may have different job orientations. For example, Holland (1976) notes studies in which the orientation of black students is more social service than scientific, although Korman, Greenhaus and Badin (1977) note that findings in the area are inconsistent. A recent study by Jones, James, Bruni and Sells (1977) of sailors in the US Navy, found that black sailors brought with them different expectations concerning jobs. They had, for example, lower expectations of satisfaction regarding jobs, which are more easily met, and hence tend to be more satisfied. They also found black sailors to be more job involved, a finding similar to that or Orpen and Ndlovu (1977) in a study of clerks in a commercial organisation in South Africa. Interestingly, Orpen and Ndlovu found black clerks to have greater higher-order needs, a finding which makes a nonsense of South Africa's racial laws in regard to black employment. A recent review by Bhagat (1979) however, comes to different conclusions concerning black/white orientation to work. Bhagat examined orientation to work in four aspects of the work ethic; (a) the good provider, (b) independence - the right to self determination, (c) success and (d) self respect - the dignity of work. He found that blacks do not associate lack of work with a sense of failure to the same extent as whites, although they did value being a good provider and hence pay. Blacks did not believe in success through work to the same extent as whites, nor did they see independence as coming through work or self-respect being dependent on work. Bhagat attributes these differences to differences in socialisation. In particular Bhagat argues that blacks are often deprived of good 'models' of success through work, and have considerable experience of discrimination and prejudice in the work situation. The negative attitude of blacks to work, therefore, reflects their lower expectations based on a realistic assessment of black experience. After all, if success in a job is likely to be difficult through lack of opportunity, it makes sense to seek life satisfactions entirely outside the job situation.

There are clearly a number of conflicting findings in the area of differences in black-white job attitudes, to some extent due, no doubt, to a failure to control for different kinds of occupations entered by the two groups. Black and white employees have different reference groups with different orientations to work which may well affect performance and attitudes. There is, however, evidence that when black and white employees are matched for occupation, then black employees can be more job-involved and can display greater higher-order needs than their white counterparts. It is unfortunately the case that because black employees have fewer opportunities, many develop negative attitudes to the Protestant work ethic at an early stage, and do not put themselves in a position to have a job with the potential for satisfaction. From the employer's point of view, of course, feelings concerning the 'work ethic' are of importance. Merrins and Garrett (1975), for example, found that on a repetitive task, those scoring high on a Protestant work ethic scale performed at a higher level than those scoring low.

Cross-cultural differences
In their review of cross-cultural issues in organisational psychology Barrett and Bass (1976) note a number of ways in which cultural differences are likely to affect productivity. At a basic level, for example, calorie deficiency may mean that in underdeveloped countries there is insufficient calorie intake for workers to produce as much as in developed countries. Thus Kerkhoven (1962) estimated that in Nigeria calorie deficiency meant that work capacity of employees was only one quarter of that of workers in more developed countries. Clearly, for workers who lack the basic physiological needs, attitudes to work are likely to be different from those in more developed countries. A study by Slocum (1971) illustrates this well. He found Mexican operatives were much more easily job-satisfied once basic family needs had been met, and were therefore much more easy to please in relation to their job, than their American counterparts who took the fulfilment of basic needs for granted, but sought fulfilment of higher-order needs. Indeed, for Mexican workers, there was little motivation to work once basic

family needs were met. In many underdeveloped countries, of course, even basic needs are difficult to meet on occasions, so that the motivation to work is very much different from their American counterparts.

An understanding of differences in attitudes to work and the context of work is of course of considerable importance in multinational companies, where management may be 'imposed' on local organisation. Unless incoming management has an appreciation of the cultural values and background regarding work, it is obvious that major conflicts are likely to result. Clearly a consideration of the different values of different cultures is well beyond the scope of this book, and indeed it must be borne in mind that local variations may involve as great an amount of difference as any cross-cultural comparison. Hulin and Blood (1968), for example, found that the attitudes of rural and urban workers in their study in the United States were considerably different, with urban workers more alienated from work and less amenable to job enrichment and to job redesign changes introduced into their organisation. Sussman (1973), whilst critical of Hulin and Blood's interpretation, also found major differences in orientation to work in a rural and an urban population. Clearly only very general statements concerning cross-cultural differences can be made with any confidence.

Bearing in mind the problems discussed above, there are a number of areas where cultural differences in relation to work are likely to operate. Apart from differences in rewards sought from the job, discussed earlier, Barrett and Bass (1976), for example, note that the relationship between work and personal life is likely to be viewed differently in different cultures, with, for example, French Canadian managers placing more stress on their family role than English Canadian managers, and Japanese workers appearing far more willing than American workers to allow that their company was 'a part of my life at least equal in importance to my personal life'.

Given the profound cultural differences in the context of work, Barrett and Bass note the value of preparing individuals who are to work overseas. A study by Ivancevich (1969) notes that problems with many overseas postings include worries about social interaction, and a study by Gruneberg, Startup and Tapsfield (1974) found that university staff moving into Wales from other areas of the United Kingdom often had problems in social adjustment which affected job satisfaction. Of particular importance is the satisfaction of the wife of an employee when moved to a new culture, and there is evidence that employee effectiveness can be directly related to the wife's satisfaction. It seems more than sensible therefore, to prepare individuals who are to work abroad by familiarising them with local attitudes to work in some depth, by ensuring that social interaction, particularly involving the wife, is facilitated as far as possible, and preparing the employee for the inevitable difficulties of adjustment that are entailed in moving from one culture to another. A number of training programmes are in fact available for facilitating individual effectiveness whilst working in different cultures. Bass (1970) and Barrett (1969), for example, report on a programme of exercises in areas such as group perceptions, salary administration, personal goals and intergroup relationships. A central bank stores data on over forty nations and norms can be drawn from the bank which allow organisations to compare their attitudes, values and behaviours.

Whilst such training programmes are likely to be of value, clearly no one set of norms is likely to give the definitive view on a culture or prescription for behaviour, if only because, within any culture, there are enormous variations, and because cultural patterns are subject to rapid change on occasion. What training programmes can perhaps best do is to sensitise the individual to the kind of problem he is likely to face, and to make him flexible in his dealings with others in the new culture.

7 Problems of Organisation Adjustment

INTRODUCTION

So far in this book, the effects of variables on such factors as productivity have been discussed. This chapter will focus on other factors of economic importance to organisations, namely absence and turnover, health problems, and industrial conflict; all aspects of poor organisational adjustment.

ABSENCE AND JOB TURNOVER

Withdrawal
One form of behaviour which has considerable economic implications for any organisation is the decision of employees to withdraw from the work situation, either temporarily by absenting themselves, or permanently by terminating their employment. The effect of absence is to disrupt work schedules and to require the organisation to employ more staff to cover for 'missing' employees. In the case of turnover, there are often considerable costs involved in training new replace-ment employees, including the employment of training staff, the cost of specialised equipment and poor initial quality and speed of work. In addition, of course, recruitment costs money in placing advertisements and in employing personnel for selection procedures. However, whilst absence is likely to be wholly undesirable for the organisation, some turnover in organisations might be thought of as healthy in removing deadwood and bringing in new blood. Indeed, Dalton and Todor (1979) argue that turnover is of positive value in encour-aging innovative behaviour and giving individuals new opportunities to develop their skills. It is also of value in putting pressure on organisations to change and grow or otherwise risk losing their employees.

  A number of workers have tried to place a figure on the costs of absence and turnover. Mirvis and Lawler (1977), for example, estimated that in a bank which they were studying, the cost of each absence was $66.45, and the cost of each termination $2522.03. Steers and Rhodes (1978), in their review of absence behaviour, estimated that in the

USA alone, absence was costing $26.4 billion. Clearly even if these figures are only remotely near the truth the cost of both absence and turnover makes their study of interest.

The actual relationship between absence and staff turnover has been the subject of considerable discussion. There are two schools of thought; one school which sees absence as a mini-form of the behaviour involved in subsequent job resignation, and the other school which sees absence as not necessarily anticipating turnover. Thus absence may occur where leaving the job is not possible, because of economic conditions, or it may be that absence and turnover may have separate causes. For example, in some occupations, leaving an organisation may be necessary for an ambitious individual who seeks advancement elsewhere. In such a case, it is unlikely there will be a history of lack of job involvement, which is sometimes associated with absence behaviour. Again, absence may be caused by illness or family commitments, which may have no implications for future job termination.

It is perhaps not surprising, therefore, that the evidence on the relationship between absence and turnover is far from clear. Whilst a number of studies (for example, Waters and Roach, 1979) have found significant, if rather low correlations between absence and turnover, Porter and Steers (1973) note that in only 6 out of 22 studies which they examined was there a relationship in the same direction between factors under study and both absence and turnover. In the study by Ingham (1970), for example, organisational size was related to absence behaviour but not to staff turnover. In other words it appears likely that in any given situation the causes of both absence and turnover are multicausal and not necessarily related to each other.

Steers and Rhodes (1978) in fact list three reasons why absence and turnover are likely to have a low relationship:

(1) absenteeism is more likely to be spontaneous and easy, job termination is likely to involve careful consideration over time;
(2) the negative consequences associated with absence are often less than those associated with termination;
(3) absence can represent a substitute form of behaviour for turnover, especially in times of economic difficulty. There would be no reason therefore to suppose that high absence was likely to be accompanied by high turnover. In view of the possible differences in causes, therefore, absence and turnover are considered separately.

Absence

One assumption that is frequently made about absence is that
it is a consequence of job dissatisfaction. However, a
number of reviews of the relationship between absence and
job satisfaction (for example, Vroom, 1964; Nicholson *et
al.*, 1976) have concluded that the relationship is either
very low or non-existent. Many of the findings are inconsistent. For example, Metzner and Mann (1953) found a relationship between satisfaction and absence for blue-collar
but not for white-collar workers, and Ilgen and Hollenback
(1977) found no real support for a relationship between job
satisfaction and absence in their study of female clerical
workers. On the other hand, some studies have reported a
significant relationship between absence and job satisfaction.
In the study of Mirvis and Lawler (1977) of bank employees, the
correlation reported (-0.81) is of course extremely high.
Such major inconsistencies certainly require an explanation.

One possible explanation put forward by Nicholson *et al.*
(1976) is that many of the studies are badly designed, and
in many cases the measures of absence and job satisfaction
used vary from study to study. Absence, for example, can
be measured in terms of days absent, frequency of absence,
or avoidable and unavoidable absence.

Steers and Rhodes (1978), in considering factors involved
in attendance, suggest a number of factors which might be
related to absence behaviour. One, for example, is job level,
where those in higher-level jobs appear less likely to absent
themselves. On the other hand, Steers and Rhodes note that in
higher-level jobs 'absence' might take more subtle forms,
such as taking time off work for 'messages', because time
will be made up working at night, taking long dinner breaks,
business rounds of golf and so on.

There is a reasonable but by no means unanimous body of
evidence to suggest that absence does decrease with greater
job interest, variety and autonomy, and a number of studies
of job enrichment do report absence declining following job
redesign (see Chapter 8). It does seem reasonable to suppose
that, all other things being equal, the more interesting
are 'on the job' factors, the less will be the relative
attractions of 'off the job' satisfactions which may lead
to absence.

Whilst the findings on job content factors reviewed by
Steers and Rhodes tend to support the view that such factors
are related to absence, Steers and Rhodes argue that the
same cannot be said for context factors, such as group size,
leadership style and satisfaction with co-workers, although
in all these cases some studies have reported a relationship.
In one case, that of promotion opportunities, there appears

to be no relationship with absence, but promotion opportunities do relate to turnover, again indicating that the two
factors have distinct causes. There are, however, a number
of context factors which do seem related to absence. For
example, in Porter and Lawler's (1965) review of organisational structure and behaviour, it was found that in ten out
of twelve studies of blue-collar workers there was a relationship between group size and absenteeism, such that the
larger the group size, the greater was absenteeism. One
important context factor which has been reported by Nicholson,
Jackson and Hawes (1978) is hours of work. Nicholson *et al*.
(1978) found, for example, that days of week and shift cycle
are both correlates of absence behaviour. Nicholson *et al*.
note that high absence for shift work may be due to the fact
that early risers have to overcome 'inertia' in order to
return to work at unsocial hours. Nor is it particularly
surprising that absence rises at weekends where work is most
likely to conflict with social arrangements.

A more important context factor which also seems to be
related to absence behaviour is pay, and Steers and Rhodes
report studies showing a direct relationship between pay
rate and absence, although more important, perhaps, is the
extent to which pay is tied to absence behaviour. Garrison
and Murchinsky (1977), for example, found that where absence
was tied to pay losses, then the more job-satisfied individuals
were absent least. Where individuals were paid during days
off, there was no relationship between job satisfaction and
absence. As Ilgen and Hollenback point out, it is unlikely
that a high degree of satisfaction with pay, security and
company policy will lead to regular attendance in an organisation where there are generous sick pay schemes. This is
certainly borne out by Davis's (1973) observations on the
Volvo auto works, where despite job redesign, absence increased by 100 per cent in five years. The cause of this,
apparently, was legislation enabling workers to stay off
the job at little cost to themselves.

Apart from voluntary absence, of course, a number of factors
are beyond the control of the organisation. Amongst these
are illness, weather conditions and family responsibilities.
As Miner and Brewer (1976) note, poor health is a primary
cause of absence, particularly 'psychological' illness such
as emotional disorders, alcoholism and drug abuse. Ill health
is also associated with increasing age, and Nicholson *et al*.
(1977) found male workers to have fewer but longer absences
with increasing age, probably reflecting increasing ill
health. Females, on the other hand, showed no such tendency.

As far as family responsibility is concerned, there is
evidence that women are absent more frequently than men,

and that family size relates to the amount of absence.

An important problem in considering the causes of absence
behaviour is the question of what is avoidable and what is
unavoidable absence. One man dying of cancer but keenly
involved in his job may continue working practically until
the end, whereas another will use his time as far as possible
with his family. One job-committed individual may struggle
through the snow on foot where another gives up because his
car is stuck. As Nicholson (1976) indicates, doctor's certi-
ficates concerning illness are rarely a satisfactory means
of assessing whether an individual is 'really' ill. There
is even a popular song about the issue of 'doctor's papers'
before a Welsh rugby international! There is evidence that
attendance will vary according to the commitment of individuals to work (for example, Smith, 1977) and the extent that
individuals hold a strong work ethic. Thus many individuals
feel that there is a moral obligation to work if possible if
one is accepting payment, and individuals who feel this way
are more likely to overcome feelings of illness and other
obstacles (see, for example, Ilgen and Hollenback, 1977).

One important question which arises is how best to deal
with absence behaviour. Two different approaches have been
taken, and both have been reported to have been successful.
One approach is to reward individuals for attendance, possibly
by paying a bonus. As noted previously, Scheflen *et al.*
(1971) found pay incentive plans to improve attendance,
especially when the group were allowed to participate in the
setting up of the scheme. More recently a study by Orpen
(1978) found that paying employees a small weekly bonus for
each week they attended work every day decreased absenteeism
in a group of female workers. On the other hand, some schemes,
though successful in reducing absence, may cost more in
incentive payments than was lost in absences (Tjersland,
1972).

The alternative approach is to use strict control procedures.
Baum (1978), for example, reports on a programme based on
legal compliance for blue-collar production and maintenance
jobs. The programme involved keeping detailed records, requiring written excuses from legitimate outside sources,
independently investigating questionable absence, counselling
workers with unauthorised absence, and disciplining unauthorised absence progressively. This programme contrasted with the
previous method of dealing with absence, which was largely
at the supervisor's discretion. The results showed a significant improvement in absence behaviour, with workers who
had high absence records the most improved. Baum argues that
as 'high absence' workers contribute a disproportionately
large amount to the total number of days lost, the fact that

the effect of a control policy was limited to this group does not matter too much. On the other hand, Baum does concede that control policies are probably not suitable for those who normally attend regularly and suggests that positive reinforcements (such as bonuses) might be more appropriate for this group.

Not all control policies for absenteeism have proved successful, however, and Nicholson (1976) reports a study in which the effect of a control policy was to change the pattern of absence behaviour. Instead of frequent short absence, there was a switch to less frequent longer absence, sanctioned by a doctor. However, Baum reports that such a switching did not occur in his study, and whilst limitations in control procedures should be noted, it should also be emphasised that they have been reported to work.

Job Turnover
Unlike the relationship between absence and job satisfaction, almost all reviews have reported a consistent relationship between job satisfaction and turnover (Porter and Steers, 1973; Price, 1977). Porter and Steers (1973), for example, note only one study out of fifteen published between 1955 and 1972 which failed to show a relationship between job satisfaction and turnover. It should be noted that most reported studies have been carried out in the USA and Price notes there are some differences between the situation in the USA and elsewhere. Turnover for example, is higher in the United States than in Europe. To this extent therefore, some caution must be exercised when generalising some of the findings reported to a European setting. Nevertheless, the sheer consistency of findings makes it likely that general statements on the relationship between turnover and various factors can be made, and studies in a British setting are supportive of American research (for example, Wild, 1970).

As well as overall job satisfaction, job context, job content and personality factors have been shown to be re- lated to turnover. One important context factor is pay, where there is ample empirical evidence that dissatisfaction with pay can result in increased turnover (see, for example, Knowles, 1964). Immediate work environment, too, appears to be a determinant of turnover. Porter and Steers (1973) note studies which have found considerate leadership to relate to turnover. However, this relationship holds true only up to a point. After a certain level of considerate leadership is reached there appears to be no relationship with turnover. Presumably other factors, such as the extent to which the individuals' other goals are fulfilled, become increasingly important.

Satisfaction with the immediate work group has been found to be related to turnover, and Price (1977) reports participation in primary work groups to be important. Where an individual feels isolated from the work group, there is an increased likelihood of termination. A study by Farris (1971), for example, found inclusion in the group to be a factor reducing turnover. A study by Evan (1963) is interesting in showing the importance of co-workers. Evan's study found that resignation amongst trainees was lower where the trainee entered a department with two or more other trainees, compared with entering a department on his own or with only one other trainee. Presumably social relationships develop which are supportive in times of stress, and which may give 'after work' social satisfactions. Porter and Steers, however, note that not all studies show the importance of group factors. It may be that where individuals obtain their satisfaction from other aspects of the job, social factors will play a less important part.

As with job context factors, a number of studies show a relationship between job content and turnover. Price (1977) in his review notes that turnover is less with increased skill level, and that blue-collar workers have a higher rate of turnover than white-collar workers. Various studies have shown task repetitiveness to be related to turnover. This is perhaps not surprising in view of the findings of Hackman and Lawler (1971) and others of a relationship between job satisfaction and the extent of job variety. On the other hand, repetitiveness is not universally disliked as was noted earlier. Where individuals are provided with a simple job, with the opportunity for considerable social interaction in pleasant surroundings and with good pay, then it may well be that job repetition is not stressful or dissatisfying. Whether some factor is dissatisfying or not depends not only on the job, but upon what the individual wants and expects from his job. Nevertheless, the evidence does suggest that in many cases turnover is higher in low-level unskilled repetitive jobs.

At least two other content aspects of the job described by Hackman and Lawler (1971) as 'core' job aspects, feedback and autonomy, have also been found to be related to turnover. Ross and Zander (1957), for example, found the extent of feedback and recognition to be related to turnover, particularly when there was a deficiency in expected feedback and recognition. Lack of autonomy, too, has been shown to be related to turnover in several studies, and Taylor and Weiss (1969) amongst others indicate that turnover is related to the perceived importance of the work performed.

The work reviewed by Porter and Steers, Price and others, quite clearly indicates the importance of job factors both intrinsic and extrinsic in inducing individuals to leave the organisation. Yet the job alone cannot be the whole story, as, in any given job, no matter how unattractive, some individuals are likely to stay. Clearly individual factors are also important.

A large number of studies point to two individual factors as of major significance in turnover, age and tenure. Price, for example, notes that younger workers are more likely to leave an organisation than older individuals. In addition he notes that tenure, that is the amount of time already spent in the organisation, was a good predictor of future resignation probability. This is hardly surprising in that those staying longer in the organisation are more likely to be satisfied with the organisation, or to feel 'locked in' because of family commitments. What is perhaps of more practical significance are the findings of Robinson (1972) and others that tenure in a previous job is predicative of tenure in the present job. As Porter and Steers note, such findings reinforce the view that some individuals are likely to be associated with job turnover. Among such individuals Porter and Steers note characteristics such as high anxiety, emotional insecurity, aggression and ambition.

Another finding of practical significance, noted earlier, is that turnover is least where the individual regards the job as giving him the opportunity to fulfil the role he wishes to fulfil. A number of studies have shown that turnover can to some extent be predicted by examining the relationship between vocational interest, as measured by objective tests, and subsequent employment. Boyd (1961), for example, found that engineers who remained longer on the job scored higher in a questionnaire on vocational interests. Again such findings are hardly surprising. If one is not employed to utilise the skill which one wants to utilise, it seems intuitively likely that one is more likely to seek a job which gives the opportunity for the use of the particular skill.

Whilst the various studies discussed point clearly to associations between job and individual factors and job termination, it still remains to be explained how the process operates. Mobley *et al.* (1978) note that the best predictor of subsequent job termination is not job dissatisfaction, but expressed intention to quit. They suggest that job dissatisfaction leads the individual to think about quitting, which leads to the next stage; assessing the alternative possibilities in a particular job market. Clearly the existing job market can materially affect the possibilities of moving,

and in a poor job market one would expect to find little
relationship between job satisfaction and resignation because
those dissatisfied will still have to stay with the organisation. Indeed in a study by Behrend (1953), it was found
that turnover decreased in all factories surveyed when unemployment increased.

In considering what leads individuals to the quitting
process, Porter and Steers point not only to actual levels
of inadequacy in the content or context of the job, but also
to the importance of failed expectations. A number of studies
have shown that where expectations concerning role function
or job context conditions are not met, there is increased
turnover. In response to this, a number of studies, for
example, Ilgen and Seely (1974) have shown that giving individuals realistic information prior to commencing the job
materially reduces subsequent turnover. In the case of Ilgen
and Seely this was done after appointment but before the job
proper commenced. Giving a realistic preview serves the function of clarifying the role the individual is expected to play
and indicating what rewards the individual can expect from
his job. When given before an appointment, a realistic preview can stop individuals,whose needs and expectations will
not be met,from joining the organisation.

Despite the large number of studies showing job dissatisfaction leading to turnover, it would be a mistake to conclude
that improving job satisfaction will eliminate turnover. Job
termination can after all be for positive as well as negative
reasons. Individuals can be perfectly satisfied with a
particular job and yet find other jobs even more attractive.
Indeed it is perhaps this 'positive' kind of turnover which
is most damaging to organisations as they are likely to lose
their most able members. Highly dissatisfied and disgruntled
members the organisation can usually do without. Porter and
Steers do note that there is a tendency for turnover to be
higher among 'ambitious' individuals. It would, of course,
be a mistake not to take on such individuals because they
are likely to leave. At least they are likely to benefit
the organisation whilst they are there.

ECONOMIC IMPLICATIONS OF 'HEALTH' PROBLEMS AT WORK

With an increasing concern for the quality of working life
of the individual, there has recently been a considerable
increase in the interest of psychologists into the effects
of stress at work. Reviews by McGrath (1976), Cooper and
Marshall (1976), Cox (1978) and Beehr and Newman (1978) have
all pointed to the detrimental effects, both physical and
mental, of stress at work. Cox (1978), for example, points

out that in Great Britain 37 million working days are lost through stress-induced psychoneurotic illness and nervous complaints. There is also considerable evidence that stress can be a causal factor in physical illness such as heart disease, bronchial asthma and diabetes mellitus amongst many others.

Perhaps the most dramatic evidence that stress can cause physical illness is in the area of coronary heart disease. Theorell (1974), for example, found that aspects of work which were stressful were reported by 41 per cent of a heart attack group compared with 17 per cent of a matched control group. A study by Buell and Breslaw (1960) also reported a potentially stressful situation relating to heart disease, in that a group of workers working over forty-eight hours per week had a significantly higher incidence of heart attacks than those working less than forty-eight hours per week. In support of the view that stress at work is likely to be associated with illness is the study of Cobb and Kasl (1972). They found that with approaching unemployment, physiological measures such as blood pressure increased; after re-employment these physiological measures associated with illness returned to normal. Of course, stress is not the only cause of heart disease; Cox (1978) notes the effects of a high-fat diet on coronary heart attacks. He notes, however, studies which tend to indicate that neither stress nor high calorie intake of themselves cause heart attacks — it is the combination of the two which is problematic.

Whilst heart disease is possibly the most dramatic consequence of stress, it is as noted above, by no means the only physical consequence. Diabetes mellitus, for example, is reported by Bradley (1979) to be affected by stress, and Totman and Kiff (1979) report that life stress affects susceptibility to common colds.

The effects of stress on mental health are also frequently documented. Ferguson (1973), for example, reports that job factors (boredom) were reported in his study to be responsible for neurotic behaviour, and Kornhauser (1965) reported that some 40 per cent of car assembly workers in his study had an unsatisfactory adjustment to life, presumably because of the mechanically paced and repetitive nature of their jobs.

In a further study on repetitive jobs, Johannson (1975) found individuals in work cycles of less than one minute suffered from depression, sleep disturbance and ulcers to a greater extent than those on a three minute cycle. Yet as Mackay and Cox (1978) note, there is a surprising absence of severe distress in many studies of repetitive work, and it may be that where there is satisfaction from security, independence and social interaction, repetitive work is not

perceived of as a source of stress. The reportedly poor
mental health of clerical workers (Warr and Wall, 1975) may
be because of the routine nature of the job, without sufficient compensation in social interaction, for example.

Despite the fact that severe mental ill health does not
seem to result from repetition *per se* in many studies, it
might well be the case that it can be stressful when combined with the mechanical pacing of the job. In the classical
study of Walker and Guest (1952) mechanical pacing and the
repetitive nature of the job were given as reasons for job
dissatisfaction, and lack of job variety has been reported
as being related to job dissatisfaction where the individual
sought higher-order fulfilment in his job (Hackman and Lawler,
1971).

As Kasl (1973) notes, however, it is difficult to interpret
findings on low-level jobs and mental health. Low-level jobs
are associated with a poor environment, low wages, and consequent family stress. Furthermore, it is possible that some
of those, at least, in low-level jobs are there because they
have 'gravitated' down, being unable to hold jobs at a higher
level. There is evidence that mental ill health is not such
a problem for the performance of low-level as for high-level
jobs (McGrath, 1976).

A number of factors in the work situation have been shown
to be related to stress, although as Beehr and Newman (1978)
note, many potential areas remain to be investigated. Among
the major factors are the nature of the task, the difficulties
individuals have in fulfilling their roles, and a personality
disposition to react to the job in terms of aggression and
competitiveness.

As noted in Chapter 4, difficulties in role performance
have been shown to be related to stress. Kahn (1974), for
example, reports role conflict to result in increased stress
and Caplan (1971) found role conflict to relate to heart
rate increases. He also found role ambiguity to be related
to anxiety and depression. Furthermore, Mackay and Cox note
the findings of the study by Cobb and Rose (1973), where air
traffic controllers with a high level of responsibility and
job load were four times more likely to have hypertension
than airmen with whom they were compared. There seems little
doubt that role strain in its various forms can be a serious
hazard to health.

Such findings are of course interesting for a number of
reasons. As far as productivity is concerned, clearly the
long term interests of organisations might be best served
by decreasing work load and role strain, so that individuals
will not absent themselves through illness. Again, the
concern of psychologists for 'quality of working life' rather

than job satisfaction *per se* receives some justification.
Although those with role strain are likely to be less job
satisfied (see, for example, Gruneberg, 1979) there is no
one to one relationship. It is quite possible for the individual to ignore the health threat through role overload and
yet enjoy his job. Whilst 'job satisfaction' and indeed
'productivity' are perfectly legitimate subjects of interest
in their own right, clearly other factors in the work situation, such as effects on health and indeed on the relationship between work and other life roles, must also be of
concern to the psychologist in industry.

Not only the situation may predispose the individual to
stress, the personality of the individual to some extent
reacts with the situation. In this connection a distinction
is often made between type A and type B personalities. The
type A personality is described by Bradley and Cox (1978) as
having an intense sustained drive to achieve self-selected
goals; to be an achiever, to have an eagerness to compete,
to have a desire for recognition and advancement, to have a
continuous involvement in a number of functions subject to
time pressure, to have a propensity to accelerate the execu-
tion of many physical and mental functions, and to have an
extraordinary mental and physical alertness. As Beehr and
Newman (1978) note, such individuals are likely to perceive
stressors in the environment to a greater extent than type
B individuals, who are not so achievement-oriented and
aggressive in their reactions to the environment.

As a number of reviewers note, there is a substantial body
of evidence that type A personalities are more likely to
suffer from heart disease (see, for example, Dembroski, 1979;
Streufert *et al.*, 1979) yet it is much more difficult to see
exactly what can, *practically* be done to help such individuals,
if 'help' is even desirable. Many of the world's leading
figures, whether scientists, or politicians or writers, have
gained eminence by producing prodigious amounts of work. It
may well be that heart disease is a risk that has to be
taken by those wishing for high levels of achievement.

In summary, stress is clearly a major problem for organisational productivity, increasing the likelihood of illness.
Apart from personality disposition, various job-related sources
of stress, such as job repetitiveness and role strain, are
often amenable to change, and should therefore be of concern
to the organisation.

Alcoholism
One major effect of stress is reported by Cox (1978) to be
increased alcoholic intake, and there can be no doubt that
problems arising from excessive alcoholic intake are of

major significance to industrial productivity. Schramm (1978),
for example, estimates the economic cost of alcoholism in
the USA at $9.3 billion in lost production alone, and Berry
and Boland (1978) estimate that alcohol-abusing workers earn
almost $10 billion less than they would if they were not
alcohol abusers. The detrimental effects of excessive alcoholic
intake arise in a number of ways. Miner and Brewer (1976),
for example, note that alcoholics have a considerable increase
in the likelihood of being involved in accidents at and away
from work. Away from work, road accident statistics strongly
support the role of alcohol as a major cause of road injury
and death. Cox notes that moderate drinkers taking three
pints of British beer are eight times more likely to be
involved in a traffic accident than those taking only $1\frac{1}{2}$
pints. Even highly skilled bus drivers have been shown by
Cohen *et al.* (1958) to have impaired judgement for driving
buses. Indeed one of the major effects of alcohol, which
obviously has implications for productivity, is that psychomotor behaviour deteriorates materially. There are, however,
other effects of alcohol excess which affect productivity,
among them being increased absence and interpersonal difficulties, all of which indicates the importance of alcoholism
for industrial productivity.

As was noted above, stress has been claimed to be a causal
factor in alcoholism. As Robinson (1976) points out, however,
it remains to be explained why most individuals who are under
stress confine their alcoholic intake within socially acceptable limits whilst others become alcoholic. He goes on to
outline a number of theories of alcoholism, the psychological,
genetic and sociological, as well as 'professional' and
everyday theories, noting the incompleteness of many. Clearly
a review of alcoholism and its causes are beyond the scope
of the present book (see, for example, Robinson, 1976, 1979
for reviews). Whatever the cause, the implications for
productivity are considerable, and industry in the USA at
least, has begun to pay serious attention to programmes of
help.

In reviewing studies of the success of alcoholic programmes
in industry, Archer (1978), reports industrial alcoholism
programmes to be relatively successful, with success rates
of about 50 per cent. This is because the prognosis for
socially stable alcoholics, that is, those with families
and jobs, is high. On the other hand, in their review of
occupational alcoholism programmes Williams and Tramortana
(1978) note the methodological inadequacies of many studies.
In particular, few studies employ control groups to assess
the extent of 'spontaneous recovery', and certain studies
may have impressive results because they select subjects

who have a high prognosis for success. Nevertheless, Williams
and Tramortana's own study showed that their treatment was
reasonably effective. The nature of treatment programmes is
obviously beyond the scope of this book, (for a fuller account
see Schramm, 1978), but it clearly is an area of potential
economic significance to organisations.

Accidents

An accident might be regarded as an unplanned event with sad
consequences. As with alcoholism, accidents at work are of
considerable financial significance. Davis and Shackleton
(1975), for example, note that about 16 million working days
are lost each year through accidents in Great Britain, whilst
the number killed at work is in the region of 1000. Kay
(1978) notes that the most frequent industrial accidents are
in handling goods, falls, and machinery accidents, with
injury to the trunk (38 per cent), fingers (20 per cent),
legs (15 per cent) and arms (9 per cent) being the most
common.

Kay (1978) divides the causes of accidents into three
categories; those caused by the individual himself; those
caused by the risks inherent in the work itself, for example,
in the application of a skill such as driving; and those
inherent in the working environment, such as lighting, noise
etc.

As far as the individual is concerned, there has long been
a theory that certain individuals are 'accident prone', that
is they have a predisposition to have accidents irrespective
of the nature of the environment, because of some deficiency
of personality. Whilst such a view has been unpopular in the
past, Miner and Brewer (1976) cite a number of studies in
which aspects of personality have been shown to be related
to accident frequency. Thus more frequent accidents are
associated with negative attitudes to work, a hatred of
superiors and other authority figures and impulsive risk-
taking. Miner and Brewer suggest that such individuals have
higher accident rates because they impulsively take risks
in order to impress others and defy authority. If this is
a cause of accidents, then there is a hopeful side in that
such a defective personality trait seems to be temporary.
Most accidents occur in the younger age group, reaching a
peak at the age of 22 years. This of course suggests that
inexperience and lack of training may account for some
accidents, but as Miner and Brewer point out, skill level
and experience is likely to be even less at ages under 22
years.

Not only personality disposition but other factors in the
individual are likely to affect the probability of having

an accident. Alcohol, for example, as noted earlier, is a
major factor in many road accidents, and increasing old age
is likely to result in poorer motor co-ordination, as evi-
denced by the steep rise in the number of deaths in old age
due to falls.

As noted above, the question of skill level is likely to
be of importance and Kay notes factors such as attention and
hand-eye co-ordination to be related to accident rate. Kay
suggests that one aspect of the relationship between skill
level and accidents occurs when there is information overload, particularly where the normal routine inflow of information is supplemented by new or unusual information. Under
such circumstances the individual will switch from a stable
routine form of behaviour to a new form, and the skill with
which this is done may determine whether or not an accident
will occur. An everyday example of this comes from driving
behaviour, where the individual's skill in dealing with an
unexpected situation, such as a child suddenly darting into
the road, can determine whether or not an accident will take
place. Skill is also important in that it is likely to affect
the rapidity with which a changing situation is identified,
as well as in terms of speed of physical reaction and the
appropriateness of the reaction.

The third class of events involved in causing accidents
is the physical context of work, such as noise, heating, lighting, and the nature of equipment design. Noise for example,
has been shown to interfere with complex cognitive tasks in
various ways (for example, Jones, 1979) and the design of
safety equipment and other machinery design changes have
clearly had a material effect in reducing accidents in coal
mines. In the late 1920s for example, over 1000 miners a
year were killed in British coal mines, compared with well
under 100 now.

It must be recognised, however, that accidents occur
because of an interaction between the environment and the
individual. Few cars are safe if the individual really wishes
to kill himself, and many potentially dangerous situations in
driving, for example, are overcome using skill. In considering
accident prevention, therefore, various workers such as
Tuttle et al. (1975) emphasise the importance of the human
operator and of shaping his attitudes to safety. Those
entering the organisation are at their most susceptible in
terms of attitude formation, so that new entrants should have
safety stressed to them at pre-employment interviews, during
job orientation and during training. In addition, new recruits
should have their initial contacts with experienced workers
who follow recommended safety procedures.

Other steps which Tuttle *et al*. suggest for improving safety include ensuring that reward systems such as pay reinforce safety, and having individuals participate in decision-making concerning safety. Miner and Brewer also note the importance of participation in decision-making for safety. They suggest that participation might be particularly useful for individuals hostile to authority. Again Tuttle *et al*. note the evidence for 'top-down' attitudes to safety, such that where individuals higher up in the organisation are safety-oriented, this is more likely to be reflected lower down. Indeed Tuttle *et al*. regard leadership influence as the beginning of improved safety. Clearly, in recommending the various courses of action that they do, Tuttle *et al*. are applying many of the findings of organisational psychology discussed in Chapters 3 and 4 to the problem of safety.

Finally, it must of course be borne in mind that positive attitudes must be complemented with training and appropriate selection of skills for jobs, as well as adequate design of equipment and the environment if safety is to be maximised.

INDUSTRIAL CONFLICT

Conflict arises in situations in which individuals and groups have different aims, and one aim can, on the face of it at least, only be obtained at the expense of others. As Kelly (1974) notes, conflict can be on at least three levels, the individual, the group and the organisational. Even in the case of the individual, there are various sources of conflict. Thus, the individual may have different goals which compete with each other. Alternatively, the goals and needs of the individual may conflict with those of the group and the organisation. Indeed it is argued by Argyris (1964) that it is the conflict between the organisational structure, with its requirements of repetitive work, and low levels of responsibility, which conflicts with the individual's need for self-actualisation.

A number of behaviours have been reported to result from conflict and the subsequent frustration of an individual's goals and needs. Lawson (1965), for example, notes that aggression, regression, and fixated, rigid behaviour, have all been reported as important reactions to frustration, although none of these reactions appears to be a necessary response to frustration. Situational factors also play a major part in determining how a person will react, and indeed what he will regard as frustrating. Within industry there is evidence that where important goals are blocked, frustrated behaviour can result, in the form of sabotage or strikes, or lack of co-operation through reduced communication

(Thomas, 1976).

It must not be thought, however, that conflict should be considered only as bad. A number of writers, such as Dubin (1965), Blake *et al.* (1964) and Kelly (1974), emphasise the positive aspects of conflict. Conflict, for example, can lead to crises, and only in crisis situations might it be possible to make changes which are necessary and desirable. Conflict, too, can lead to the facing of problems which are present but not expressed, and which cannot be solved until they are acknowledged. Being presented with a conflict which requires co-operation for its solution can also lead to novel solutions, and co-operation in problem-solving can help to induce feelings of trust in antagonistic groups. Blake *et al.* (1964) give various examples of this in their consideration of conflict in industry.

Even for the individual, however, conflict can have positive effects. Strikers, for example, often report feelings of excitement and enjoyment (Stagner, 1956). At a group level, the study reported by Sherif (1966) showed that intergroup conflict led to higher feelings of morale, and greater group cohesion. Sherif's experiment involved taking groups of boys in a boys' camp and introducing conflict by means, for example, of competitive games. Although the positive effects of increased morale and cohesion can be regarded as positive, Sherif also found negative effects in terms of increased intergroup hostility. One clear practical implication of this research is that competitiveness between groups can be problematic where co-operation is later required.

As Kelly notes, Sherif's demonstration that conflict could be induced by the situation shows that it is not necessarily helpful to look on conflict in terms of neurotic personalities. Indeed many writers go further and argue that conflict is endemic to organisations in rapidly changing economic and technological conditions. The introduction of new machinery, for example, is likely to affect the way a job is done, or indeed whether the job remains at all. Furthermore, there are built-in conflicts of interest in many organisations, perhaps the most serious problem involving conflict of interest in the distribution of rewards. The evidence that the majority of strikes are about money (Lawler, 1971) would appear to bear this out to some extent.

As Thomas (1976) notes, given that conflict can be a source of good as well as bad, and given also the fact that conflict is endemic to organisations, the present emphasis is not on the elimination of conflict, but on its constructive management.

Thomas, in his review, points out that groups in conflict have a number of possible orientations towards one another.

These orientations are:-

(1) competitive - a desire to win at the other's expense;
(2) accommodative - a desire to satisfy the other without
     consideration for oneself, perhaps because of an
     interest in the long-term nature of the relationship;
(3) sharing - incomplete satisfaction for both parties -
     splitting the difference;
(4) collaborative - a desire to fully satisfy both parties,
     involving a problem-solving approach;
(5) avoidance - withdrawing contact from each other.

As far as the competitive orientation is concerned, described
by Blake *et al.* as the 'win-lose' situation, parties in a
conflict will seek to influence each other by the use of
power, such as formal power (pulling rank) or coercive power
such as striking. However, there are several undesirable
features of win-lose situations played to the bitter end.
The loser, for example, may well suffer from a sense of
bitterness and grievance, and the original source of conflict
is likely to remain. For the loser, as Blake *et al.* point
out, consequences can involve replacement of representatives
as a consequence of intragroup conflict and frustration. On
the other hand, the winning representatives are generally
consolidated in their position and become more influential.
     Various other approaches, short of win-lose, are often
adopted. Accommodation may involve yielding completely on a
particular issue, because of a wish to maintain good long-
term relationships, even though it may well lead to defeat
in later conflict situations. Compromise (split the difference)
is another approach which ensures that whilst no one wins,
at least the other party does not completely lose face. This
too is the advantage of a 'fate' approach, in which complex
issues have been reportedly solved by a toss of the coin.
Where no compromise seemed possible, the toss of the coin
allowed the loser to claim that it was not his fault that
he lost.
     At the other extreme from the win-lose situation, is the
collaborative approach to conflict, which Blake *et al.* describe as an attempt at problem-solving, rather than merely
accommodating different points of view or having a trial of
strength. For problem-solving to occur, both groups have to
have a vested interest in the outcome, and both must be
interested in developing final positions that represent the
convictions of both.
     There are various advantages of collaborative problem-
solving. In the first place, if it is successful, both parties
benefit rather than one losing, hence the general level of

self-esteem is raised. Secondly, in problem-solving, individuals are likely to be more flexible in their approach to
particular problems, and to incorporate ideas from the other
group in the final solution, often giving a creative novel
solution unseen by either party before problem-solving
commenced.

To the extent that this occurs, conflict can be regarded
as creative and useful. Again a problem-solving approach must
involve communication between groups, listening to the point
of view of others and seeking similarities as well as differences, rather than stating rigidly-fixed positions which
emphasise differences between the parties. Conflicts of the
win-lose variety have a major disadvantage of often being
bad for the victor as well as for the vanquished. In some
strikes, for example, it may take years to make up the high
loss in total earnings with the little extra gained in a
percentage increase. When people are collaborating, the cost
of the conflict to each party is minimised.

Blake *et al.* suggest a number of stages in the collaborative
approach. The first stage involves a common problem definition.
Thus the problem is not defined beforehand but is developed
through intergroup contact, possibly by group representatives.
This stage involves a joint assessment of facts. As Blake
et al. note, even 'facts' may be different for two groups in
conflict, before and after joint assessment. After this stage
has been completed, a range of alternative solutions is
developed by representatives of those in conflict which are
carefully worked through without initially arriving at fixed
positions. This allows each sub-group to see the others'
frame of reference and permits identification of alternatives
not obvious to either. Only after possible solutions have
been put forward and examined in terms of their own merits,
is it desirable to proceed to an evaluation stage where each
solution is considered in relation to others, if necessary
ranking each solution in sequence from best to worst. (See
Blake *et al.* for fuller details of the various stages.)

Blake *et al.* argue that this kind of procedure produces
facts, not misunderstandings, to serve as the bases for
finding solutions. Given the comments made earlier about the
advantages of this kind of approach, the question arises as
to why the competitive approach is ever adopted, never mind
frequently adopted. Thomas (1976) suggests a number of influences in the direction of competitive conflict.

In the first place, combatants in disputes often are disposed by their personalities to try to defeat their opponents,
and competition is noted by many writers to be a characteristic
of many aspects of Western society. From our earliest school
days we are urged to compete, to beat our rivals, so it is

hardly surprising that this approach becomes ingrained in
our everyday styles of coping with life.

The personality explanation, however, is likely at best to
be a partial explanation, if only because from our earliest
school days we are also taught to consider the other person's
point of view, to have feelings of justice and equity, and
not to kick an opponent when he is down. In conflict situations, therefore, it is necessary to explain why this kind
of behaviour takes second place to the alternative of a
competitive 'win at all costs' approach.

One possible reason is that in many conflict situations,
representatives of groups take part in bargaining, and
representatives are subject to a number of social pressures.
Thomas (1976), for example, notes that group leaders have a
vested interest in maintaining hostile relationships with
the 'outgroup' where there is the danger of hostility between
group members. As Sherif noted, there is increased group
cohesion and morale when in conflict with another group.
Again, as Blake *et al.* note, this higher cohesion may well
disappear when the external threat is removed, if there is
otherwise little to keep the group together. Blake *et al.*
also note some of the other social pressures on representatives; where, for example, the representative changes his
position he risks being thought of as a traitor, where he
wins in a win-lose situation he is regarded as a hero. In
other words, the representative who moves his position to
take account of objective facts is in danger of losing his
group, and hence his power base.

Apart from these 'social' factors making for competitive
bargaining, other situational factors may also point bargaining in the same direction. Where, for example, the goal
is important or where there are scarce resources so that one
must win at the other's expense, both in the short and the
long term there is more likely to be competitive bargaining.
Finally, the rules and procedures for bargaining within an
organisation may be so formalised that a problem-solving
approach becomes more difficult, and an adversary relationship
is almost imposed.

Given that so much of industrial conflict is of a win-lose
variety, and given the costs of failure are high for both
sides, many conflicts are resolved by taking it to a third
party, either a mediator or an arbitrator. A mediator will
normally take an active role in trying to bring the sides
together, by seeking a solution acceptable to both, although
his solution is often not binding on either party. An arbitrator, on the other hand, is a presumed impartial judge,
whose judgement is normally accepted as binding on both
parties before they enter arbitration.

As Thomas notes, whilst mediation is likely to focus on a problem-solving approach in which both sides retain responsibility for the decision, arbitration often leaves the underlying hostility unaltered, and leaves the losing party feeling that the arbitration was unfair. Far from being an ideal solution, therefore, arbitration is best looked on as a last resort where problem-solving attempts have failed.

Strikes

Clearly an extreme example of industrial conflict is the strike, in which one party to the conflict seeks to exert its coercive power by withdrawing its labour and consequently halting the production process. As Stagner (1956) notes, contrary to popular belief, striking is not a frequent phenomenon, although strikes are dramatic and do receive considerable attention from the press. It would be a mistake, however, to assume that because any one individual group rarely strikes the effect of strikes is exaggerated by the press. Given the interdependence of organisations in industry, a strike anywhere in the chain is likely to be highly disruptive. Thus in the car industry in Great Britain, a strike in shipping, the docks, the steel industry, road or rail transport, electricity supply, coal and component manufacturers amongst others, could disrupt manufacturing, without mentioning the disruption caused by strikes in the car assembly industry itself. Nevertheless, it does remain true that days lost through strike action represent a relatively small total of days lost.

The actual cause of strikes is incompletely understood. Kornhauser *et al.* (1954) report that some industries are more strike prone than others, and indicate mining as the most strike prone industry. Clearly, however, the extent of strike-proneness changes from time to time and from country to country. In Great Britain, for example, there has been no serious strike in the coal mining industry since 1974, whereas some conveyor belt industries, in particular the car industry, have suffered considerably. Conclusions on strike causes, therefore, based on the strike prone nature of particular industries are problematic, particularly as the mere threat of a strike might be enough to attain desired ends. On the other hand, it is also too glib to assume that the stress and boredom brought about by conveyor belt technology induces strikes. Lawler (1971), for example, reports that 'money' is the major given reason for striking, and it may be that financial factors alone are responsible for increased striking in the car industry and reduced striking in the coal industry. Furthermore, the assumption that continuous process industries are less strike prone than others has recently been questioned by Gill (1979) on the basis of survey data. He found that, irrespective of size, continuous process industries reported a higher level of strike activity.

On the other hand, as Stagner points out, strikes are likely to occur because of a complex of factors, including aggression and the perceived probability of achieving goals through strikes. Obviously critical is whether a strike can be seen as having an important effect. In the only strike in which we have taken part, lecturers had to be asked if they had been on strike, as no one could distinguish those on strike from those working! It must be added that this is because of the complex nature of a university teacher's role, rather than because they never work anyway!

It would, however, be incorrect to assume any one to one relationship between job satisfaction and strike behaviour. In national strikes involving industries, individuals in any one organisation may be perfectly satisfied, but strike because of feelings of obligation and solidarity. Such national strikes may be called because of the state of labour relations, or by trends in wage settlements in other comparable industries not being matched in a particular case. Again Stagner notes that strikes tend to increase in time of increasing prices, perhaps as a response to the individual workers' standard of living being threatened. As noted above, such factors may have little to do with job satisfaction as such. On the other hand, the study by James (1951) does suggest that strikes can involve considerations of job satisfaction over a range of job facets. James (1951) also noted that in a strike which he examined, strikers differed from non-strikers in their dissatisfaction with their boss, their workweek, their promotion opportunities and their seniority rights.

Clearly strikes are not a desirable state of affairs. Apart from lost production and lost wages, the frustration and hostility induced can, as Blake *et al.* note, have its aftermath once the strike is over. In the loser's camp, the effect is lowered morale, and often replacement of representatives with those thought better able to attain group goals, an action which may lead to further problems in the future. On the other hand, like any other conflict, it is possible to utilise the opportunity to make radical changes, and to seek a new beginning. At the very least a strike highlights a failure in normal relationships which both sides should seek to rectify.

8 Job Redesign

A large number of schemes have been put forward in recent
years as aids to improved productivity. Some have been seized
on by enthusiastic consultants as panaceas for a myriad of
organisational problems and even academics have become en-
amoured by various techniques without taking due account of
the evidence for their efficacy. There is, needless to say,
no panacea, no scheme which will do good to all organisations
in all circumstances. A number of schemes have been shown
to have some value in some circumstances, and five of these
approaches to job redesign are considered in this chapter.
They are: flexible working hours; management by objectives;
Scanlon plan; job enrichment; socio-technical systems design
(autonomous working group). It must be stressed, however,
that the following outlines are intended to give the reader
a brief account of the various programmes, and are not intended as cook-book recipes for organisational change.

FLEXIBLE WORKING HOURS (FWH)

Cummings and Molloy (1977) define flexible working hours as
'an arrangement whereby employees have a degree of freedom
in choosing the hours they will work each day'. In most
schemes the day is divided up into core time, when the
employee must be present, and flexible time, normally at
the beginning and the end of the day, when the employee is
free to choose when he will start and when he will finish,
always providing that he works a certain minimum number of
agreed hours during the week or month. For example, an
employee must be contracted to work for 160 hours for a four-
week period. He may be required to work every day between
10.00 a.m. and 12.00 and between 2.00 p.m. and 4.00 p.m.,
but may have the freedom to start work at 7.00 a.m. to 10.00
a.m. or finish at any time between 4.00 p.m. and 7.00 p.m.
In this way an employee might be able to carry out forty
hours per week by working the first three days from 7.00 a.m.
to 1.00 p.m. and from 2.00 p.m. to 6.00 p.m., and working

on the last two days from 10.00 a.m. to 1.00 p.m. and from
2.00 p.m. to 4.00 p.m.

Clearly the advantage to the employee is that he can plan
his working week with his leisure and family activities in
mind, although as flexible hours are not imposed, the employee can work normally if he wishes. While the basic
flexible working hours arrangement involves a core time, a
flexible working time, and an agreed number of contracted
hours over a given period, most schemes advocate increasing
flexibility by allowing individuals to build up credit hours
over a contract period, which can then be carried over to
be set against individuals who go into debit, if personal
circumstances make it desirable to take off more than usual
time in any accounting period. The flexibility of both credit
and debit hours is limited, however, in order that it will
not lead to overload or underload amongst other employees
in any given period. Even core time is not sacrosanct in
some schemes, although here the flexibility is much more
limited and would normally operate only in special circumstances. At first sight FWH would have a great deal to re-
commend it, both from the point of view of employees, who,
as noted above, gain greater control over their leisure
times, and for employers, where staggering working hours
might well mean the longer use of expensive equipment, and
better management-employee relations, as employees are able
to take part in decision-making concerning their own working
hours. Furthermore, bad time keeping is eliminated as each
individual chooses his own starting and stopping time.

Another major advantage claimed for flexible working hours
arrangements in the scheme introduced by Messerschmitt (MMB)
was that it got rid of the problems of congestion at the
beginning and at the end of the day. Management in the organisation noted that a great deal of effort at the end of the
working day was given over to problems of how to avoid the
inevitable traffic jams when work stopped, and indeed the
flexible working hours movement started as a result of MMB's
introduction of the flexible working hours system in order
to overcome this problem. For MMB, itself, the introduction
of flexible working hours was seen by employees as creating
a better balance between work and private life, and easing
travel problems. Wade (1973) reports that management were
more than happy with the arrangement, claiming it saved
some £16,000 per month in increased productivity and lower
absenteeism.

Empirical Evidence
Since the case of MMB, a number of studies have been conducted on flexible working hours. Wade (1973), for example,

reports on studies conducted at Lufthansa's head office in
Cologne, where eighteen months after the introduction of
FWH, 96 per cent of personnel reportedly liked the system,
and 39 per cent of managers reported their department's
efficiency to have increased compared with 3 per cent who
reported that it had gone down. In a more recent study,
Schein, Maurer and Novak (1978) found that supervisors perceived flexible working hours to have a positive effect on
productivity, employee honesty, unit administration, employee
time, handling and employee work habits. Thus, for example,
57 per cent of respondents·reported productivity increases
and 87 per cent perceived their employees as working satis-
factorily with less supervisory coverage. In reviewing six
such studies, Cummings and Molloy note that all six reported
improvements in attitudes, five reported increases in
productivity and four reported reductions in absence and
staff turnover. One reason given by Golembiewski and Proehl
(1978) for reduced absence is that individuals who are going
to be late would often, in normal circumstances, take the
day off with an illness excuse, rather than face a 'hassle'
with their supervisor. FWH removes the need for this. Cummings
and Molloy note, however, that almost all studies are deficient in important respects. Most fail to use control groups
to ensure that outside factors are not responsible for changes.
Furthermore, many fail to present adequate statistics so that
the real significance of the changes reported cannot be
assessed. In this respect, findings on flexible working hours
are similar to those on job enrichment, discussed later. The
findings of these studies therefore suggest, but do not
adequately demonstrate, that *under the right circumstances*
flexible working hours can benefit both the employee and the
productivity of the organisation.

  Legge (1974) points out what some of the right and wrong
circumstances might be. She notes that technology, the labour
market, disputes procedures and structural characteristics of
the organisation can materially affect whether or not FWH is
appropriate. As far as technology is concerned, it is obviously
more appropriate to work a flexible working hours system where
each individual is to some extent independent of others. It
is often quite easy, for example, for a computer programmer
to work flexible hours, as his preparation can be usually
carried out independently of others. On the other hand, where
a job requires the back-up services of other individuals, and
if their services are essential to the performance of others,
working flexible hours is much more problematic. The problem
of interdependence of jobs can to some extent be overcome if
the jobs involved are relatively routine and require little
training, as it is then relatively easy to provide cover for

the individual who is not present. On the other hand, FWH is much more problematic if an individual has a unique skill which others need to utilise in order to perform their own work.

As far as the labour market is concerned, as Legge points out, low turnover and low absence make it considerably easier to arrange cover for the flexible part of the working day. Again arrangements, once made, are likely to be stable where the workforce is stable, but to require far more organisation and administration where the turnover of staff is rapid. It might be pointed out, however, that one of the main objectives of FWH is to reduce both absence and staff turnover.

One major problem with FWH is the question of overtime. As Legge notes, in theory the need for overtime disappears since hours in excess of standard can be compensated for by building up credit balances so that the employee can have extra hours off work. Furthermore, arrangements can be made for overtime work where the employee is specifically asked by his supervisor to work specific extra hours. Yet undoubtedly some of the savings attributable to FWH come from savings in overtime payments. Wade (1973), for example, notes one organisation where £45,000 was saved in one year through reduction in overtime payments alone. This, as Legge points out, is a serious problem for employees who rely on overtime payments for a substantial part of their pay packet, and must be carefully dealt with in any attempt to introduce FWH. Clearly, where overtime is not normally worked, the problem is less acute.

As far as structural job characteristics are concerned, Legge argues that white-collar jobs are often more amenable to FWH than blue-collar jobs. Partly this is because white-collar jobs are often more independent of other workers, partly overtime working and the efficient utilisation of expensive capital equipment is less of a problem. Again a female workforce is thought more likely to be amenable to FWH as this gives women more flexibility in dealing with domestic problems.

Because FWH is more appropriate to white-collar jobs of certain types, the introduction of FWH, even if successful for the part of the organisation where it is appropriate, may cause problems elsewhere. By giving one group of employees 'extra' privileges, it is quite possible to induce feelings of inequity elsewhere, particularly in the production part of the organisation. Wade (1973) notes this problem, but claims it can be overcome. He cites the case of the Swiss company Sandoz AG. Whilst the flexible time system for white-collar workers could not be introduced for production personnel, the latter were permitted to choose a starting time for shifts, within limits, and all employees were paid on a monthly basis. The time clock, too, was abolished and each employee was made responsible for completing his time recording sheet, which had to be agreed by an immediate superior.

One major potential problem of FWH does not seem to have materialised in most cases. Given that FWH is almost always applied to white-collar workers, and that accurate time-keeping is an essential aspect of a successful scheme, it might be thought that status-conscious white-collar workers would be sensitive about any formal method of time keeping, such as clocking in. In fact considerable attention has been given to this problem, and most studies report that time keeping, if *properly* introduced is not a problem, although if badly handled can alienate staff (Wade, 1973).

Wade reports on two successful schemes for time keeping. One involved the use of manual recording. Here a British company used a time sheet on which staff entered the time they were ready to start work, when they finished work, and the total hours worked. This kind of 'honour' system, Wade notes, is compatible with the increased responsibility given to staff. It is also the cheapest way of doing things and might be most appropriate in situations where management can easily check staff movements.

'Clocking in' systems vary in kind from those which note start and finish times, to those developed by Hengstler (see Wade, 1973). Hengstler's time-recording equipment does not record a starting and finishing time, but does record the cumulative total of hours worked. The main psychological advantage of this is that it removes the feeling of being spied on to keep proper time. Clearly the recording equipment costs money, although organisations using the system often claim that the capital outlay is soon recouped in increased productivity.

Assuming that a particular firm wishes to introduce a FWH system, all advocates insist that a careful programme of introduction is essential. Steps suggested for introduction by Cummings and Molloy (1977) include an initial feasibility study to ensure that the plan is likely to be successful. As noted above, FWH is likely to be more appropriate the more independent the jobs are, the more stable the labour market, the less overtime is worked, where the jobs are white-collar, where the labour force is predominantly female, where the unions are co-operative and where work flow is appropriate to flexible working hours. Of course with ingenuity any one of these difficulties might well be overcome with a co-operative workforce.

Wade, for example, notes that in the scheme adopted by Pilkington Glass, service, technology and engineering

departments were successfully involved in the greater use of
expensive equipment. Wade warns that management must be quite
clear about the kind of FWH arrangement it wants before
consultations take place. Appropriate core time, flexible
time, band widths (that is, starting and finishing times),
credit/debit carry over, contracted hours, time off core
time, policy on overtime, recording methods, and length and
scope of the project and its assessment, must be established.
This is an interesting point, since many advocates of FWH
suggest that it is an opportunity to involve employees in
decision-making. As Golembiewski and Proehl (1978) note,
however, almost all schemes are imposed from the 'top' down.
Participation, if it occurs, occurs later.

Like all management schemes, FWH appears to be a useful
scheme for some organisations in some situations, although
the scientific evidence for its usefulness is not particularly
well documented. In many ways, however, it is an easier
scheme to introduce than others as it involves less fundamental change to the role of the individuals, particularly
managers, than, say, job enrichment. If the scheme fails,
furthermore, it is relatively easy to go back to a normal
timing system, without much disruption to the structure of
the organisation. As with the introduction of all new schemes,
its success depends critically on how it is introduced as
much as what is introduced. With goodwill on both sides,
difficulties can be relatively easily put right. Where,
however, there is initial mistrust, FWH might well be seen
as a chance for getting more out of the workers, controlling
their movements more rigidly by introducing a time clock,
and reducing earnings by reducing overtime.

The Forty Hour Week
Related to rescheduling work hours through flexible working
hours is rescheduling the number of working days per week.
The most popular of these has been the ten hours, four-work-
days per week scheme and, as with FWH, a number of studies
have reported its successful implementation. As with FWH too,
the experimental evidence is by no means adequate, with many
studies failing to use control groups or very adequate
statistical analysis. A number of studies have found no effect,
but, perhaps most worrying of all, a number of studies have
reported negative effects. Nord and Costigan (1973), for
example, found that workers, whilst initially favourable,
later reported negative effects on home life. Wade (1973),
too, reports on a study in which many employees were unhappy
with the system, these being mostly married staff with young
children. It does appear, therefore, that such a system has
the opposite effect from FWH in making home life and work

life incompatible for some employees.

Another major problem reported by Wade is that of employee fatigue. He notes that many employers adopting the four-day-week have problems of worker fatigue at the end of the day.

Nevertheless Wade notes one consultant report that it took the workforce about six months to adjust to the new work schedules. This conflicts with other studies which have found no long-term changes in productivity, and a worsening of attitudes. However, whilst there are clear indications that the four-day ten-hour work week is not a universal panacea, there are undoubtedly instances where the adoption of the system appears to have been successful. Wade (1973), for example, reports on one successful company. Productivity rose by more than 15 per cent in the first year and has risen to 20 per cent since then (after eight years). Workers have had higher wages, in some cases up to 30 per cent more. Mechanical breakdowns are reduced because maintenance staff have every Friday for repairs and general servicing. Absenteeism is reduced as is turnover, and job attitudes seem to be highly favourable.

As with so many organisational changes, it is almost impossible to say why this particular scheme has been successful while others have failed. It could, for example, have been that better machinery maintenance leads to greater continuous production, which in turn leads to greater earnings. Financial rewards, in other words, resulting from mechanical improvements may have been a major factor in improving attitudes. Similarly absence may have been reduced because the financial loss for one day's absence is greater when less days are worked per week.

Many companies which have tried the four-day system do report satisfaction with it. Poor (1970), for example, found that twenty-two out of twenty-seven companies who had used the system had had good experiences with it. Yet it would be foolish to initiate such a programme without taking account of the practical problems; that it can be severely disruptive, that it can lead to worker fatigue and in practical terms is unlikely to be popular with unions who have succeeded in establishing a normal working day of eight hours. As with any system, if it is to be introduced, it should only be done so after full consultation, where the workforce is willing to adapt to social changes involved, and where the management must be tolerant of worker fatigue until employees adapt to the new time schedules. As with FWH, it is obviously desirable to define the scope and length of the project and to agree to an assessment of its value after a trial period, with the possibility of reverting back if the scheme is unsuccessful. In the case of the four-day week this is

particularly important, since at least one study, that of
Ivancevich and Lyon (1977) reported short-term improvements
which disappeared after two years.

MANAGEMENT BY OBJECTIVES

One management scheme which incorporates a number of principles discussed earlier in the book is management by objectives (MBO). Much of the initial impetus for MBO was provided
by Drucker (1954) and by McGregor (1960). Drucker pointed to
the importance of managers having clear objectives that
support the objectives of those in higher positions in the
organisation. McGregor argues that by establishing performance goals for employees after reaching agreement with
superiors, the problems of appraisal of performance are
minimised. MBO in essence involves the setting out of clearly
defined goals of an employee in agreement with his superior.
Carroll and Tosi (1973), in an extensive account of MBO, note
its following characteristics:

(1) the establishment of organisational goals;
(2) the setting of individual objectives in relation to
     organisational goals;
(3) a periodic review of performance as it relates to
     organisational goals;
(4) effective goal-setting and planning by top management;
(5) organisational commitment;
(6) mutual goal-setting;
(7) frequent individual performance reviews;
(8) some freedom in developing means of achieving objectives.

It can be seen, therefore, that MBO involves the principles
of goal-setting, feedback and participation, factors which
have been shown to be related to improved performance. It
would not be surprising, therefore, if MBO were to prove to
be an effective means of improving productivity.

The Empirical Evidence
Whilst a large number of studies have been reported on MBO,
and many report improvements in performance, it is often
difficult to assess exactly what causes improvement because
of the large number of organisational changes that are often
made simultaneously. A study by Raia (1965, 1966) did show
the effects of MBO on performance. Raia showed that following
the introduction of an MBO programme, productivity increased
by over 6 per cent. However, it appears that the effectiveness of the programme started to decline after a period of
time, in line with the findings of Ivancevich (1977) on goal-

setting. One problem in the Raia study was that foremen
felt they were not properly participating in the MBO programme, and Latham and Yukl (1975) note the failure of many
MBO programmes because of lack of management enthusiasm.

   That MBO programmes can have difficulties does not of
course mean that MBO is an ineffective means of improving
productivity where it is appropriately applied, properly
conducted and where organisational members have a commitment
to its success. Ivancevich (1974) reports on just such a
study, in which plants were compared which had, or did not
have, positive reinforcement from top management for the
MBO programme. Furthermore, only in the plant with positive
reinforcement was there an operating committee consisting
of managers from each level in the hierarchy who met each
month to consider problems of operating the programme. The
production levels of product and marketing departments were
monitored for a three-year period after the introduction of
MBO. Two important findings emerged. First, performance
increased in the first six months in both groups where MBO
was initiated. However, the longer lasting effects over
thirty-six months were only sustained in the group where
there was positive reinforcement and where there was an
organising committee which dealt regularly with the operation of the programme. Whilst Ivancevich acknowledges that
the study must be treated with caution, because of the relatively small numbers of supervisors involved, the fact that
in this and in other studies (for example, Raia, 1965;
Meyer *et al.*, 1965), there were significant effects following
MBO, does give further encouragement to the view that the
findings of researches on goal-setting can be implemented
successfully within a management programme, although some
problems must be borne in mind.

   One major problem noted by Carroll and Tosi (1973) is that
in many studies managers report being burdened with paperwork, as they are required to set out, in writing, agreed
goals. Because time demands for paperwork are felt to be
excessive, passive resistance to the scheme sometimes sets
in. Wickens (1968) also notes other causes of MBO failure.
These include the establishment of conflicting objectives,
rapidly changing market conditions which mean that objectives have to be rapidly re-assessed, and a failure to
integrate MBO with other organisational programmes. Wickens
also notes that MBO might be more appropriate for some kinds
of organisation than for others, in that, for example, long-
range corporate planning is inherently more difficult in
firms involved in small-unit and small-batch production than
for those in large-batch and mass production. In small-batch
production, for example, managers are able to plan only a

fairly short way ahead, and must do so in close co-operation
with others. Wickens gives other examples of difficulties of
MBO, such as frequent design modifications delaying production
and invalidating sales forecasts. Thus MBO is not likely to
succeed where long-term overall objectives are rather loose,
where departmental objectives are flexible and short term,
and are frequently revised at irregular and unpredictable
intervals. Whilst these comments are probably more appropriate for small-batch and unit product organisations, clearly
some of these problems are likely to apply to every organisation. This is particularly true for the problem of changing
circumstances invalidating specific objectives, and external
factors influencing the probability of the individual achieving his goals.

One factor which is likely to affect the long-term success
of MBO involves management philosophy towards its employees.
In particular, it is important to consider the question of
what rewards should flow to employees consequent on improved
performance. The notion that individuals will derive sufficient satisfaction from achieving organisational goals alone
seems naive in view of the complex role of money as a reward.
Failure to reward employees, by, for example, increased
salaries, may be interpreted as inequitable, or at least as
a failure of top management to give recognition to the individual's achievements. This effect of failing to reward
productivity in a job enrichment experiment has been noted
by Locke, Sirota and Wolfson (1976).

The existing philosophy of the organisation, too, may make
the introduction of MBO difficult. Wickens (1968) notes that
in organisations used to autocratic management, moves to
increase participation are viewed with apathy and even
hostility. Not only might increased participation be seen
as not legitimate, where organisations are autocratic, individuals might have lost interest in the goals of the
organisation and managers might find it almost impossible to
change managerial styles of a lifetime.

Implementation
In considering how to implement an MBO scheme, Carroll and
Tosi (1973) note that a number of problems must be resolved
before any programme can be successfully implemented. For
example, there must be integration with other components of
the formal structure such as manpower planning. There must
be consideration of the manner in which goal-setting will
take place, whether left entirely to the employee and his
superior or formalised. The question of the nature of performance evaluation must be considered; should it be by
oral interview only, or should it be recorded. What should

be the content of the performance appraisal, how frequently should it be conducted and to whom should the contents be communicated. These are all noted by Caroll and Tosi to be important questions which must be settled before an MBO programme can be successfully implemented. Consideration must also be given to managerial resistance to the amount of time involved in developing, preparing and communicating the goals and objectives of the organisation and to allowing subordinates to participate in decision-making. The latter sometimes gives rise to feelings of erosion of authority and to problems of face-to-face interaction in the performance review.

THE SCANLON PLAN

Like management by objectives, the Scanlon plan is another programme which seeks to improve productivity by incorporating a number of principles which have been shown to improve productivity. In the Scanlon plan (SP), individuals participate in decision-making concerning goals, they make suggestions concerning productivity and receive group bonuses on the basis of productivity increases. SP, therefore, involves participation in decision-making, goal-setting, incentive payments and group working.

The Scanlon plan takes its name from Joseph Scanlon, a union officer in a Pennsylvania steel mill. During the depression, when his firm was threatened with going out of business, Scanlon persuaded his company to seek the aid of employees in reducing waste and improving efficiency. The philosophy behind the Scanlon plan is that many employees are able to make a constructive contribution to their work situation when they are consulted and motivated. In other words, organisations are wasting a considerable amount of valuable talent by not utilising the human resources available.

However, the opportunity to participate in helping the organisation to increase productivity is unlikely to be successful unless it is coupled with an equitable treatment and financial or other reward for any productivity improvement, and participation and equitable reward is the essence of the Scanlon plan. SP does normally involve more than this however, and Cummings and Molloy (1977) note that group interaction is an important element in SP. Group cohesion and group motivation is increased by allocation of rewards on a group basis and by employee participation in the setting of group objectives.

Motivation to perform well under the Scanlon plan is seen to be due to a number of factors. Participation in decision-

making of importance to the individual is seen to increase
the individual's feeling of having control over his environment (autonomy). Being consulted by others is also likely to
increase his feelings of self-esteem, especially in situations
where his suggestions are adopted and lead to greater productivity and financial reward. Receiving bonus payments as
a consequence of improved productivity of the group is seen
to be rewarding directly specific achievements, and increases
the feeling of equity concerning financial reward. Because
of a greater emphasis on group achievement, satisfaction
with social aspects of the work situation is increased and
individual competition lessened, while at the same time
beneficial co-operation is increased. Again the SP requires
greater responsibility for decisions concerning the setting
of goals, determining of production methods, and indeed having
new members and selecting supervisors. As noted earlier
(Chapter 4), goal-setting and successful achievement of
goals is likely to increase levels of aspiration for future
goals, whilst increasing the variety and meaningfulness of
jobs is likely to increase satisfaction with work, if not
productivity (see also Chapter 4).

The Empirical Evidence
What then is the evidence for the success of the SP, what
are its advantages and disadvantages? A large number of
reported studies claim productivity improvements as a result
of SP, although many studies are case studies in which there
are no experimental controls and where statistical evidence
is again somewhat wanting. Furthermore, as Cummings and
Molloy (1977) point out, SP is almost universally supplemented
by a wide range of changes also intended to improve productivity. For example, task variety is often increased,
training is often given and feedback on performance improved.
    Despite reservations, Cummings and Molloy present evidence
from eight studies to show that, following SP, there were
increases in both quantity and quality of productivity and
improvements in absence and turnover, and Locke *et al.* (1980)
note that in all but two of fourteen studies they consider,
performance improvements are reported. Locke *et al.* give
16 per cent as the average productivity improvement for the
Scanlon plan, although some studies report improvements of
well over 30 per cent. Again many of the SP programmes have
been going for a number of years, so that unlike some other
systems, the improvements do not seem to be merely transient.
    Yet as with other systems, SP is by no means universally
successful and a number of failures of SP have been reported.
Hackman (1977) notes that in one review of forty-four studies
of SP, thirty were successful whilst fourteen were not. One

factor noted by Hackman to be a factor in failure was that
productivity payments were less under Scanlon than under
the former incentive plan. A study by Gray (1971) of SP in
a motor plant in Scotland also indicates the difficulties
which might be encountered. One problem which arose in the
study involved the increase in job flexibility. Employees
resented being moved from one job to another, especially
when this movement meant a lowering in skill level. Gray
also found that bonus levels were not seen as adequate and
for this reason suggestions fell. Inequity might have been
felt by the workers when it was felt that insufficient
material rewards were flowing from the system.

   Another reported failure is the study of Gilson and
Lefcowitz (1957). Failure here was attributed to a management
philosophy which was against participation, and to a dis-
interested workforce which did not really identify with the
goals of organisation. Katzell and Yankelovich (1975) note
that where SP has failed, it has been due to major flaws in
the design or implementation of adequate bonus schemes or
adequate participation procedures, and Cummings and Molloy
(1977) also emphasise that SP cannot be grafted on to
organisations where attitudes and practices are inconsistent
with Scanlon philosophy, and so may be inappropriate for
many organisations. Other factors noted by Katzell and
Yankelovich to be essential for the success of SP include
the ability of the company to absorb increased production,
should it arise, and the necessity, in a large organisation,
of co-ordinating the goals of different groups.

   The question of co-ordination within an organisation is
very important where increases in productivity in one
department are not matched by the increases in others. Apart
from difficulties produced by bottlenecks, there is the
ever-present danger of feelings of resentment over equity
of payment for different groups, and the risk of competition
between groups growing up. Again Hackman (1977) notes that
the success of SP depends on employees seeing a relationship
between what they do and their rewards. The larger the
organisation, the more difficult this becomes. He notes that
most successful SPs have been in organisations of under 500
employees, although White (1979) found no relationship between the success of SP and organisational size.

   Hackman also points out that SP is likely to be inappropriate in organisations where performance history is difficult
to measure and good performance measures are difficult to
obtain, perhaps in organisations where rapid changes are
occurring. Administrative costs too, tend to be high with
SP and in some cases so high as to make SP inappropriate.
Finally, as Cummings and Molloy point out, for SP to have

DATE DUE

DEC 0 5 1996			

a chance of success the possibility must exist that employees can influence productivity to a significant extent. This is not always the case, as for example in some industries, where productivity is basically determined by technology.

That there have been a number of failures of SP does not of course mean that the plan is valueless. Whilst the evidence for the value of SP rests on studies which have individual limitations, the number of studies reporting success makes it probable that under appropriate circumstances, SP can be successful. It is not possible to say, however, why SP is successful, given the large number of factors varied at any one time. Indeed it is not clear that productivity increases following SP are due to increased work motivation at all. It might well be that much of the increase in productivity comes from the adoption of better working practices suggested by the workforce, under conditions where they too will benefit from increased productivity. Alternatively it may be that when the workforce believes it will benefit equitably from increased productivity, then it will be less resistant to the introduction of new machinery which will of itself increase productivity. Of course, from the point of view of the organisation, it perhaps does not matter too much why productivity is increasing as long as it does.

In summary, the SP seems to be successful in some companies in some situations, perhaps because it allows employees to relate their efforts to tangible rewards and because it allows employees to participate in decision-making concerning important aspects of their work. It is, however, not entirely clear why SP works, as many changes normally take place simultaneously during the implementation of SP, and it may be that increased work motivation on the part of the workforce has little to do with increased productivity. Thus productivity may increase because of the adoption of practical suggestions for work improvement or it may be that the promise of increased remuneration makes the workforce less resistant to the introduction of new, more productive machinery. Of course, even if this were to be the case, SP could still be regarded as a successful programme for increasing productivity.

Whilst the discussion on SP has been in terms of increased productivity, one possible advantage of the scheme is that it sometimes appears to be accompanied by increased job satisfaction. In their review of eight SP studies, Cummings and Molloy note that six report improvements in quality of working life, although the research designs leave a great deal to be desired. It seems reasonable, however, to conclude that the evidence suggests that both productivity and job satisfaction can be improved in appropriate cases.

JOB ENRICHMENT

Probably the most widely discussed method of job redesign
is job enrichment in which jobs are redesigned to take account
of the higher-order needs of individuals. Thus those in
enriched jobs have increased autonomy to make decisions,
increased variety, increased identity and meaningfulness
and increased feedback.

Much of the impetus for job enrichment has come from the
work of Herzberg (1966), who sees the intrinsic aspects of
the job as vital to increased satisfaction and production.
Whilst his theoretical position is somewhat problematic
(see Chapter 2), his work has had an influence on later
workers such as Hackman and Lawler (1971) who sought to
identify those aspects of the job which were correlated
with satisfaction and productivity.

Job enrichment as a job redesign strategy should be distinguished from job rotation, in which the employee is
moved from one job to another, in order to increase job
variety. For example, on Monday the employee might perform
Job A, on Tuesday, Job B and so on. Some writers are critical
of this as a job redesign strategy in that they regard it
as just the addition of more boring jobs to the one the
employee already holds. Furthermore, from the point of view
of productivity, it may be that the loss of production
involved in training new individuals up to an adequate
standard in new jobs does not compensate for any motivational
gains through reducing the amount of boredom on the job.
Again job rotation may disrupt ongoing workgroups from which
the individual derives his satisfaction at work, and may
therefore reduce, rather than increase job satisfaction.
Nevertheless, where job rotation is wanted by employees,
there seems little reason to oppose its introduction, provided it does not materially disrupt productivity over the
long term.

Related to job rotation is vertical job enlargement, where
the individual has more jobs or operations added to the ones
he already has. Thus instead of doing Job A only, he is
required to undertake Job B and C at the same time. Again
many writers object to this job enlargement on the same
grounds as they object to job rotation, as being an increase
in the number of boring jobs individuals are required to do.
However, Walker and Guest (1952) noted in their study that
the greater the number of operations an individual performed,
the greater was job satisfaction. It may well be therefore
that in some situations vertical job enlargement does increase satisfaction. As with the other features of job design,
one might expect individual differences in reaction to

increased job variety. For those who get their satisfaction
at work from social interaction, say, increased job variety
might involve more concentration on the job and less time
for social interaction, with a consequent increase in job
dissatisfaction.

For Herzberg (1966) and many other workers, however, the
essence of job redesign is job enrichment in which not only
job variety, but autonomy, meaningfulness, task significance
and feedback are essential elements in the new job. Such
jobs aim to go beyond increasing job satisfaction, which
might be attained by satisfying lower-order needs, to allowing
an individual to apply skills to the performance of his job
and thus fulfil his higher order needs (see, for example,
Hackman and Lawler (1971)).

Empirical Evidence
As was noted in Chapter 4, evaluation of the relationship
between core job aspects and productivity is problematic.
Apart from a low correlation between core aspects and quality
of productivity, little evidence is produced by Hackman and
Lawler (1971) or later studies, to show a significant
relationship, and Herzberg's theoretical position is, as
was noted earlier, more than somewhat problematic. If job
enrichment works, therefore, in relation to productivity,
it has little sound empirical or theoretical background.
For this reason it is necessary to be more than usually
cautious in evaluating evidence.

There is little doubt that on the face of it, a substantial number of studies show evidence of improved productivity
and satisfaction as a result of job enrichment. Yet it is
equally clear that a large number of studies suffer from
flaws sufficiently great to discount their value as evidence
of the efficacy of job enrichment. Fein (1974), for example,
notes that defects in the famous studies of Walton at Topeka
(1972) of Ford at AT and T (1969), and of Texas instruments,
make it unlikely that conclusions can be drawn from any of
these studies. In the case of Topeka foods, a new plant was
set up in which only one in ten job applicants was selected
in five screening interviews. Such highly selected and
highly motivated employees are unlikely to be typical of
the normal employees facing managers in established ongoing
organisations. In the case of the AT and T studies, jobs
were redesigned to take the place of poorly designed jobs
so that practically any change would have improved productivity, and at Texas instruments pay was raised by 46 per
cent and benefits worth one third of pay were added, making
any improvements found as likely to be due to pay increases
as to job design.

Apart from these well-known studies, numerous reviews have pointed to the inadequacies of most studies to date, for example, Katzell and Yankelovich (1975), Cummings and Molloy (1977), and Locke *et al.* (1980). Cummings and Molloy (1977), for example, note that many studies fail to have adequate controls for all the threats to validity. Many studies involve small numbers of employees, many fail to provide adequate statistical evidence, and some studies are problematic in that the workers selected for job enrichment programmes differ systematically from those used as controls. For example, in a study by Alderfer (1969) the 'best' blue-collar workers were selected for a job enrichment programme.

Another major problem with the interpretation of job redesign studies is illustrated by Locke, Sirota and Wolfson (1976) in their research on the job enrichment of a group of clerical workers in a government agency. One can regard the Locke *et al.* study as well designed. It incorporates control groups, uses adequate statistical analysis and involves substantial job changes which can be regarded as enriching the job. Job redesign resulted in an increase in productivity of 21.5 per cent, although interestingly,job satisfaction did not increase. Yet the important point is that the increased productivity may have had little to do with the motivational aspects of job enrichment, but rather to result from better manpower utilisation. Where, for example, a job involves individual A opening mail which is passed on to individual B who then sorts it for individual C, it is obvious that where all three are involved in the opening of mail,its sorting and subsequent processing, there will be less of a bottleneck from A to B. What looks like the effects of increased variety and autonomy, is in fact the effect of better manpower utilisation.

An interesting feature of Locke *et al.*'s study is that there was no improvement in job satisfaction following job enrichment. Locke *et al.* attribute this to a failure of management to reward increased productivity with increased payments. Whilst Locke *et al.* argue that this shows the workforce to be instrumental in its approach to work, it seems reasonable to point out that many people feel unjustly treated if higher productivity is not rewarded. Money is as much a token of recognition of good work, as a financial reward in its own right. It is therefore interesting to note that in a number of studies which report the successful implementation of job enrichment, workers were financially rewarded for increased productivity (for example, Alderfer, 1969). There is one recent study (Orpen, 1979) in which job redesign led to improvements in attitude without increasing financial rewards. In this study, however, productivity did

not improve. The task was similar to that of the Locke *et al*. study, and Orpen attributes the failure to find productivity improvements to increased disorganisation in work methods and to individuals wishing to try out different jobs. It might well be, however, that had there been financial incentives, then the employees would have sought to increase productivity as well as improve satisfaction.

Other problems of interpretation of the job enrichment studies include the problem of improved training following the introduction of new machinery, and Hawthorne effects, where improvements may be due to the special attention employees are receiving.

Despite the many problems in interpretation, reviewers do consistently show that job enrichment studies 'work'. Cummings and Molloy (1977), for example, in a review of twenty-eight cases, found productivity improvements reported in 54 per cent of cases, quality improvements reported in 61 per cent of cases and attitudes improved in 64 per cent of cases. Lawler (1969) found higher quality of production to be reported in all ten of the studies he examined, and quantity to be increased in four studies. Locke *et al*. (1980), in examining thirteen of the least flawed studies they could find, found productivity increases averaging 17 per cent and found 92 per cent to show some productivity improvement. Katzell and Yankelovich (1975), on the basis of their review, also conclude that despite many reservations productivity improvements have been shown in about 50 per cent of cases.

To the extent that job enrichment *per se* is a factor in increased productivity, it still remains the case that it is not likely to be equally applicable to all organisations. Katzell and Yankelovich (1975), for example, note a number of questions which must be asked before considering the implementation of job enrichment. These involve assessing whether the organisational climate is favourable, whether the technology is suitable and whether the workforce is likely to be adaptable to organisational change. Rief and Monczka (1974) have also looked at the pre-conditions of a favourable application of job enrichment, which they divide into job design factors, psychosocial environment, technology and management.

Job Design Factors. Under this heading, Rief and Monczka (1974) note that jobs which are to be redesigned should have the potential for increased variety. A prerequisite for this is that there should be a large number of parts, tools and controls and that the workflow can be modified to meet individual requirements. Autonomy, too, as previously noted, requires that there are a variety of operations, procedures

and so on, which are not determined by the technology or
the supervisor, so that the employee can have some discretion
over how he performs his job. This is obviously related to
the question of responsibility, for without allowing the
individual more responsibility in decision-making, autonomy
is a meaningless concept. Where it is not possible to give
autonomy without seriously affecting productivity and work
scheduling, then job enrichment becomes more problematic to
apply. Katzell and Yankelovich (1975) note that the question
of flexibility of work is one of the more difficult ones
for management, as it is easy to be convinced that technological structure is not amenable to change. Whilst this may
be truer in high technology industries than in other organisations, a number of studies have shown that even with
seemingly impossible technology, change is sometimes possible.
Sirota and Wolfson (1972), for example, enriched the jobs
of machine workers tending a silicon wafer slicing machine
in an electronics factory. Enrichment involved giving the
employees training in maintenance, and giving authority to
change slicing blades when they thought it appropriate. They
were also given feedback on their performance. Sirota and
Wolfson report that as a result of the enrichment programme
production increased and attitudes of employees improved.
There was a saving of the time of maintenance men who were
now free to concentrate on more complex problems.

Rief and Monczka also note that the potential for two other
core job aspects, task identification and feedback, require
the possibility that jobs can be designed so that the value
of the task can be made apparent. Feedback is of course
essential if the individual is to be able to see the value
of his contribution. Characteristics of the job which make
feedback difficult include situations where information
cannot readily be provided because of cost or technical
problems. Again a limitation in making the task more 'whole',
and therefore more meaningful, is that making a task too
large may result in role strain and role overload (Chapter
4).

Context factors are also considered by Rief and Monczka.
They note that job enrichment may be more suitable for tasks
where co-operation amongst a group is required, where context
factors in general are perceived as satisfactory and where
payment is not solely based on output. Katzell and Yankelovich
(1975) also note the importance of context factors being
satisfactory before job enrichment can be implemented. They
note that if pay, for example, is perceived as very inadequate
then job design changes are likely to be seen as management's
way of avoiding adequate financial rewards. Even more important than pay, however, is the question of job security.

A number of writers have noted that where job enrichment
leads to increased productivity which cannot be disposed of,
this will lead to a reduction of the workforce. No rational
employee will work harder when the effect of this is to
work himself out of a job.

Psychosocial Environment. Rief and Monczka note a number of
factors under this heading which relate to the employee's
willingness and ability to enjoy job enrichment. As noted
in Chapter 7, one factor of major importance is whether the
work ethic is favourable for job enrichment. Hulin and Blood
(1968), for example, note differences between urban and rural
workers in their attitudes towards jobs, with those from rural
areas reacting more favourably towards job redesign programmes.
Sussman (1973) has questioned the conclusion that those from
urban backgrounds do not react favourably to job enrichment,
although even he noted differences in reactions to programmes
of job change as between urban and rural workers. Hulin and
Blood (1968) argue that alienation from their work is the
main reason for unfavourable reactions to job enrichment,
and it appears intuitively likely that where employees have
suffered poor psychological and physical conditions for years,
job enrichment programmes are likely to be greeted with
suspicion.

Related to the question of alienation from work is the
question of what motives employees do have for working. Rief
and Monczka argue that where employees have higher-order job
needs, job enrichment is more likely to succeed. This view
is shared by Hackman and Oldham (1976) who also argue that
higher-order needs moderate the relationship between core
job aspects and productivity.

One characteristics of a workforce which is likely to
determine whether or not they will be receptive to jobs able
to fulfil higher-order needs is the age and educational level
of the workforce. The more highly educated the workforce,
the more they are likely to have expectations regarding
fulfilment of higher-order needs at work. A younger workforce
is also likely to be more flexible in its approach to work
and hence more amenable to job changes. More important than
age, however, may be the length of time the individual has
been with the organisation and in a particular job within
the organisation. Katz (1978) found that when employees
joined an organisation they were far more concerned with
establishing themselves as acceptable and competent than with
deriving satisfaction from 'core' job characteristics such
as autonomy. Indeed Katz found that for new employees, there
was a strong negative relationship between the amount of
autonomy and job satisfaction. New employees, on the other

hand, do require feedback on performance and acceptance, so
that satisfactory social relationships are of importance.
For those who are newly promoted within the organisation,feed-
back on performance was also found to be the most important
factor in relation to satisfaction. It therefore seems that,
when undertaking job enrichment programmes, employers should
appreciate the insecurities engendered, and concentrate on
giving feedback on performance rather than giving immediate
autonomy. After all, who, on their first flight as a trainee
pilot, would welcome the instructor baling out with the
parting words of 'it's all yours'.

In considering who might be most amenable for job enrichment programmes, Katz found the highest relationship between
satisfaction and core job aspects to be with employees who
had been in the organisation from four months to three years,
and indeed after fifteen years on the same job in the organisation, the satisfaction - core job aspects correlation was
near zero. Employees who have been with the organisation for
about two years have therefore overcome the initial pre-
occupation with being seen as competent, and are not yet so
'set' in their ways that they do not see job changes as
threatening or undesirable.

A final psychosocial characteristic noted by Rief and
Monczka but often ignored by other writers is the skill level
of the workforce. Even if employees are happy with enriched
jobs, this is not necessarily to the advantage of the organisation if there is a lack of ability to carry out new skills
effectively. At least one case is known to the authors in
which an explosion occurred in a chemical plant following
job redesign because of the lack of skill in an employee.
Furthermore, if job enrichment places skill demands on the
employee which are beyond his capabilities, then not only
is efficiency likely to be threatened, the employee is likely
to become unhappy through role overload. (See Chapter 4.)

Technology. Rief and Monczka argue that technological features
favourable to job enrichment include situations where workers
rather than technology are responsible for output, where
technological costs involved in change are low and where
technology is available to facilitate change. The question
of the nature of technology has been discussed earlier, where
it was noted that even where technology seemed too rigid to
change and was determining productivity, change was sometimes
possible with careful thought. The question of cost and
availability of new technology is clearly important, since
to redesign jobs which may not result in improved productivity
is clearly a major gamble where costs are high. On the other
hand, it is interesting to note that Lupton and Tanner (1980)

found job enrichment to occur mostly because of the introduction of new technology rather than the other way round.
Lupton and Tanner, for example, found that in many well-
known European job enrichment programmes which have been
held up as examples of ways of improving the quality of work
life, changes were mainly carried out by organisations in
response to demands for product change. In other words new
technology became the opportunity to enrich jobs, rather
than resulting from the concept of job enrichment.

Management. Obviously, for job enrichment to have a chance
to succeed, management must be favourably disposed towards
the major organisational changes implied. As participation
in decision-making is essential to job enrichment, this
involves a willingness on the part of management to devolve
decision-making to employees at lower levels, to concern
itself with the utilisation of human resources both for
productivity purposes and for the benefit of employees, and
to be instrumental in ensuring democratic styles of supervisory behaviour.

Of major importance, as Katzell and Yankelovich point out,
is that goodwill exists between management and employees, as
problems will inevitably arise which will be interpreted as
exploitation where there is a history of mistrust. Trust,
of course, depends on a history of fair dealing on context
factors such as security and pay, on working conditions and
on relationships between management and unions, and in general
on ensuring that the welfare of employees has been attended
to.

In summary, a large number of factors, including the nature
of the job, the nature and characteristics of the workforce,
the history of management-employee relations and the attitude
of management all are likely to determine whether job enrichment is going to 'take' in a particular organisation. As no
organisation is likely to have everything 'going for it',
clearly the problem is one of weighing up the likelihood of
job enrichment being advantageous.

SOCIO-TECHNICAL SYSTEMS THEORY (autonomous working group)

Job enrichment programmes, such as those using the job
characteristics model of Hackman *et al.*, are generally
concerned with the enrichment of the individual's job, and
see this coming about through changing the characteristics
of the job itself. Socio-technical systems theory views job
change in the broader context of the individual as a social
being, interacting with the ongoing technology, and seeks
to optimise both the social and technical aspects of the job.

Working in groups with autonomy over decision-making concerning the job is thus a corner-stone of socio-technical systems theory (SST). Technological arrangements which enhance this form of working are another. SST also regards it as essential to provide the individual with wide job variety, the possibility of learning, the possibility of individual decision-making in regard to the job, and to allow the individual to feel that the job leads to some kind of desirable future (Cherns, 1976). SST also, of course, regards it as important to provide the individual with a meaningful present, by assigning to the group a significant and worthwhile 'whole' piece of work. In other words, the job should provide for variety, autonomy and meaningfulness, core job aspects as defined by Hackman *et al.* (1975). Indeed, Kelly (1978) points out that to the extent that many socio-technical theorists utilise the job characteristics model, there is a considerable overlap with other job design approaches. The main difference is perhaps in emphasising group as opposed to individual job design. This group emphasis does, however, contain major implications. First, reward for performance is normally based on group performance rather than individual performance. Second, in order to be autonomous, groups have to be given authority to make decisions concerning work scheduling, the assignment of individuals to tasks, and internal quality control. Third, job variety comes in the form of each group member using a number of skills, which allows for group flexibility in tackling problems.

Socio-technical systems theory emerged with the work of Trist and Bamforth (1951) on the effects of new technology on the efficiency of coal-mining. The effect of the new technology was to change the nature of the job. Before the new technology small groups worked at all the tasks necessary for coal-getting. This clearly involved a high degree of social interaction, variety and a fair degree of autonomy. The introduction of machinery resulted in a specialisation of labour, and the operations for coal-getting became spread over three shifts. The changes resulted in less social interaction, less autonomy, less task variety and also had the consequence of reducing productivity and increasing absence. Following a redesign of the job to take account of social factors at work, including the reintroduction of group working, production and morale again rose.

As a result of their studies Trist and Bamforth argued that production systems could not be seen as either technical systems or as social systems, but had to be seen in terms of both, hence the term socio-technical systems. Given that both social and technical systems were involved in production,

Trist and Bamforth argued that effective performance was a
function of joint-optimising of the social and technical
systems. As noted above, from the point of view of the social
system, the optimum organisation was seen to be the autonomous working group, a group of employees who possess all
the skills necessary to produce and to quality-control its
output as well as allocate labour.

Kelly (1978), in an analysis of socio-technical systems
theory, notes that the next major theoretical development
is associated with the work of Rice (1953), where again
workers were organised into groups. It is interesting to
note that in the Rice study, group interdependence was
reinforced with a group payments system. Productivity rose
considerably although quality initially fell as workers
traded quality for quantity. Another point of note in the
Rice study was that work became more specialised rather than
less.

As Kelly points out, the approach of Rice differs somewhat
from the later work of Norwegian investigations discussed by
Emery and Thorsrud (1975). The Norwegian work was far more
concerned with job design factors and whilst the earlier and
later writers all emphasise the importance of groups, there
is perhaps a major difference in the newer emphasis on work
itself.

To the extent that group working is emphasised in socio-
technical systems theory, Cummings and Molloy argue that it
has two advantages over more traditional task designs at
the individual job level. First, many jobs require inter-
dependent tasks which go beyond the capabilities of one man,
and designing individual jobs does not take account of social
interactions. Second, the job undertaken by the group as a
whole allows for more task flexibility for individual group
members. Thus individuals are free to switch their efforts
to where they are most needed at any one point in time and
are free to make rapid judgements about such matters. In-
equalities of work load are also ironed out because of the
possibility of each man being able to undertake every group
task. This allows the pace of work of the whole group to be
raised. Kelly (1978) regards the value of socio-technical
systems to being in just this intensification of labour
which allows for a raising of workloads.

Empirical Evidence
There have been a number of studies on socio-technical
systems theory and a review of sixteen of these studies by
Cummings and Molloy (1977) suggests that they frequently
increase productivity. Thus 93 per cent reported definite
effects on productivity, 88 per cent on costs, 86 per cent

quality improvements, 73 per cent withdrawal improvements
and 70 per cent attitude improvements. As the reviewers
note, however, in all the studies a number of simultaneous
changes were made, making it difficult to determine exactly
why the reported change had taken place. For example, in a
substantial number of cases considered by Cummings and
Molloy, pay systems were altered, as well as changes being
made in autonomy, variety, feedback, training and so on.
Kelly (1978) notes that pay as a mechanism of labour intensification has been 'greatly underestimated in SST and that
changes in output and product quality could be accounted for
more plausibly and parsimoniously by reference to changes in
pay incentives'. Kelly directs these remarks at the studies
of Trist on coal miners and more particularly the study of
Rice, where improvements in quantity of productivity were
gained at the expense of loom maintenance with a consequent
increase in damage to raw materials. Kelly suggests that
this can reasonably be accounted for by the desire of workers
on incentive payments to reach production targets. Whilst
Kelly admits that the evidence on payments is not conclusive,
the fact that in several studies the workers themselves
claimed pay was an important incentive makes the interpretation at least plausible. Hackman (1977) also noted that pay
incentive schemes are important for the success of SST in
that successful systems almost invariably involve group
payments rather than individual incentives. This, argues
Hackman, is because group payment systems reduce interpersonal conflict and increase co-operation amongst the workforce. However, in one recent study by Wall (1980) of a
newly created working group, pay was found not to be an
important factor. Nevertheless Wall showed considerable
performance improvements consequent upon the introduction
of a workgroup.
   Apart from the problems of interpretation discussed above,
many of the studies of SST reviewed by Cummings and Molloy
suffered from methodological defects and many failed to
report the statistical significance of their findings. Again,
as with job enrichment studies, the possibility of 'Hawthorne'
effects, (where productivity is likely to increase because
of the greater interest of management in the workers), is
an ever present possibility. Again, productivity may increase
because of the more *efficient* utilisation of men and machines,
as Kelly notes, rather than because of increased motivation
to work brought about by the autonomous work group *per se*.
Indeed in a number of studies, initial work organisation was
so poor that practically any kind of systematic reorganisation would have increased productivity. In this connection
it is interesting to note that in almost half the studies

reviewed by Cummings and Molloy, further job training was given, again increasing the likelihood of better utilisation of manpower in relation to technical systems. A final factor which may affect productivity is that in the majority of studies, workers in (SST) designs were volunteers. Such individuals are clearly likely to be more highly motivated to work under the changed conditions and at the very least one must be cautious of generalising the findings to non-volunteer groups.

As with the performance improvements consequent on job enrichment, it might be argued that why socio-technical systems theory works is not so important as the fact that it does, although in many cases it is much more the social than the technical system which has been 'optimised'. Kelly (1978), for example, points out that in the studies of Rice and Trist the problem was to bring recalcitrant social systems into line, and that the emphasis was on machine utilisation. Indeed in the Rice study and others there was a subordination of worker autonomy to economic imperatives.

As with all job redesign schemes, SST is clearly more suited to some situations rather than others. Hackman (1977), for example, suggests that group-based work is desirable where meaningful individual work is not possible. In such situations a group might be able to take responsibility for a meaningful piece of work where an individual could only take a small segment of the work. Hackman (1977) notes that groups are desirable where high interdependence among workers is required. Cummings and Molloy (1977) in fact also note that SST has mostly been applied in material processing industries, which allows discrete task grouping and where clear product outcome is easily established. Kelly (1978) also notes a characteristic of SST application is that it very often involves high process uncertainty, and that this is just the situation where flexible group working is likely to be most effective. In other words, SST is most suitable where precise specification of duties and workload in the style of Taylor would be counter-productive because fluctuations in workflow frequently arise. As Kelly notes, SST allows for variance in production to be evenly distributed amongst group workers. In other words Kelly argues that the achievement of SST has been to discover the limiting conditions-high process uncertainty-of scientific management. The implication of this is not that SST is generally applicable. In many other industries such process variability does not apply. In Kelly's terminology only in certain industries does group working lead to an intensification of labour.

Hackman also notes that successful application of SST

depends on individuals having a high expressed need for
social interaction. This is an important point since by no
means everyone gains satisfaction from working in a team on
complex tasks. Many individuals, for example, prefer to
achieve on their own perhaps because of a highly developed
need for achievement.

As Hackman notes, designing jobs for groups is by no means
a guarantee of increased productivity. Groups which 'take'
and become cohesive can just as easily develop norms for
low as for high productivity. High productivity will only
become the goal of the group where the group task is seen as
meaningful to the group as a whole and where the group sees
itself as equitably treated. Where, for example, group members see themselves as unfairly paid, the effect of being a
highly cohesive group may be to put pressure on group members
to reduce their productivity. Again as Hackman notes, con-
stituting groups is unlikely to lead to increased productivity
in situations where social rewards are considered important
and productivity rewards unimportant by group members. In
such a situation the energy of group members is likely to
be taken up in social interaction as in the case of the two
girls in the Hawthorne experiment who had to be dismissed
for talking too much. Finally, the potential for benefiting
from training is important as autonomous group work demands
that each individual learns an array of skills. Where such
skills are expensive to impart or where a low level of skill
is dangerous, in for example chemical processing, then
clearly the advantages of SST must be carefully considered.

SUMMARY AND CONCLUSIONS

All the job redesign programmes discussed in this chapter
have a number of features in common. All report successful
application of their systems. In all cases there are reported failures and it is clear that their successful application is limited to certain situations which are specifically
suited to their characteristics. In all cases it is difficult
to assess why, if they are successful, their success is
achieved, and in all cases it is likely that a number of
factors extraneous to the specific change process are responsible for improvement. Thus, for example, further job
training is a prerequisite of some job changes. Again all
programmes involve participation by employees in decision-
making, and in some of the programme changes discussed,
improved performance may be a consequence of technological
and manpower utilisation changes resulting from employee
suggestions. On the other hand the work of Lupton and Tanner
(1980) suggests that some improvements may be due to tech-

nological changes introduced by management which requires new manpower organisation. In all cases of job redesign the scientific status of many of the successful studies is questionable to some extent, so that whilst the number of reported successes makes it likely that there are real chances of benefit to organisations consequent on job re-design, the findings must be treated with caution and the value of any proposed programme to a particular organisation must be assessed with care.

9 Performance Appraisal

INTRODUCTION

Previous chapters have considered the ways in which an understanding of psychology can contribute to the more efficient
use of human resources. An implicit assumption has been that
changes in individual performance can be measured in a
relatively simple and straightforward way. Unfortunately
performance appraisal can be anything but simple, and in
this chapter the problems of performance appraisal are
considered.

THE PURPOSE OF PERFORMANCE APPRAISAL

In their useful review, Cummings and Schwab (1973) note that
performance appraisal has two main functions, evaluative and
developmental.

The evaluative function involves the use of performance
assessment to make decisions concerning promotion, transfer
and dismissal. Such decisions are normally based on whether
performance comes up to explicit or implicit standards. In
addition, performance appraisal is used evaluatively in
assessing the working of selection and placement schemes,
and of training procedures for teaching skills within the
organisation.

The second, developmental, function of performance assessment involves helping individuals to improve their performance by identifying areas for improvement. Unlike the
evaluative function, which is often seen as threatening by
employees, the developmental function of performance appraisal can be seen to be useful by giving the individual
relevant information regarding achievement and advancement.
Obviously a developmental approach also allows for the
discussion of problems with a view to providing help in
overcoming them.

Assessing employee performance is clearly essential to the
adequate functioning of the organisation. As many writers
have noted, however, effective performance appraisal is

fraught with problems. Decoutiis and Petit (1978), for
example, note three classes of problem:

(1) problems involving the motivation of raters (and
    employees);

(2) problems involved in relation to appropriate standards
    for making judgements;

(3) problems involved in the rater's ability to use
    information.

The motivation of employees

As far as employees are concerned, one major problem of
evaluation is that any evaluation is likely to have implications for organisational rewards and punishments. There
is therefore, as Porter, Lawler and Hackman (1975) note, a
pressure to provide misleading information. Employees who
are concerned with advancement, for example, have a vested
interest in covering up mistakes. Another common distortion
of performance arises in situations where performance standards are being set. Employees have a vested interest in
setting standards below that which is easily achieved, so
that they need not work too hard in order to achieve the
standard, and in some cases to achieve bonus rates for
'overproduction' relative to the standard.

   Even in its developmental aspects, performance appraisal
is sometimes seen as problematic by the employee. This is
particularly true of negative feedback from the supervisor,
and Meyer *et al.* (1965) found that employees who were given
negative feedback became defensive, and indeed productivity
later fell. To give an individual negative feedback is to
threaten his self-esteem, particularly if the negative
feedback is on personality traits rather than the achievement
of objective goals.

Rater motivation

As Porter, Lawler and Hackman (1975) note, it is not only
the subordinate who finds performance appraisal unpleasant.
Superiors, too, often find the process irksome and unpleasant, and will vary the amount of effort and the accuracy
of their assessment according to the situation. For example,
Decoutiis and Petit (1978) note that appraisal for organisational administrative purposes is less accurate than when
it is required for developmental purposes, and where the

reports are confidential they are more accurate than when they are open to employee inspection. This last finding probably reflects the fact that superiors do not enjoy having to give employees negative feedback any more than employees like to receive it. Apart from making the employee unhappy, negative feedback might, as noted above, make him defensive and unco-operative in future, and Patton (1960) notes that this is particularly likely where assessment is based on traits rather than objective performance. Even where objective criteria are used, however, performance appraisal is looked on with unease by raters and, in the absence of pressure to the contrary, there is a tendency to abandon performance appraisal (Porter *et al.*, 1975).

Appropriate standards for judgements

As Decoutiis and Petit (1978) note, the availability of appropriate standards of performance and methods of appraisal materially affect the superior's motivation in assessing performance. For example, the more that performance assessment is based on job information, the more easily it is understood; and the more it is perceived of as being adequate, the greater will be the rater motivation. Unfortunately a large number of factors make the provision of adequate information problematic.

One major problem with performance assessment is that often no suitable 'objective' criterion is readily available. This is particularly true where the individual to be assessed is a member of a group, and where group productivity is the only measure of output. 'Objective' criteria in the form of quantity of output is also problematic where productivity is affected by factors other than the individual's efforts, such as variations in demand for the product or if the machinery breaks down frequently. 'Quantity' is also clearly an inappropriate measure of productivity when dealing with individuals whose skills are qualitatively rather than quantitatively important, as, for example, when considering the industrial relations personnel or innovators in industry. Whilst 'quality' is more difficult to measure than quantity, it is sometimes possible to measure it objectively in, for example, assessments of the number of faults committed, or 'rejected' products. Unfortunately, this kind of 'objective' criterion is not always possible for individuals such as the manager, the scientist or the production engineer.

A second major problem with appropriate standards for judgements is that the performance being assessed is not normally unidimensional. In other words, a number of factors have to be considered in deciding whether or not performance is effective. Many jobs, for example, involve a large number

of dimensions. A sales manager, in addition to achieving sales, and being aware of the changing nature of his product, must be skilled at motivating his workforce and in dealing with other parts of the organisation to ensure the smooth transaction from orders to delivery. Yet it is clear even in this example that high skills in one area do not necessarily imply high skills in others. The sales manager who was promoted because his manner resulted in high sales, may be most unsuited for dealing at an interpersonal level with an unmotivated workforce. The fact that performance is multidimensional, therefore, leads to the possibility of dysfunctional consequences in situations where only scme aspects of necessary performance are rewarded by the crganisation. In the experiment of Rice (1953), for example, following job redesign there was an improvement in quantity but a deterioration in quality of production because bonus payments depended on quantity rather than quality.

How different performance aspects should be weighted together and what aspects should be emphasised, depends on the reason for the performance appraisal. For example, where promotion is being considered it may be that skills not necessary on the present job but vital for success in the promoted job should be given priority. Where equitable payments systems are being considered, however, all those aspects necessary for adequate performance, and not just quantity should be considered.

Clearly the ways in which the importance of different dimensions are combined to give an overall weighting is a major problem in performance appraisal. Even when it is desirable to do so it may still be extremely problematic if an adequate assessment of performance is difficult. Job analysis, which overcomes some of the problems discussed above, will be considered presently.

Problems of the individuals' ability to use information
As Latham, Wexley and Pursell (1975) note, those making assessments of others tend to make systematic errors of various kinds. Being human, supervisors are likely to assess their subordinates under the influence of personal relationships, and may find it difficult to be too critical about their friends when reporting to others. More important, perhaps, any one individual is likely to be systematically biased, either regarding all his geese as swans or all his swans as geese! A third possibility, chosen perhaps by those not too confident of their own judgement, is to place all subordinates in the middle range of performance, thus minimising the chance of a gross error.

Individual bias

There is some evidence that individuals vary in their ability
at making judgements, at least of the personality characteristics of others. Thus good emotional adjustment and intelligence are noted by Taft (1955) to be characteristics
related to good judgement. Clearly individuals with personality and adjustment problems may have biases against making
good and unprejudiced judgements, and Cummings and Schwab
(1973) note that willingness to do a conscientious job of
appraising is a prerequisite of good assessment which will
vary from individual to individual. As noted earlier, the
perceived importance of the assessment might well be a
factor in conscientiousness of appraisal. Decoutiis and
Petit (1978), in their review of individual factors in
assessment, note that whether stressing goal attainment or
individual characteristics of the ratee, rater style is
related to rater ability, with rater ability being higher
where the stress is on goal attainment. They also noted
rater status was important; the lesser the status difference
of rater and ratee, the greater the accuracy of assessment.
Borman (1977) in fact found that 17 per cent of variance in
accuracy of ratings can be attributed to characteristics of
raters, such as dependability and stability.

OVERCOMING PROBLEMS OF PERFORMANCE ASSESSMENT

Motivational problems of raters and subordinates

As was noted earlier, a major problem for both raters and
subordinates involves difficulties in interpersonal interaction as a result of negative evaluation. In considering
how to deal with assessment problems, therefore, it is
useful to distinguish between evaluative and developmental
aspects of the assessment process, since they have different
implications for interpersonal behaviour.

Meyer *et al.* (1965) advocate carrying out the evaluative
and the developmental aspects at different times, so that
when dealing with development, negative criticism is avoided
and the appraisal process concentrates on both identifying
those aspects of performance where improvements are desirable
and considering by what methods agreed goals can be achieved.
Nevertheless, despite a temporal separation, there is an
inherent conflict between the superior's role as a judge of
performance and purveyor of rewards and punishments on the
one hand, and as a counsellor and friend on the other. Few
people would be misled by the supervisor concentrating on
the attainment of goals if the implication was that these
goals ought to have been attained. Whilst negative feedback

can be reduced, it is unlikely that it can be eliminated
where the supervisor acts as both evaluator and counsellor.
Furthermore, as is noted in Chapter 3, negative feedback can
be useful in providing valuable information, provided that
the negative emotional effects of negative feedback do not
outweigh the positive informational effects.

Bassett and Meyer (1968) note the problems of negative
feedback as causes of defensiveness, and conducted a study
to show how it might be overcome to some extent. Rather than
have a performance review based on the supervisor's assessment, performance appraisal and its discussion was based on
a self review by the employee. Thus the responsibility for
the performance review and the initiative of appraisal
discussion was in the hands of the employee, and this cast
the role of the superior as that of counsellor. Their study
provided evidence that such an approach was favoured by
managers. There was also evidence of less defensive behaviour,
and 'on the job performance' was likely to show improvement
after self review discussion, particularly of low-rated
employees. Nevertheless, self-review appraisal was not seen
as satisfactory by all employees, particularly those with a
low 'need' for independence.

Appropriate standards for judgements
Before any assessment of adequate performance is possible,
it is necessary to establish the goals which the employee
is required to meet and to decide whether the individual has
attained these goals. Job analysis is the concern of the
former, performance evaluation is the concern of the latter.
They are considered in turn.

Job analysis Job analysis is defined by Salvendy and
Seymour (1973) as 'the methodology employed in collation and
analysis of job relevant data'. Salvendy and Seymour note
that adequate job analysis involves techniques taken not
only from psychology, but also from industrial engineering,
physics, physiology and ergonomics, and that job analysis
that relies on only one of these approaches is likely to be
defective. However, a comprehensive account of job analysis
is beyond the scope of this book, and for a detailed account
the reader is referred to such texts as Salvendy and Seymour
(1973). From a psychological perspective, job analysis
information is collated by using a number of techniques,
such as interviews and questionnaires, technical conferences
involving group troubleshooting or brainstorming, work
participation methods, and the analysis of accidents and
near accidents. An extension of this last technique to an

analysis of all critical incidents whether resulting in good or bad performance, has been suggested by Cummings and Schwab (1973). The purpose of these techniques is of course to collect information on such factors as the nature of the task, the duties and responsibilities associated with the job, the machine and tools which need to be used, and the conditions of work, such as physical surroundings, etc. All of these factors have to be considered in making decisions about what it is reasonable to expect of an employee. It is self-evident, for example, that employees using new, efficient, machinery can be expected to produce more, as can employees working under reasonable physical conditions and with clear duties and responsibilities.

Exactly what duties and responsibilities are expected of the individual in a particular job is often problematic. As noted previously, a major problem with assessing satisfactory performance is that a job consists of a number of tasks, and the interrelationship and importance of each task must be assessed. Successful fulfilment of some aspects of the job are clearly of more importance than success in others, so that the different tasks must be weighted in coming to an assessment of satisfactory job performance. Again, as noted earlier, this weighting will normally be determined by the ultimate goals of the department and organisation. For example, if quantity rather than quality of production is important, more weight might be given to speed than to accuracy of operation and so on.

Obviously, the lower the level of job or the more identifiable the performance outcome, the easier it becomes to make a job analysis which will identify the appropriate skills and how they should be carried out. Even here, however, allowance must be made for the context in which the job takes place, such as the physical condition of work, the amount of training received, the quality of supervision and so on.

In high-level jobs or where output is not easily identifiable as that of one individual, such as in higher-level management tasks, the problems are clearly complex and good job behaviour is difficult to specify beforehand. Nevertheless, overall objectives can usually be specified and the extent to which a manager reaches these is the basic criterion of his success. A football manager, for example, has a large number of tasks, from overseeing coaching, planning strategy, signing on good players and getting rid of poor ones, making team selection and promoting the name of the team, amongst others. It is almost impossible to specify how he should behave in relation to these activities; whether

he is successful or not is determined solely by whether his team wins. Nevertheless, for most tasks, some critical behaviours can be identified, and success or failure can be judged in relation to performance on these tasks. As noted above, critical job aspects must be established and the behaviours associated with successful completion of these job aspects identified before one is in a position to evaluate the individual's performance. As noted earlier, use can be made of techniques such as the critical incident technique to classify behaviour which is 'good' and which is 'bad'. In high level jobs, 'experts' can be asked to supply criteria by which they would classify work as good or bad. Because of the difficulties in defining good job performance in high-level jobs, emphasis is often given to those job aspects which are administratively easier to assess, as for example, in the quantity of goods sold.

Evaluating performance As Cummings and Schwab (1973) note, the purpose of performance appraisal will determine the method of performance appraisal used. For developmental aspects of performance appraisal, where the purpose of the exercise is to improve performance through self-learning, formal appraisal techniques involving a number of superiors is not appropriate. Rather the aim is to involve the employee in problem-solving concerning difficulties in performance, and the appraisal of performance is therefore non-evaluative. Indeed the emphasis is not on past performance at all but rather on future performance, so that an analysis of past performance is only relevant to the extent that it facilitates future performance. An example of this difference in an educational setting would be the difference between the assessment of class essays and of term examinations. The purpose of class essays is to reveal problems that the student has in understanding the topic and presenting his work in an appropriate way. The essay normally has a number of constructively critical comments appended to it by the tutor, pointing out problems and highlighting good points, and the mark at the end of the essay is merely an indication of what that performance would have been evaluated at under examination conditions. An examination essay, however, is marked with the object of assessing the individual's performance at a particular point in time, and making administrative decisions, such as what class of degree the individual student should be awarded. Such assessment is normally much more final, and it normally involves a number of examiners and does not necessarily seek to improve performance on future occasions.

METHODS OF APPRAISAL

A number of procedures have been developed in order to deal
with the judgemental aspects of performance appraisal. One
class of procedures for example, has been developed in order
to compare individuals at particular levels within the
organisation. Such comparisons are often necessary when, for
example, promotion is to take place.

Ranking technique
In order to compare one individual with another a common
procedure is to rank each individual to be evaluated in
terms of their overall effectiveness, starting with the most
effective and working down to the least effective. Thus, for
example, the most effective individual in a group of 12 is
rated as 1, the second most effective 2 and the least effective 12. One major advantage of ranking procedures is that
by forcing the evaluator to make a choice between the competence of different individuals, systematic tendencies to
rate each employee as either of high or low ability are
overcome. Whilst ranking procedures are relatively simple
and straightforward, those that rely on one global dimension
being ranked are probably oversimplifying the appraisal
process. As was noted earlier, job success is almost invariably multi-dimensional. On the other hand, if one has to
make a choice between two individuals for promotion, some
kind of 'final' single measure has to be given so that a
relative judgement can be made. This kind of problem again
highlights what was stressed earlier, that the most appropriate appraisal system depends on the purpose to which it
is put. Clearly a global ranking is of little use in giving
feedback in order to improve performance any more than a
mark at the end of an essay. On the other hand, the relative
merits of individuals as assessed by performance appraisal
is only one factor in deciding administrative policies such
as promotion. Unions, for example, place stress on seniority.
At least promotion on the basis of seniority is objective,
and overcomes problems of the subjective nature of performance appraisal in organisations where there is mistrust.
  There is, of course, no theoretical reason why the problems
of global ranking cannot be overcome by having ranked assessments on several factors. This might be most appropriate
where placement of a number of trainees is being considered,
so that individuals can be allocated to departments where
their relative strengths lie. One major limitation of ranking
techniques, however, is that they cannot easily be used when
large numbers of individuals have to be assessed, as the
problems of comparing large numbers of individuals one with

another becomes extremely complex.

Rating techniques

Comparative techniques obviously assess individual performance in relation to others. In many situations, however, it
is more appropriate to assess performance in relation to an
absolute standard. Typical of techniques designed to assess
absolute standards are rating scales, where evaluators are
asked to rate on a scale, perhaps from one to seven, how
competent an individual is at an aspect of his job. For
example, if 7 were very poor and 1 were excellent, a rating
of 2 would indicate good performance on a particular job
aspect. As with rankings it is possible to have ratings both
on overall effectiveness and on effectiveness in different
job aspects.

Ratings have the advantage over ranking in showing not only
relative positions of individuals, but the absolute value of
these relative positions. Even if an individual were the
poorest salesman of a group of ten, he might still be seen
as good at his job. Also, of course, where individuals are
more or less indistinguishable in terms of competence, no
distinction is forced on the assessor.

Behaviourally anchored scales

Cummings and Schwab (1973) note that conventional rating
scales suffer from problems of reliability and validity. For
example, they allow the rater to make systematic errors, such
as rating all of his subordinates at too high or too low a
level. In order to overcome this problem to some extent,
behaviourally anchored rating scales have been developed in
which a particular rating is described in terms of appropriate behaviour. For example, an *extremely* good grocery
clerk would be one who in terms of knowledge, knew the price
of each item and could rapidly identify mislabelled items, a
good clerk would be aware of items which fluctuated in price,
whereas a *poor* clerk might take up his time talking to
customers or other clerks. Porter *et al.* (1975) argue that
this kind of rating scale can yield better ratings and lead
to clearer job definitions, as well as reduce the problem of
systematic biasing. Again Cummings and Schwab argue that
behaviourally anchored scales have value in terms of feedback
to employees in that it makes clear why ratings have been
assigned in the way they have. It also seems likely that such
scales will reduce differences between raters, as they are
assessing behaviour on the same basis. It does seem clear
that behaviourally anchored scales are preferable to conventional scales, although of course they take more time to

develop. There are, needless to say, numerous other techniques and variations on techniques described above, for
making judgements of individual performance. Weighted check-
lists, for example, list a large number of behaviours, and
assign a value to each behaviour according to how important
it is to good performance, as previously determined by
judges. Another technique is the critical incident technique,
in which incidents thought critical to good or bad performance
are classified into a number of categories. The employee is
then assessed in terms of positive or negative incidents that
feature in each category. This clearly is a form of continuous assessment, and it might be resisted by those who feel
that their behaviour is being permanently monitored.

Whilst many of the techniques outlined above can assist to
some extent in developmental aspects of assessment as noted
earlier, objectives-oriented techniques are probably more
suited to this function. Objectives-orientated approaches
such as management by objectives (MBO) seek to tailor the
evaluation process to criteria set for each individual as an
individual, rather than in relation to other individuals or
in relation to any absolute standard. Obviously MBO goals
cannot be entirely independent of objective criteria, as
absolute good performance must guide what the individual has
set as an appropriate goal for himself. MBO also has problems, however, as was noted in Chapter 8.

The individual's ability to use information
In considering the problems of the individual in utilising
the information available to him, it was noted that raters
often made systematic errors in evaluating their subordinates,
either rating them at too high or too low a level. Again it
was pointed out that interpersonal factors sometimes affected
the accuracy of raters.

One way of reducing problems of interpersonal relationships
caused by the judgemental aspect of performance appraisal, is
to have that appraisal shared amongst a number of individuals,
rather than being the sole responsibility of one person. In
this way negative assessment cannot be attributed to one
individual.

Whilst using more than one individual to evaluate performance has a number of advantages it also has some disadvantages. Where one individual has an intimate knowledge of
performance and other assessors do not, then the question of
relative weights to be given to judgements in the case of
rater disagreement becomes a problem. Whilst immediate
superiors may be biased in the ways described above, they are
likely to have a more intimate knowledge of performance. As

Cummings and Schwab note, lack of knowledge about the individual evaluated is a serious source of error. Whilst evaluation by a group may have advantages over evaluation by one
individual, therefore, it clearly is not problem free.

Appraisal by peers and subordinates

One alternative to appraisal by superiors noted by Cummings
and Schwab is appraisal by peers. This operates best, it is
suggested, in situations where peers are not in competition
for rewards, where there is a high level of interpersonal
trust and where performance outcomes are equally available
to peers. Such situations are not common, needless to say,
in highly competitive organisations, and in many situations
peer assessment places the peer in conflict in deciding
between truth and friendship. It also places him in conflict
where maximising the evaluation of a peer may reduce the
chances of maximising his own career opportunities. There
can be few organisations where the possibility does not
exist of competition for advancement among peers.

Subordinate assessment

Even more threatening than peer appraisal in some ways is
appraisal by subordinates. Not only may it be perceived of
as not legitimate by both superior and subordinate, it may
well be that the superior will distort his behaviour to
favour subordinate reports at the expense of good organisational functioning. The supervisor who is kind and
tolerant of bad workmanship may receive high subordinate
ratings, but may not be acting in the best interests of the
organisation. Again, the subordinate may not be in the best
position to assess the value of the superior's performance
as, for example, in the case of a teacher who may deal with
the interesting aspects of the subject at the expense of the
more difficult or routine but fundamental aspects.

Not only is subordinate evaluation seen as threatening to
the superior, subordinates themselves sometimes regard this
form of appraisal as threatening because of the power that
the superior has to take action against the individual who
presents a critical report. Of course, to some extent
anonymity can help in this situation, but the fear of being
found out may well be inhibiting. The many problems with
subordinate assessment make it unsuitable in most cases.

SUMMARY AND CONCLUSIONS

Performance appraisal is fundamental to the adequate functioning of organisations, for purposes of rewarding and

punishing, promotion and placement, training and developing employees. From the point of view of the individual, performance appraisal gives feedback as to how he is perceived of by the organisation, and indeed performance appraisal is one way in which the organisation shows it is taking an interest in the individual. Where performance appraisal is absent, the implication is that the individual is not of sufficient value or interest to the organisation to spend effort on.

One major problem with performance appraisal is of course its subjective nature, which leads to conflicts in interpretation and acceptance. Whilst trait approaches to performance appraisal, such as in terms of responsibility, have given way to assessments of job performance following job evaluation, it nevertheless remains true that systematic errors of judgement are likely to occur, and that raters will fail to take full acount of the behaviours and achievements relevant to adequate overall performance.

A major problem pointed out by Whisler (1958) in relation to appraisal for development is that there is often a conflict of interest between the objectives of the organisation and that of the individual. Whisler notes the lack of payoff for a superior in developing the skills of his subordinate above an adequate level. Normal organisational rewards go to what the superior himself achieves, and developing the capacities of others can be a time-consuming and relatively unrewarded activity.

Bibliography

Adams, J.S. and Jacobson, P.R. (1964) 'Effects of wage inequities on work quality', *Journal of Abnormal and Social Psychology*, 69, 19–25.

Alderfer, C.P. (1969) 'Job enlargement and the organizational context', *Personnel Psychology*, 22, 418–26.

Anastasi, A. (1968) *Psychological Testing* (3rd edn) (New York: Macmillan).

Andrews, J.D.W. (1967) 'The achievement motive and advancement in two types of organisation', *Journal of Personality and Social Psychology*, 6, 163–9.

Archer, J. (1978) 'Occupational alcoholism: A review of issues and a guide to the literature', in C.J. Schramm (ed.), *Alcoholism and its Treatment in Industry* (Baltimore: Johns Hopkins University Press).

Argyris, C. (1964) *Integrating the Individual and the Organisation* (New York: Wiley).

Argyle, M., Gardner, G. and Cioffi, I. (1958) 'Supervisory methods related to productivity, absence and labor turnover', *Human Relations*, 11, 23–40.

Arvey, R.D. (1972) 'Task performance as a function of perceived effort – performance and performance-reward contingencies', *Organizational Behaviour and Human Performance*, 8, 423–33.

Atkinson, J.W. (1964) *An Introduction to Motivation* (Princeton, New Jersey: Van Nostrand).

Atkinson, J.W. and Reitman, W.R. (1956) 'Performance as a function of motive strength and expectancy of goal attainment', *Journal of Abnormal and Social Psychology*, 53, 361–6.

Azer, N.Z., McNeil, P.E. and Leung, H.C. (1972) 'Effects of heat stress on performance', *Ergonomics*, 15, 681–91.

Baddeley, A.D., Cuciaro, W.J., Egstrom, G.H., Weltman, G. and Willis, M. (1975) 'Cognitive efficiency of divers working in cold water', *Human Factors*, 17, 446–54.

Bardwick, J.M. (1971) *Psychology of Women* (New York: Harper and Row).

Bare, A.C. (1978) 'Staffing and training: Neglected supervisory functions related to groups performance',

Personnel Psychology, 31, 107-17.

Barrett, G.V. (1969) 'The international research graphs on management information systems', in N.J. Blood Jr. (ed.), *Management Science in Planning* (New York: TAPPI).

Barrett, G.V. and Bass, B.M. (1976) 'Cross cultural issues in industrial and organizational psychology', in M.D. Dunnette (ed.), *Handbook of Industrial and Organizational Psychology* (Chicago: Rand McNally).

Barrow, J.C. (1976) 'Worker performance and task complexity as causal determinants of leader behaviour style and flexibility', *Journal of Applied Psychology*, 61, 433-40.

Bartol, K. (1974) 'Sex differences in job orientation: a re-examination', *Proceedings of National Academy of Management* (Seattle).

Bass, B.M. (1970) 'Men planning for others', *Journal of Applied Behavioural Science*, 6, 151-71.

Bassett, G.A. and Meyer, H.H. (1968) 'Performance appraisal based on self review', *Personnel Psychology*, 21, 421-30.

Baum, J.F. (1978) 'Effectiveness of an attendance control policy in reducing chronic absenteeism', *Personnel Psychology*, 31, 71-81.

Becker, L.J. (1978) 'Joint effect of feedback and goal setting on performance', *Journal of Applied Psychology*, 63, 428-33.

Beehr, T.A. (1976) 'Perceived situational moderators of the relationship between subjective role ambiguity and role strain', *Journal of Applied Psychology*, 61, 35-40.

Beehr, T.A. and Newman, J.E. (1978) 'Job stress, employee health and organizational effectiveness: A facet analysis, model and literature review', *Personnel Psychology*, 31, 655-99.

Behrend, H. (1953) 'A note on labour turnover in an industrial factory', *Journal of Industrial Economics*, 2, 58-64.

Benson, A.J., Huddleston, H.F. and Rolfe, J.M. (1965) 'A psychophysiological study of compensatory tracking on a digital display', *Human Factors*, 7, 457-72.

Berkowitz, L. (1954) 'Group standards, cohesiveness and productivity', *Human Relations*, 7, 509-19.

Berlew, D.E. and Hall, D.T. (1966) 'The socialization of managers: Effects of expectations on performance', *Administrative Science Quarterly*, 11, 207-23.

Berry, R.E. and Boland, J. (1978) 'Work related costs of alcohol abuse', in C.J. Schramm (ed.), *Alcoholism and its Treatment in Industry* (Baltimore: Johns Hopkins University Press).

Bhagat, R.S. (1979) Black-white ethnic differences in

identification with the work ethnic: Some implications
for organizational integration', *Academy of Management
Review*, 4, 381-91.
Blake, R.R., Shephard, H.A. and Mouton, J.S.   (1964)
Managing Intergroup Conflict in Industry (Houston: Gulf
Publishing).
Borman, W.C.   (1977)   cited by Kane, J.S. and Lawler, E.E.
in B. Staw *Research and Organisational Behaviour*, 1979
(Greenwich, Connect.:   J.A.I. Press).
Bowen, H.M.   (1968)   'Diver performance and the effects of
cold', *Human Factors*, 10, 445-64.
Boyd, J.B.   (1961)   'Interests of engineers related to
turnover, selection and management', *Journal of Applied
Psychology*, 45, 143-9.
Bradley, C.   (1979)   'Psychophysiological effects of
stressful experiences and the management of diabetes
mellitus', in D.J. Oborne, M.M. Gruneberg and J.R. Eiser
(eds.), *Research in Psychology and Medicine*, vol I
(London: Academic Press).
Bradley, C. and Cox, T.   (1978)   *Stress* (London: Macmillan).
Bradley, J.V.   (1967)   'Tactual coding of cylindrical knobs',
Human Factors, 9, 483-96.
Bragg, J.E. and Andrews, I.R.   (1973)   'Participative
decision making: An experimental study in a hospital',
Journal of Applied Behavioural Science, 9, 727-35.
Bray, D.W., Campbell, R.J. and Grant, D.L.   (1974)   *Formative
Years in Business: A Long Term A.T and T Study of
Managerial Lives* (New York: Wiley).
Brayfield, A.H. and Crockett, W.H.   (1955)   'Employee atti-
tudes and employee performance', *Psychological Bulletin*,
52, 396-424.
Brief, A.P. and Oliver, R.L.   (1976)   'Male-female differ-
ences in work attitudes among retail sales managers',
Journal of Applied Psychology, 61, 526-28.
Broadbent, D.E.   (1954)   'Some effects of noise on visual
performance', *Quarterly Journal of Experimental Psycho-
logy*, 6, 1-5.
Broadbent, D.E.   (1957)   'Effects of noise on behaviour',
in C.M. Harris (ed.), *Handbook of Noise Control* (New
York: McGraw-Hill).
Bromley, D.B.   (1966)   *The Psychology of Human Ageing*
(Harmondsworth: Penguin).
Buckhout, R.   (1964)   'Effects of whole body vibration on
human performance', *Human Factors*, 6, 157-63.
Buell, T. and Breslow, L.   (1960)   'Mortality from coronary
heart disease in Californian men who work long hours',
Journal of Chronic Disease, 2, 615.
Camman, C. and Lawler, E.E.   (1973)   'Employee reactions to

a pay incentive plan', *Journal of Applied Psychology*, 58, 163-72.

Campbell, J.P., Dunnette, M.D., Lawler, E.E. and Weik, K.E. (1970) *Managerial Behaviour, Performance and Effectiveness* (New York: McGraw-Hill).

Campbell, J.P. and Pritchard, R.D. (1976) 'Motivation theory in industrial and organizational psychology', in M.D. Dunnette (ed.), *Handbook of Industrial and Organizational Psychology* (Chicago: Rand McNally).

Campion, J.E. (1972) 'Work sampling for personnel selection', *Journal of Applied Psychology*, 56, 40-4.

Caplan, R.D. (1971) cited in T. Cox (1978) *Stress* (London: Macmillan).

Carrell, M.R. and Dittrich, J.E. (1978) 'Equity theory: The recent literature, methodological considerations and new directions', *Academy of Management Review*, 3, 202-10.

Carroll, S.J. and Tosi, H.L. (1973) *Management by Objectives. Application and Research* (New York: Macmillan).

Centers, R. and Bugental, D.E. (1966) 'Intrinsic and extrinsic job motivation among different segments of the working population', *Journal of Applied Psychology*, 50, 193-7.

Cherns, A. (1976) 'The principles of sociotechnical design', *Human Relations*, 29, 783-92.

Christ, R.E. (1975) 'Review of analysis of colour coding research for visual displays', *Human Factors*, 17, 542-70.

Clarke, R.O., Fatchett, D.J. and Roberts, B.C. (1972) *Worker Participation in Management in Britain* (London: Heinemann).

Clarke, R.S., Hellon, R.F., and Lind, A.R. (1958) 'The duration of sustained contractions of the human forearm at different muscle temperatures', *Journal of Physiology*, 143, 454-73.

Clelland, S. (1955) *Influence of Plant Size on Industrial Relations* (Princeton, New Jersey: Princeton University Press).

Cobb, S. and Kasl, S.V. (1972) 'Some medical aspects of unemployment', in G.M. Shatto (ed.), *Employment of the Middle-aged; Papers from Industrial Gerontology Seminars* (Springfield: C. Thomas).

Cobb, S. and Rose, R.M. (1973) 'Hypertension, peptic ulcers and diabetes in air traffic controllers', *Journal of the American Medical Association*, 224, 489.

Coch, C.L. and French, J.R.P. (1948) 'Overcoming resistance to change', *Human Relations*, 1, 512-32.

Cohen, J., Dearnaley, E.J. and Hansel, C.E.M. (1958) 'The risk taken in driving under the influence of alcohol',

British Medical Journal, 1, 1438.

Cooper, C.L. (1978), 'Work Stress', in P. Warr (ed.), *Psychology at Work* (Harmondsworth: Penguin).

Cooper, C.L. and Marshall, J. (1976) 'Occupational sources of stress: A review of the literature relating to coronary heart disease and mental ill health', *British Journal of Occupational Psychology*, 49, 11-28.

Cox, T. (1978) *Stress* (London: Macmillan).

Cross, D. and Warr, P. (1971) 'Work group composition as a factor in productivity', *Industrial Relations Journal*, 2, 3-13.

Cummin, P.C. (1967) 'TAT correlates of executive perform-ance', *Journal of Applied Psychology*, 51, 78-81.

Cummings, T.G. and Molloy, E.S. (1977) *Improving Pro-ductivity and The Quality of Working Life* (New York: Praeger).

Cummings, L.L. and Schwab, D.P. (1973) *Performance in Organisations* (Glenview, Illinois: Scott, Foresman).

Dalton, D.R. and Todor, W.D. (1979) 'Manifest needs of stewards - propensity to file a grievance', *Journal of Applied Psychology*, 64, 654-9.

Dashevsky, S.G. (1964) 'Check-reading accuracy as a function of pointer alignment, patterning and viewing angle', *Journal of Applied Psychology*, 48, 344-7.

Davis, D.R. and Shackleton, V.J. (1975) *Psychology and Work* (London: Methuen).

Davis, L.E. (1973) 'Job redesign on the assembly line: Farewell to blue-collar blues?', *Organizational Dynamics*, 1, 51-67.

Decoutiis, T. and Petit, A. (1978) 'The performance appraisal process: A model and some testable propositions', *Academy of Management Review*, 3, 89-96.

Dembroski, T.M. (1979) 'Cardiovascular reactivity in type A coronary prone subjects', in D.J. Oborne, M.M. Gruneberg and R.J. Eiser (eds.), *Research in Psychology and Medicine*, vol I (London: Academic Press).

Drucker, P. (1954) *The Practice of Management* (New York: Harper).

Dubin, R. (1965) in Dubin, R., Homans, G.C., Mann, F.C. and Miller, D.C. *Leadership and Productivity* (Scranton: Chandler).

Dunham, R.D. (1978) 'Shift work: A review and theoretical analysis', *Academy of Management Review*, 2, 624-34.

Dunn, H.K. and White, S.D. (1940) 'Statistical measurements on conversational speech', *Journal of the Acoustic Society of America*, 11, 278.

Dunnette, M.D. (1976) 'Aptitudes, abilities and skills',

in M.D. Dunnette (ed.), *Handbook of Industrial and Organizational Psychology* (Chicago: Rand McNally).

Elliott, C.D. (1971) 'Noise tolerance and extraversion in children', *British Journal of Psychology*, 62, 375-80.

Emery, F.E. and Thorsrud, E. (1975) *Democracy at Work* (Canberra: Australian National University).

Evan, W.M. (1963) 'Peer-group interaction and organizational socialization: A study of employee turnover', *American Sociological Review*, 28, 436-40.

Farris, G.F. (1971) 'A predictive study of turnover', *Personnel Psychology*, 24, 311-28.

Farris, G.F. and Lim, F.G. (1969) 'Effects of performance on leadership cohesiveness, influence, satisfaction and subsequent performance', *Journal of Applied Psychology*, 53, 490-7.

Fein, M. (1974) 'Job enrichment: A re-evaluation', *Sloan Management Review*, 15, 69-88.

Ferguson, D. (1973) 'A study of occupational stress', *Ergonomics*, 16, 649-64.

Fleishman, E.A. (1962) 'The description and prediction of perceptual motor skill learning', in M. Glaser (ed.), *Training Research and Education* (Pittsburg: University of Pittsburg Press).

Fletcher, H. and Munson, W.A. (1937) 'Relation between loudness and masking', *Journal of Acoustical Society of America*, 9, 1-10.

Ford, R.W. (1969) *Motivation through the Work Itself* (New York: American Management Association).

Fox, J.G. (1971) 'Background music and industrial efficiency - a review', *Applied Ergonomics*, 2, 70-3.

Fox, J.G. and Embrey, E.D. (1972) 'Music - an aid to productivity', *Applied Ergonomics*, 3, 202-5.

Fry, L.W. (1976) 'The maligned F.W. Taylor: A reply to his many critics', *Academy of Management Review*, 124-9.

Gardner, G. (1977) 'Is there a valid test of Herzberg's two factor theory?', *British Journal of Occupational Psychology*, 50, 197-204.

Garrett, J.W. (1971) 'The adult human hand: some anthropometric and biomechanical considerations', *Human Factors*, 13, 117-31.

Garrison, K.R. and Murchinsky, R.M. (1977) 'Attitudinal and biographical predictions of incidental absenteeism', *Journal of Vocational Behaviour*, 10, 221-30.

Gibbs, C.B. and Brown, I.D. (1955) 'Increased production from information incentive in a repetitive task', Report no. 730, M.R.C.A.P.U., Great Britain.

Gilbert, M. and Hopkinson, R.G. (1949) 'The illumination

of the Snellen chart', *British Journal of Opthamology*, 33, 305-10.

Gill, C. (1979) 'Research Note: Continuous-process technology and industrial conflict', *Industrial Relations Journal*, 10, 69-72.

Gill, C.G. and Warner, M. (1979) 'Managerial and organisational determinants of industrial conflict - chemical industry case', *Journal of Management Studies*, 16, 56-69.

Gilson, T.Q. and Lefcowitz, M.J. (1957) 'A plant-wide productivity bonus in a small factory: Study of an unsuccessful case', *Industrial and Labor Relations Review*, 10, 284-96.

Goldthorpe, J., Lockwood, D., Bechofer, F. and Platt, J. (1968) *The Affluent Worker* (Cambridge University Press).

Golembiewski, R.T. and Proehl, C.W. (1978) 'A survey of the empirical literature on flexible working hours', *Academy of Management Review*, 3, 837-53.

Goodman, P.S., Rose, J.H. and Fircon, J.E. (1970) 'Comparison of motivational antecedents of the work performance of scientists and engineers', *Journal of Applied Psychology*, 54, 491-5.

Graen, G., Orris, J. and Johnson, T.W. (1973) 'A developmental study of the assimilation of new people into various office worker roles within a large public university', *Journal of Vocational Behaviour*, 3, 395-420.

Gray, R.B. (1971) 'The Scanlon plan - a case study', *British Journal of Industrial Relations*, 9, 291-310.

Grether, W.F. (1949) 'Instrument reading. The design of long-scale indicators for speed and accuracy of quantitive readings', *Journal of Applied Psychology*, 33, 363-72.

Grether, W.F. (1971) 'Vibration and human performance', *Human Factors*, 13, 203-16.

Griffin, M.J. and Lewis, C.H. (1978) 'A review of the effects of vibration on visual acuity and continuous manual control. Part 1: Visual acuity', *Journal of Sound and Vibration*, 56, 383-413.

Gruneberg, M.M. (1970) 'Scholastic aptitude and attainment related to employment choice: A study of senior secondary school leavers in Scotland', *The Vocational Aspect of Education*, 22, 159-86.

Gruneberg, M.M. (1979) *Understanding Job Satisfaction* (London: Macmillan).

Gruneberg, M.M., Startup, R. and Tapsfield, P. (1974) 'The effect of geographical factors on job satisfaction of university teachers', *Vocational Aspects of Education*, 26, 25-9.

Guignard, J.C. and King, P.F. (1972) 'Aeromedical aspects of vibration and noise', *AGARD*, no. 151.

Guion, R.M. and Gottier, R.F. (1967) 'Validity of person-
ality measures in personnel selection', *Personnel Psycho-
logy*, 20, 135-64.
Hackman, J.R. (1976) 'Group influences on individuals',
in M.D. Dunnette (ed.), *Handbook of Industrial and
Organizational Psychology* (Chicago: Rand McNally).
Hackman, J.R. (1977) 'Work design', in J.R. Hackman and
J.L. Suttle , *Improving Life At Work* (Santa Monica:
Goodyear Publishing).
Hackman, J.R. and Lawler, E.E. (1971) 'Employee reactions
to job satisfaction characteristics', *Journal of Applied
Psychology*, 55, 259-86.
Hackman, J.R., Oldham, G., Janson, R. and Purdy, K. (1975)
'A new strategy for job enrichment', *California
Management Review*, 17, 57-71.
Hackman, J.R. and Oldham, G.R. (1976) 'Motivation through
the design of work: Test of a theory', *Organizational
Behaviour and Human Performance*, 15, 250-79.
Hackman, J.R. and Suttle, J.L. (1977) *Improving Life at
Work* (Santa Monica: Goodyear Publishing).
Haines, R.F. and Gilliland, K. (1973) 'Response time in
the full visual field', *Journal of Applied Psychology*,
58, 289-95.
Hall, D.T. and Lawler, E.E. (1970) 'Job characteristics
and pressures and the organizational integration of
professionals', *Administrative Science Quarterly*, 15,
271-81.
Harrell, T.W. and Harrell, M.S. (1945) 'Army general
classification test scores for civilian occupations',
Educational and Psychological Measurements, 5, 229-39.
Harvey, E. (1968) 'Technology and the structure of
organizations', *American Sociological Review*, 33, 247-59.
Heneman, H.G. and Schwab, D.P. (1972) 'An evaluation of
research on expectancy theory predictions of employee
performance', *Psychological Bulletin*, 78, 1-9.
Herzberg, F. (1966) *Work and the Nature of Man* (Cleveland:
World Publishing).
Herzberg, F. (1968) 'One more time: How do you motivate
employees?', *Harvard Business Review*, 46, 53-62.
Herzberg, F., Mausner, B. and Snyderman, B. (1959) *The
Motivation to Work* (New York: Wiley).
Hespe, G. and Wall, T. (1976) 'The demand for participation
among employees', *Human Relations*, 29, 411-28.
Hickson, D.J. (1961) 'Motives of workpeople who restrict
their output', *Occupational Psychology*, 35, 111-29.
Hitt, W.D. (1961) 'An evaluation of five different
abstract coding methods exp IV', *Human Factors*, 3, 120-30.

Hockey, G.C.R.   (1972)   'Effects of noise on human efficiency
   and some individual differences', *Journal of Sound Vi-
   bration*, 20, 299-304.
Hoffman, L.W.   (1976)   'Fear of success in 1965 and 1974:   A
   follow up study', *Journal of Consulting and Clinical
   Psychology*, 42, 353-8.
Hoffman, M.A. and Heimstra, N.W.   (1972)   'Tracking perform-
   ance with visual auditory or electrocutaneous displays',
   Human Factors, 14, 131-8.
Hoffman, M.L.   (1977)   'Personality and social development',
   Annual Review of Psychology, 28, 295-321.
Holland, J.K.   (1976)   'Vocational preferences', in M.D.
   Dunnette (ed.), *Handbook of Industrial and Organizational
   Psychology* (Chicago: Rand McNally).
Homans, G.C.   (1965) in R. Dubin., G.C. Homans, F.C. Mann
   and D.C. Miller, *Leadership and Productivity* (Scranton:
   Chandler Publishing).
Hopkinson, R.G. and Collins, J.B.   (1970)   *The Ergonomics of
   Lighting* (London: McDonald Technical and Scientific).
Horner, M.   (1972) 'The motive to avoid success and changing
   aspirations of college women', in J.M. Bardwick (ed.),
   Readings on the Psychology of Women (New York: Harper and
   Row).
Hoyenga, K.B. and Hoyenga, K.T.   (1979)   *The Question of Sex
   Differences* (Boston: Little, Brown).
Hulin, C.L. and Blood, M.R.   (1968)   'Job enlargement,
   individual differences and worker response', *Psychological
   Bulletin*, 69, 41-65.
Hundal, P.S.   (1969)   'Knowledge of performance as an incen-
   tive in repetitive industrial work', *Journal of Applied
   Psychology*, 53, 224-6.
Ilgen, D.R., Fisher, C.D. and Taylor, M.S.   (1979)   'Conse-
   quences of individual feedback in behaviour in organ-
   izations', *Journal of Applied Psychology*, 64, 349-71.
Ilgen, D.R. and Hollenback, J.C.   (1977)   'The role of job
   satisfaction in absence behaviour', *Organizational
   Behaviour and Human Performance*, 19, 148-61.
Ilgen, D.R. and Seely, W.   (1974)   'Realistic expectations
   as an aid in reducing voluntary resignations', *Journal of
   Applied Psychology*, 59, 452-5.
Ingham, G.   (1970)   *Size of Industrial Organization and
   Worker Behaviour* (Cambridge University Press).
Ivancevich, J.M.   (1969)   'Perceived need satisfactions of
   domestic versus overseas managers', *Journal of Applied
   Psychology*, 53, 274-8.
Ivancevich, J.M.   (1974)   'Changes in performance in a
   management by objectives programme', *Administrative*

Science Quarterly, 19, 563-74.

Ivancevich, J.M. (1977) 'Different goal setting treatments and their effects on performance and job satisfaction', *Academy of Management Journal*, 20, 406-19.

Ivancevich, J.M. and Donnelly, J.H. (1975) 'Relation of organizational structure to job satisfaction, anxiety stress and performance', *Administrative Science Quarterly*, 20, 272-80.

Ivancevich, J.M. and Lyon, H.L. (1977) 'The shortened workweek: A field experiment', *Journal of Applied Psychology*, 62, 34-7.

James, J. (1951) 'An experimental study of tensions in work behaviour', *University of California Publications in Culture and Society*, 2, 203-42.

Johansson, G. (1975) 'Psychophysiological stress reactions in the sawmill: A pilot study', in B. Ager (ed.), *Ergonomics in Sawmills and Woodworking Industries* (Stockholm: National Board of Occupational Safety and Health).

Jones, A.P., James, L.R. and Bruni, J.R. (1975) 'Perceived leadership behaviour and employee confidence in the leader as moderated by job involvement', *Journal of Applied Psychology*, 60, 146-9.

Jones, A.P., James, L.R., Bruni, J.R. and Sells, S.B. (1977) 'Black white differences in work environment perceptions and job satisfaction and its correlates', *Personnel Psychology*, 30, 5-16.

Jones, D.M. (1979) 'Stress and memory', in M.M. Gruneberg and P.E. Morris (eds.), *Applied Problems in Memory* (London: Academic Press).

Kahn, R.L. (1956) 'The prediction of productivity', *Journal of Social Issues*, 12, 41-9

Kahn, R.L. (1974) 'Conflict ambiguity and overload: Three elements in job stress', in A. Maclean (ed.), *Occupational Stress* (Springfield: Charles Thomas).

Kahn, R.L., Wolfe, D.M., Snoek, J.E. and Rosenthal, R.A. (1964) *Organisational Stress: Studies in Role Conflict and Ambiguity* (New York: Wiley).

Karasek, R.A. (1979) 'Job demands, job decision latitude and mental strain - implications for job redesign', *Administrative Science Quarterly*, 24, 285-308.

Kasl, S.V. (1973) 'Mental health and work environment: An examination of the evidence', *Journal of Occupational Medicine*, 15, 509-18.

Katz, R. (1978) 'Job longevity as a situational factor in job satisfaction', *Administrative Science Quarterly*, 23, 204-23.

Katzell, R.A. and Yankelovich, D. (1975) *Work, Pro-*

ductivity and Job Satisfaction (New York: The Psychological Corporation).

Kay, H. (1978) 'Accidents: Some facts and theories', in P.B. Warr (ed.), *Psychology at Work* (Harmondsworth: Penguin).

Kelly, C. (1968) *Manual and Automative Control* (New York: J. Wiley).

Kelly, J. (1974) *Organizational Behaviour* (Homewood, Illinois: Irwin Inc.).

Kelly, J.E. (1978) 'A reappraisal of sociotechnical systems theory', *Human Relations*, 31, 1069-99.

Kerkhoven, C.L.M. (1962) 'The cost price of food calories for heavy work', *Ergonomics*, 5, 53-65.

Kim, J.S. and Hamner, W.C. (1976) 'Effect of performance feedback and goal setting on production and satisfaction in an organizational setting', *Journal of Applied Psychology*, 61, 48-57.

King, N. (1970) 'Clarification and evaluation of the two factor theory of job satisfaction', *Psychological Bulletin*, 74, 18-31.

Klein, S.M. and Maher, J.R. (1966) 'Educational level and satisfaction with pay', *Personnel Psychology*, 19, 195-208.

Knowles, M.C. (1964) 'Personal and job factors affecting labour turnover', *Personnel Practice Bulletin*, 20, 25-37.

Korman, A.K. (1966) '"Consideration", "initiating structure" and organizational criteria - a review', *Personnel Psychology*, 19, 349-62.

Korman, A.K. (1977) *Organizational Behaviour* (Engelwood Cliffs: Prentice Hall).

Korman, A.K., Greenhaus, J.H. and Badin, I.J. (1977) 'Personnel attitudes and motivation', *Annual Review of Psychology*, 28, 175-96.

Kornhauser, A. (1965) *Mental Health and the Industrial Worker* (New York: J. Wiley).

Kornhauser, A., Dubin, R. and Ross, A.M. (eds.) (1954) *Industrial Conflict* (New York: McGraw-Hill).

Kryter, K.O. (1970) *The Effects of Noise on Man* (New York: Academic Press).

Kuhlin, R.G. (1963) 'Needs, perceived needs satisfaction and satisfaction with occupation', *Journal of Applied Psychology*, 47, 56-64.

Kurke, M.I. (1956) 'Evaluation of a display incorporating quantitative and check reading characteristics', *Journal of Applied Psychology*, 40, 233-6.

Latham, G.P. and Baldes, J.J. (1975) 'The 'practical' significance of Locke's theory of goal setting', *Journal of Applied Psychology*, 60, 122-4.

198   INDUSTRIAL PRODUCTIVITY

Latham, G.P., Mitchell, T.R. and Dossett, D.L. (1978) 'Importance of participative goal setting and anticipated rewards on goal difficulty and performance', *Journal of Applied Psychology*, 63, 163-71.

Latham, G.P., Wexley, K.N. and Pursell, E.D. (1975) 'Training managers to minimize rating errors in the observation of behaviour', *Journal of Applied Psychology*, 60, 550-5.

Latham, G.P. and Yukl, G.A. (1975) 'A review of research on the application of goal setting in organizations', *Academy of Management Journal*, 18, 823-45.

Lawler, E.E. (1969) 'Job design and employee motivation', *Personnel Psychology*, 22, 426-35.

Lawler, E.E. (1970) 'Job attitudes and employee motivation: Theory, research and practice', *Personnel Psychology*, 23, 223-37.

Lawler, E.E. (1971) *Pay and Organizational Effectiveness* (New York: McGraw-Hill).

Lawler, E.E. and O'Gara, P.W. (1967) 'Effects of inequity produced by underpayment on work output, work quality and attitudes towards work', *Journal of Applied Psychology*, 51, 403-10.

Lawler, E.E. and Porter, L.W. (1969) 'The effects of performance on job satisfaction', *Industrial Relations*, 8, 20-28.

Lawrence, P.R. and Lorsch, J.W. (1967) *Organization and Environment* (Boston: Harvard Business School).

Lawson, R. (1965) *Frustration: The Development of a Scientific Concept* (New York: Macmillan).

Lee, R.A. and King, A.I. (1971) 'Visual vibration response', *Journal of Applied Psychology*, 30, 281-6.

Legge, K. (1974) 'Flexible working hours - panacea or placebo', *Management Decisions*, 12, 264-80.

Leventhal, G.S., Michael, S.J. and Sanford, C. (1972) 'Inequity and interpersonal conflict: Reward allocation and secrecy about rewards as methods of preventing conflict', *Journal of Personality and Social Psychology*, 23, 88-102.

Lewin, K., Lippitt, R. and White, R.K. (1939) 'Patterns of aggressive behaviour in experimentally created social climates', *Journal of Social Psychology*, 10, 271-99.

Licklider, J.C.R. (1948) 'The influence of interaural phase relations upon the masking of speech by white noise', *Journal of Applied Psychology*, 20, 510-19.

Likert, R. (1955) cited in R. Dubin., G.C. Homans, F.C. Mann and D.C. Miller *Leadership and Productivity* (Scranton: Chandler).

Lippitt, G. (1961) 'How to get results from a group', in

L. Bradford (ed.), *Group Development* (Washington D.C.: National Training Laboratories).

Locke, E.A. (1968) 'Towards a theory of task performance and incentives', *Organizational Behaviour and Human Performance*, 3, 157-89.

Locke, E.A. (1976) 'The nature and causes of job satisfaction', in M.D. Dunnette (ed.), *Handbook of Industrial and Organizational Psychology* (Chicago: Rand McNally).

Locke, E.A. and Bryan, J.F. (1969) 'Knowledge of score and goal level as determinants of work rate', *Journal of Applied Psychology*, 53, 59-65.

Locke, E.A., Feren, D.B., McCaleb, V.M., Shaw, K.N. and Denny, A.T. (1980) 'The relative effectiveness of four methods of motivating employee performance', in K.D. Duncan, M.M. Gruneberg and D. Wallis (eds.), *Changes in Working Life* (London: Wiley).

Locke, E.A. Sirota, D. and Wolfson, A.D. (1976) 'An experimental case study of the successes and failures of job enrichment in a government agency', *Journal of Applied Psychology*, 61, 701-11.

Lockhart, J.M. (1968) 'Extreme body cooling and psychomotor performance', *Ergonomics*, 11, 249-60.

Lockhart, J.M. and Keiss, M.O. (1971) 'Auxiliary heating of the hands during cold exposure and manual performance', *Human Factors*, 13, 457-65.

Lodahl, T.M. (1964) 'Patterns of job attitudes in two assembly technologies', *Administrative Science Quarterly*, 8, 482-519.

Lodahl, J.M. and Kejner, M. (1965) 'The definition and measurement of job involvement', *Journal of Applied Psychology*, 49, 24-33.

Lott, A.J. and Lott, B.E. (1965) 'Group cohesiveness as interpersonal attraction', *Psychology Bulletin*, 65, 259-309.

Loveless, N.E. (1962) 'Direction-of-motion stereotypes: A review', *Ergonomics*, 5, 357-383.

Lovesey, E.J. (1975) 'The helicopter - some ergonomic factors', *Applied Ergonomics*, 6, 139-46.

Lupton, T. and Tanner, I. (1980) in K.D. Duncan, M.M. Gruneberg and D. Wallis (eds.), *Changes in Working Life* (London: Wiley).

McCormick, E.J. (1976) *Human Factors in Engineering and Design* (New York: McGraw-Hill).

MacKay, C. and Cox, T. (1978) 'Stress at work', in T. Cox *Stress* (London: Macmillan).

McFarland, R.A. (1956) 'Functional efficiency, skills and employment', in J.E. Anderson *Psychological Aspects of*

Ageing (Washington: American Psychological Association).

McGrath, J.E. (1976) 'Stress and behaviour in organisations', in M.D. Dunnette (ed.), *Handbook of Industrial and Organizational Psychology* (Chicago: Rand McNally).

McGregor, D. (1960) *The Human Side of the Enterprise* (New York: McGraw-Hill).

Mackworth, N.H. (1950) 'Researches on the measurement of human performance', HRC Special Report Series 268 (London: HMSO).

Mann, F.C. and Williams, L.K. (1962) 'Some effects of changing work environments in the office', *Journal of Social Issues*, 18, 92-101.

Marriott, R. (1949) 'Size of working group and output', *Occupational Psychology*, 23, 47-57.

Marriott, R. (1957) *Incentive Payments Systems* (London: Staples Press).

Maslow, A.H. (1943) 'A theory of human motivation', *Psychological Review*, 50, 370-96.

Meister, D. (1976) *Behavioural Foundations of Systems Development* (New York: J. Wiley).

Merrins, M.R. and Garrett, J.B. (1975) 'The Protestant work ethic scale as a predictor of repetitive work performance', *Journal of Applied Psychology*, 60, 125-7.

Metzner, H. and Mann, F. (1953) 'Employee attitudes and absence', *Personnel Psychology*, 6, 467-85.

Meyer, H.H., Kay, E. and French, J.R.P. (1965) 'Split roles in performance appraisal', *Harvard Business Review*, 43, 123-9.

Miller, D.C. (1965) in R. Dubin, J.C. Homens, F.C. Mann and D.C. Miller *Leadership and Productivity* (Scranton: Chandler Publishing).

Miller, E. (1979) 'Memory and ageing', in M.M. Gruneberg and P.E. Morris (eds.), *Applied Problems in Memory* (London: Academic Press).

Miller, R.F. (1978) 'Worker self-management in Yugoslavia. The current state of play', *Industrial Relations Journal*, 20, 264-85.

Miner, J.B. and Brewer, J.F. (1976) 'The management of ineffective performance', in M.D. Dunnette (ed.), *Handbook of Industrial and Organizational Psychology* (New York: Rand McNally).

Mirvis, P.H. and Lawler, E.E. (1977) 'Measuring the financial impact of employee attitudes', *Journal of Applied Psychology*, 67, 1-8.

Misshawk, M.J. (1971) 'Supervisory skills and employee satisfaction', *Personnel Administration*, 34, 29-33.

Mobley, W.H., Honner, S.O. and Hollingsworth, A.T. (1978)

'An evaluation of precursors of hospital employee turnover',
Journal of Applied Psychology, 63, 408-14.

Moore, T.G. (1976) 'Controls and tactile displays', in
K.F. Kraisse and J. Moraal (eds.), *Introduction to Human
Engineering* (Verlag TUV).

Morse, N.C. and Reimer, E. (1956) 'The experimental change
of a major organizational variable', *Journal of Abnormal
and Social Psychology*, 52, 120-9.

Morton, R. and Provins, K.A. (1960) 'Finger numbness after
acute local exposure to cold', *Journal of Applied Psychology*, 15, 149-54.

Murrell, K.F.H. (1970) *Ergonomics* (London: Chapman and
Hall).

Murrell, H. and Humphries, S. (1978) 'Age, experience and
short term memory', in M.M. Gruneberg, P.E. Morris and
R.N. Sykes (eds.), *Practical Aspects of Memory* (London:
Academic Press).

Murrell, K.F.H. and Kingston, P.M. (1966) 'Experimental
comparison of scalar and digital micrometers', *Ergonomics*,
9, 39-47.

Napier, R.W. and Gershenfeld, M.K. (1973) *Groups: Theory
and Practice* (Boston: Houghton Mifflin).

Newcomb, T.H. (1958) 'Attitude development as a function
of reference groups: The Bennington study', in E.E.
Maccoby, T.H. Newcomb and E.L. Hartley (eds.), *Readings
in Social Psychology* (New York: Holt, Rinehart and
Winston).

Nicholson, N. (1976) 'Management sanctions and absence
control', *Human Relations*, 29, 139-51.

Nicholson, N., Brown, C.A. and Chadwick-Jones, J.K. (1976)
'Absence from work and job satisfaction', *Journal of
Applied Psychology*, 61, 728-37.

Nicholson, N., Brown, C.A. and Chadwick-Jones, J.K. (1977)
'Absence from work and personal characteristics', *Journal
of Applied Psychology*, 62, 319-27.

Nicholson, N., Jackson, P. and Hawes, G. (1978) 'Shift-
work and absence: An analysis of temporal trends', *Journal
of Occupational Psychology*, 51, 127-38.

Nixon, J.C. and Glorig, A. (1961) 'Noise induced permanent
threshold shift at 2000 cfs and 4000 cfs', *Journal of the
Acoustic Society of America*, 33, 904-8.

Nord, W.R. and Costigan, R. (1973) 'Worker adjustment to
the four day week: A longitudinal study', *Journal of
Applied Psychology*, 58, 60-66.

Opsahl, R.L. and Dunnette, M.D. (1966) 'The role of
financial compensation in industrial motivation',
Psychological Bulletin, 66, 94-118.

Organ, D.W.   (1977)   'A reappraisal and reinterpretation of
the satisfaction - causes - performance hypothesis',
Academy of Management Review, 2, 46-53.

Orpen, C.   (1978)   'Effects of bonuses for attendance on the
absenteeism of industrial workers', *Journal of Organisational Behaviour Management*, 1, 118-24.

Orpen, C.   (1979)   'The effects of job enrichment on employee
satisfaction, motivation, involvement and performance: A
field experiment', *Human Relations*, 32, 189-217.

Orpen, C. and Ndlovu, J.   (1977)   'Participation, individual
differences and job satisfaction amongst black and white
employees in South Africa', *International Journal of
Psychology*, 12, 31-8.

Patchen, M.   (1965)   'Some questionnaire measures of employee
motivation and morale', *Institute for Social Research
Monograph*, 41, 1-70.

Patton, A.   (1960)   'How to appraise executive performance',
Harvard Business Review, 38, 63-70.

Payne, R. and Pugh, D.S.   (1976)   'Organizational structure
and climate', in M.D. Dunnette (ed.), *Handbook of Industrial and Organizational Psychology* (Chicago: Rand
McNally).

Pepler, R.D.   (1958)   'Warmth and performance: An investigation in the tropics', *Ergonomics*, 2, 63-88.

Poor, R. (1970)   *4 Days, 40 Hours* (Cambridge, Mass.: Bursk
and Poor).

Porter, L.W. and Lawler, E.E.   (1965)   'Properties of
organization structure in relation to job attitudes and
behaviour', *Psychological Bulletin*, 64, 23-51.

Porter, L.W., Lawler, E.E. and Hackman, J.R.   (1975)
Behaviour in Organizations (New York: McGraw-Hill).

Porter, L.W. and Steers, R.M.   (1973)   'Organizational work
and personal factors in employee turnover and absenteeism',
Psychological Bulletin, 80, 151-76.

Poulton, E.C.   (1977)   'Continuous intensive noise masks
auditory feedback and inner speech', *Psychological
Bulletin*, 84, 977-1001.

Poulton, E.C.   (1978)   'A new look at the effects of noise:
A rejoinder', *Psychological Bulletin*, 85, 1069-79.

Price, J.L.   (1977)   *The Study of Turnover* (Ames: Iowa
State University Press).

Pritchard, R.D.   (1969)   'Equity theory: A review and
critique', *Organizational Behaviour and Human Performance*,
4, 76-211.

Pritchard, R.D., Dunnette, M.D. and Jorgenson, D.D.   (1972)
'Effects of perceptions of equity and inequity on worker
performance and satisfaction', *Journal of Applied*

Psychology, 56, 75-94.

Pritchard, R.A. and Karaseck, B.W. (1973) 'The effects of organizational climate on managerial job performance and job satisfaction', *Organizational Behaviour and Human Performance*, 9, 126-46.

Rabinowitz, S. (1975) cited in S. Rabinowitz and D.T. Hall 'Organizational research on job involvement', *Psychological Bulletin*, 84, 265-88.

Rabinowitz, S. and Hall, D.T. (1977) 'Organizational research on job involvement', *Psychological Bulletin*, 84, 265-88.

Raia, A.P. (1965) 'Goal setting and self control: An experimental study', *Journal of Management Studies*, 2, 32-53.

Raia, A.P. (1966) 'A second look at management by goals and controls', *California Management Review*, 8, 49-58.

Rice, A.K. (1953) 'Productivity and social organization in a weaving shed', *Human Relations*, 6, 297-329.

Rief, W.E. and Monczka, R.M. (1974) 'Job redesign - contingency approach to implementation', *Personnel*, 51, 18.

Rizzo, J.R., House, R.J. and Lirtzman, S.I. (1970) 'Role conflict and ambiguity in complex organization', *Administrative Science Quarterly*, 15, 150-63.

Robinson, D.A. (1976) *From Drinking to Alcoholism* (New York: John Wiley).

Robinson, D.A. (1979) *Alcohol Problems, Reviews, Research and Recommendations* (London: Macmillan).

Robinson, D.D. (1972) 'Prediction of clerical turnover in banks by means of a weighted application blank', *Journal of Applied Psychology*, 56, 282.

Rodger, A. and Cavanagh, P. (1962) 'Training occupational psychologists', *Occupational Psychology*, 36, 82-8.

Roethlisberger, F.J. (1941) *Management and Morale* (Cambridge, Mass.: Harvard University Press).

Roethlisberger, F.S. and Dickson, W.J. (1939) *Management and the Worker* (Chicago: Harvard University Press).

Ronan, W.W., Latham, G.P. and Kinne, S.B. (1973) 'Effects of goal setting and supervision on worker behaviour in an industrial situation', *Journal of Applied Psychology*, 58, 302-7.

Rose, M. (1978) *Industrial Behaviour: Theoretical Development since Taylor* (Harmondsworth: Penguin).

Ross, I.C. and Zander, A. (1957) 'Need satisfactions and employee turnover', *Personnel Psychology*, 10, 327-38.

Rosseger, R. and Rosseger, S. (1960) 'Health effects of tractor driving', *Journal of Agricultural Engineering Research*, 5, 241-75.

Ruch, W.A. and Hershauer, J.C. (1974) *Factors affecting productivity,* Occasional Papers no. 10 (Temple, Arizona: College of Business Administration, Arizona State University).

Runnion, A., Johnson, T. and McWhorter, J. (1978) 'The effects of feedback and reinforcement on truck turnaround time in materials transportation', *Journal of Organisational Behaviour Management,* 1, 110-7.

Russek, H.I. and Zohman, B.L. (1958) 'Relative significance of heredity, diet and occupational stress in C.H.D. of young adults', *American Journal of Medical Science,* 253, 266.

Saleh, O. and Otis, J.L. (1964) 'Age and level of job satisfaction', *Personnel Psychology,* 17, 425-30.

Salvendy, G. and Seymour, W.D. (1973) *Prediction and Development of Industrial Work Performance* (New York: John Wiley).

Scheflen, K.C., Lawler, E.E. and Hackman, J.R. (1971) 'Long term impact of employee participation in the development of pay incentive plans', *Journal of Applied Psychology,* 55, 182-6.

Schein, V.E., Maurer, E.H. and Novak, J.F. (1978) 'Supervisors reactions to flexible working hours', *Journal of Occupational Psychology,* 51, 333-7.

Schneider, B. and Olsen, K. (1970) 'Effort as a correlate of organizational reward system and individual values', *Personnel Psychology,* 23, 313-26.

Schneider, B. and Snyder, R.A. (1975) 'Some relationships between job satisfaction and organizational climate', *Journal of Applied Psychology,* 60, 318-28.

Schramm, C.J. (ed.) (1978) *Alcoholism and its Treatment in Industry* (Baltimore: Johns Hopkins University Press).

Schuler, R.S. (1975) 'Sex, organisation level and outcome importance: Where the differences are', *Personnel Psychology,* 28, 365-75.

Schuler, R.S. (1977) 'Role conflict and ambiguity as a function of task-structure-technology interaction', *Organizational Behaviour and Human Performance,* 20, 66-74.

Schwab, D. and Cummings, L.L. (1970) 'Theories of performance and satisfaction', *Industrial Relations,* 9, 408-30.

Seligman, C. and Darley, J.M. (1977) 'Feedback as a means of decreasing residential energy consumption', *Journal of Applied Psychology,* 62, 363-8.

Sherif, M. (1966) *Group Conflict and Co-operation: Their Social Psychology* (London: Routledge and Kegan Paul).

Shipley, P. (1980) 'Technological change, working hours and individual well being', in K.D. Duncan, M.M. Gruneberg

and D. Wallis (eds.), *Changes in Working Life* (London: John Wiley).

Shoenberger, R.W. (1974) 'An investigation of human information processing during whole-body vibration', *Aerospace Medicine*, 143-53.

Siegal, A.L. and Ruh, R.A. (1973) 'Job involvement, participation and decision making, personal background and job behaviour', *Organizational Behaviour and Human Performance*, 9, 318-27.

Simons, C.W. and Roscoe, S.N. (1956) 'Altimeter studies part II. A comparison of integrated versus separated displays', *Technical Memo no. 435* (Culver City, California: Hughes Aircraft).

Singleton, T. (1960) 'An experimental invesigation of speed controls for sewing machines', *Ergonomics*, 3, 365-76.

Sirota, D. and Wolfson, A.D. (1972) 'Job enrichment: Surmounting the obstacles', *Personnel*, 4, 8-19.

Slocum, J.W. (1971) 'A comparative study of the satisfaction of American and Mexican operators', *Academy of Management Journal*, 14, 89-97.

Smith, F.J. (1977) 'Work attitudes as predictors of specific day attendance', *Journal of Applied Psychology*, 62, 16-9.

Smith, H.C. and Wakeley, J.H. (1972) *Psychology of Industrial Behaviour* (New York: McGraw-Hill).

Sobel, I. (1970) 'Economic changes and older worker utilisation patterns', in P.M. Paillat and M.E. Bunch (eds.), *Age, Work and Automation* (Basel: Karger).

Stagner, R. (1956) *Psychology of Industrial Conflict* (New York: Wiley).

Startup, R. and Gruneberg, M.M. (1973) 'The academic as administrator and policy maker', *Higher Education Review*, 6, 45-53.

Steers, R.M. (1975) 'Task-goal attributes in achievement and supervisory performance', *Organizational Behaviour and Human Performance*, 13, 392-403.

Steers, R.M. (1977) *Organizational Effectiveness. A Behavioural View.* (Santa Monica: Goodyear).

Steers, R.M. and Mowday, R.T. (1977) 'The motivational properties of tasks', *Academy of Management Review*, 2, 645-58.

Steers, R.M. and Porter L.W. (1974) 'The role of task-goal attributes in employee performance', *Psychological Bulletin*, 81, 434-52.

Steers, R.M. and Rhodes, S.R. (1978) 'Major influences on employee attendance: A process model', *Journal of Applied Psychology*, 63, 391-407.

Streufert, S., Streufert, S.C., Dembroski, T.M. and
MacDougal, H.M. (1979) 'Complexity, coronary prone be-
haviour and psychological response', in D.J. Oborne, M.M.
Gruneberg and R.J. Eiser (eds.), *Research in Psychology and
Medicine*, vol I (London: Academic Press).
Sussman, G.I. (1973) 'Job enlargement: Effects of culture
on worker responses', *Industrial Relations*, 12, 1-15.
Sutermeister, R.A. (1976) *People and Productivity* (New
York: McGraw-Hill).
Taft, R. (1955) 'The ability to judge people', *Psycho-
logical Bulletin*, 52, 1-23.
Taylor, F.W. (1911) *Principles of Scientific Management*
(New York: Harper and Row).
Taylor, K. and Weiss, D. (1969) 'Prediction of individual
job turnover from measured job satisfaction', *Research
Report 22* (University of Minnesota Work Adjustment
Project, Minneapolis).
Taylor, P.J. (1967) 'Individual variations in sickness
absence', *British Journal of Industrial Medicine*, 24,
169-77.
Teichener, W.H., Areas, E. and Reilly, R. (1963) 'Noise
and human performance, a psychophysiological approach',
Ergonomics, 6, 83-97.
Terborg, J.R. and Miller, H.E. (1978) 'Motivation, be-
haviour and performance: A closer examination of goal
setting and monetary incentives', *Journal of Applied
Psychology*, 63, 29-39.
Theoroll, T. (1974) 'Life events before and after onset
of a premature myocardial infarction', in B.P. Dohrenwerd
and B.P. Dohrenwerd (eds.), *Stressful Life Events: Their
Nature and Effects* (New York: Wiley).
Thomas, J.C. (1965) 'Use of piezoacceletometer in studying
eye dynamics', *Journal of The Optical Society of America*.
Thomas, K. (1976) 'Conflict and conflict management', in
M.D. Dunnette (ed.), *Handbook of Industrial and Organ-
izational Psychology* (Chicago: Rand McNally).
Tjersland, T. (1972) *Changing Worker Behaviour* (New York:
Manpower Laboratory AT and T).
Totman, R.G. and Kiff, J. (1979) 'Life stress and suscep-
tibility to colds', in D.J. Oborne, M.M. Gruneberg and
R.J. Eiser (eds.), *Research in Psychology and Medicine*,
vol I (London: Academic Press).
Trist, E.L. and Bamforth, K.W. (1951) 'Some social and
psychological consequences of the longwall method of coal
getting', *Human Relations*, 4, 1-38.
Turner, A.N. and Lawrence, P.R. (1965) *Industrial Jobs
and the Worker* (Cambridge, Mass.: Harvard University
Press).

Tuttle, T.C., Dachler, H.P. and Schneider, B. (1975)
  'Organizational psychology', in B.L. Margolis and W.H.
  Kroes (eds.), *The Human Side of Accident Prevention*
  (Springfield, Ill.: C.H. Thomas).
Umstot, D.D., Bell, C.H. and Mitchell, T.R. (1976) 'Effects
  of job enrichment and task goals on satisfaction and
  productivity: Implications for job design', *Journal of
  Applied Psychology*, 61, 379-94.
Van Zelst, R.H. (1952) 'Validation of a sociometric
  regrouping procedure', *Journal of Abnormal and Social
  Psychology*, 47, 299-301.
Vroom, V.H. (1959) 'Some personality determinants of the
  effects of perception', *Journal of Abnormal and Social
  Psychology*, 59, 322-27.
Vroom, V.H. (1962) 'Ego involvement, job satisfaction and
  job performance', *Personnel Psychology*, 15, 159-77.
Vroom, V.H. (1964) *Work and Motivation* (New York: John
  Wiley).
Vroom, V.H. (1976) 'Leadership', in M.D. Dunnette (ed.),
  Hardbook of Industrial and Organizational Psychology
  (Chicago: Rand McNally).
Vroom, V.H. and Yetton, P.W. (1973) *Leadership and Decision
  Making* (Pittsburgh: University of Pittsburgh Press).
Wade, M. (1973) *Flexible Working Hours in Practice*
  (Epping, Essex: Gower Press).
Walker, C.R. and Guest, R.H. (1952) 'The man on the
  assembly line', *Harvard Business Review*, 30, 71-83.
Wall, T. (1980) 'Group work redesign in context: A two-
  phase model', in K.D. Duncan, M.M. Gruneberg and D. Wallis
  (eds.), *Changes in Working Life* (London: Wiley).
Wall, T.D., Clegg, C.W. and Jackson, P.R. (1978) 'An
  evaluation of the job model', *Journal of Occupational
  Psychology*, 2, 183-96.
Wall, T. and Lischeron, J.A. (1977) *Worker Participation:
  A Critique of the Literature and some Fresh Evidence*
  (London: McGraw-Hill).
Wall, T.D. and Stephenson, G.M. (1970) 'Herzberg's two-
  factor theory of job attributes: A critical evaluation
  and some fresh evidence', *Industrial Relations Journal*,
  1, 41-65.
Walton, R.A. (1972) 'How to counter alienation in the
  plant', *Harvard Business Review*, May-June, 12.
Warr, P. and Wall, T. (1975) *Work and Well Being*
  (Harmondsworth: Penguin).
Waters, L.K. and Roach, D. (1979) 'Job satisfaction,
  behavioural intention and absenteeism as predictors of
  turnover', *Personnel Psychology*, 32, 393-8.

Weed, S.E., Mitchell, T.R. and Moffitt, W. (1976) 'Leadership style, subordinate personality and task type as
predictors of performance and satisfaction with supervision', *Journal of Applied Psychology*, 61, 58-66.

Wegel, R.C. and Lane, C.E. (1924) 'The auditory masking of
a pure tone by another and its probable relation to the
dynamics of the inner ear', *Physics Review*, 23, 266-85.

Welford, A.T. (1976) *Skilled Performance: Perceptual and
Motor Skills* (Illinois: Scott, Foresmen).

Wernimont, P.F. and Fitzpatrick, S. (1972) 'The meaning of
money', *Journal of Applied Psychology*, 56, 218-26.

Whisler, T.L. (1958) 'Performance appraisal and the organisation man', *Journal of Business*, 31, 19-27.

White, J.K. (1979) 'Scanlon Plan: Causes and correlates
of success', *Academy of Management Journal*, 22, 292-312.

White, E.S., Mitchell, T.R. and Bell, C.H. (1977) 'Goal
setting, evaluation, apprehension and social cues as
determinants of job performance and job satisfaction in a
simulated organization', *Journal of Applied Psychology*,
62, 665-73.

Wickens, J.D. (1968) 'Management by objectives: An
appraisal', *Journal of Management Studies*, 5, 365-79.

Wild, R. (1970) 'Job needs, job satisfaction and job behaviour of women manual workers', *Journal of Applied
Psychology*, 54, 157-62.

Wilkinson, R.T. (1978) 'Hours of work and the twenty-four
hour cycle of rest and activity', in P.B. Warr (ed.),
Psychology at Work (Harmondsworth: Penguin).

Williams, R.L. and Tramortana, J. (1978) 'Evaluation of
occupational alcohol programmes', in C.J. Schramm (ed.)
Alcohol and its Treatment in Industry (Baltimore: Johns
Hopkins University Press).

Winer, J.S. and Hutchinson, J.C. (1945) 'Hot humid environment: Its effect on the performance of a motor coordi-
nation task', *British Journal of Industrial Medicine*, 2,
154-7.

Wing, J.F. (1965) 'Upper thermal tolerance limits for
unimpaired mental performance', *Aerospace Medicine*, 36,
960-4.

Woodward, J. (1965) *Industrial Organization: Theory and
Practice* (London: Oxford University Press).

Wrege, C. and Perroni, A. (1974) 'Taylor's pig tales: A
historical analysis of Frederick W. Taylor's pig iron
experiments', *Work Study and Management Services*, 564-75.

Yukl, G.A. and Latham, G.P. (1978) 'Interrelationship
among employee participation, individual differences,
goal difficulty, goal acceptance, goal instrumentality

and performance', *Personnel Psychology*, 31, 305–23.

Zander, A. and Newcomb, T. (1967) 'Group levels of aspiration in united fund campaigns', *Journal of Personality and Social Psychology*, 6, 157–62.

Author Index

Subject Index